# THE DANUBE

# Landscapes of the Imagination

# THE DANUBE

## A CULTURAL HISTORY

Andrew Beattie

OXFORD
UNIVERSITY PRESS

2010

# OXFORD
## UNIVERSITY PRESS

Oxford University Press, Inc., publishes works that further
Oxford University's objective of excellence
in research, scholarship, and education.

Oxford New York
Auckland Cape Town Dar es Salaam Hong Kong Karachi
Kuala Lumpur Madrid Melbourne Mexico City Nairobi
New Delhi Shanghai Taipei Toronto

With offices in
Argentina Austria Brazil Chile Czech Republic France Greece
Guatemala Hungary Italy Japan Poland Portugal Singapore
South Korea Switzerland Thailand Turkey Ukraine Vietnam

Published by Oxford University Press, Inc.
198 Madison Avenue, New York, New York 10016

www.oup.com

Oxford is a registered trademark of Oxford University Press

Co-published in Great Britain by Signal Books

Library of Congress Cataloging-in-Publication Data
Beattie, Andrew.
    The Danube : a cultural history / Andrew Beattie.
      p. cm.—(Landscapes of the imagination)
    Includes bibliographical references and indexes.
    ISBN 978-0-19-976834-9 (hardcover : alk. paper)—ISBN 978-0-19-976835-6 (pbk. : alk. paper)
1. Danube River--History.   2. Danube River—Description and travel.
3. Danube River Valley—History.   4. Danube River Valley—Civilization.
5. Danube River Valley—History, Local.   6. Danube River Valley—Description and travel.
I. Title.
    DB446.B39 2011
    949.6—dc22      2010029648

Design & production: Devdan Sen Images: © Andrew Beattie: 3, 25, 30, 34, 38, 44, 49, 51, 59, 76, 82,
87, 115, 144, 160, 163, 182, 195, 221, 242; dreamstime.com: 1, 22, 63, 79, 104, 117, 126, 137, 148,
177, 185, 188, 239, 251; Elaine Galloway: 208, 231, 241, 248; istockphoto.com: 65, 72, 108, 111, 228;
Wikipedia Commons: 5, 17, 55, 85, 99, 134, 175, 191, 204, 211, 213, 217, 232, 234
Printed in the United States of America
on acid-free paper

# *Contents*

## Introduction

# "THE KING OF THE RIVERS OF EUROPE"

The sentiment is right, of course; but cartographers and geographers would seek to disagree with these words written by Napoleon. The Danube may be the prince of European rivers, but, unfortunately for poets, writers and romantics, it is not the king. That title belongs to the Volga, the great river of western Russia that drains into the Caspian Sea and is a full 500 miles longer than the Danube, Europe's second longest river (and the 25th longest in the world). Patrick Leigh Fermor, one of the most famous writers associated with the Danube, remarked that the Volga is "almost too far away to count" when faced with this unarguable but uncomfortable fact of geography. For, in popular imagination at least, the Danube *is* Europe's longest river. And even if the Danube's length does not make it top class, its historical, artistic and literary associations more than compensate: for no other river in the world can match the Danube for the sheer historical richness of the cities and landscapes through which it passes.

Over a course of 1,777 miles, from its source in Germany's Black Forest to its delta on the Romanian and Ukrainian shores of the Black Sea, the river forms a backdrop to momentous historical events that stretch from the foundation of the earliest Mesolithic settlements in Europe to the Nato bombing of the former Yugoslavia. Empires have risen and fallen along its length, as the Macedonians, the Romans, the Habsburgs, the Ottomans and the Nazis have all fought for control of land through which the river passes. Myth and reality have blended along the river to form a cocktail of legend: Jason and the Argonauts were supposed to have sailed along its reaches, as were the characters in the epic medieval poem *The Song of the Nibelungs*.

Forming a background to these legends and stories is some of the most spectacular river scenery anywhere in the world: from cavernous gorges to vast plains, from snow-bound forested valleys to marshes that teem with an extraordinary variety of birdlife. The variety of the landscapes through which the Danube flows matches that of its historical and cultural legacy; not surprisingly, the river has been a source of inspiration for cultural

figures from the composer Johann Strauss to the painter Albrecht Altdorfer, and for writers and poets as diverse as Patrick Leigh Fermor and Friedrich Hölderlin. And yet—particularly in recent centuries—the Danube's familiar cultural legacy has been a Germanic one, confined to the upper and middle courses of the river. Only in contemporary times has a unified culture emerged that applies to the river in its entirety—endowing the river with a legacy that chimes with the momentous political changes that continue to engulf central and south-eastern Europe.

## From the Black Forest to the Black Sea

The Danube is one of the most venerable features of European geography; the mountains where its waters rise are newcomers to the scene in comparison. Sixty million years ago the river flowed into an ancient sea, the Tethys, which covered much of what is now south-eastern Europe. At that time Europe was welded together with North America and Asia to form one giant continent known as Laurasia. Then Laurasia broke apart and the Alps and the Carpathians erupted in an arc across Europe, splitting the Tethys Sea in two; soon the Danube was flowing into an inland sea that geologists have named the Paratethys, whose sea floor now forms the plains of modern-day Hungary. As the Paratethys filled, its waters needed an outlet: in time, a deep spillway, the Iron Gates gorge, was cut through the southern limb of the Carpathians, and the waters poured through the new opening and forged a new path that took the river almost as far as Asia. Slowly, as the continents reconfigured themselves, the Paratethys dried up completely, while the original Tethys shrunk to form the Mediterranean and the Caspian Seas.

By this time, around three million years ago, the Danube's familiar course was set firm across the continent: the river's headwaters rose in the eastern Alps and the Black Forest, its middle course took it across the great plains of central Europe, and at the end of its journey its sluggish waters formed a magnificent delta as the river finally drained into the Black Sea. (The Danube's general direction of flow, from west to east, sets it apart from all the other major rivers of Europe, which tend to orientate themselves north-south.) But like all rivers, the course followed by the river today is a temporary one: aeons into the future, as the old mountain chains are worn down and new ones rise in their place, and as new seas are created and old ones dry up, the river's course will renew itself again.

A long course that sweeps a river from snowy mountains to windswept continental plains inevitably experiences extremes in weather. In spring, snowmelt in the Alps can cause catastrophic floods of biblical proportions along the Danube; in summer, violent thunderstorms that build in the torrid heat of the continent are the source of yet more misery. The severe inundation along the upper course of the river in August 2002, which left one hundred people dead and caused an estimated US$10 billion worth of damage, was merely the most recent flood to have blighted the lives of those who, for thousands of years, have made their homes alongside this capricious river. No wonder the sixteenth-century German cartographer and cosmographer Sebastian Münster, in his multi-volume text book *Cosmographia,* claimed that the Danube originated as a drainage channel for Noah's Flood. Even when the river is not in flood, the melting snow and fierce rains create a high discharge and a strong current that is the curse of navigators; and to make matters worse, the river often freezes over during the harsh east European winters. A bitter, howling blast from Russia can shut a solid lid of ice over the surface of the water in the course of a single December night, cracking the hulls of ships like walnuts.

But as winter gives way to spring the ice slowly thaws and the river bursts into life again. The writer Patrick Leigh Fermor witnessed the spectacle of the spring thaw on the Danube for himself during his epic walk beside the river in 1934. "All at once the water was crowded with racing fragments [of ice]," he wrote in his book *Between the Woods and the Water.* "It was no good trying to keep pace: jostling triangles and polygons rushed past, cloudier at the edges each day and colliding with a softer impact until they were as flimsy as wafers; and at last, one morning, they were gone."

Despite the freezing winters and the violent current, the Danube is home to an abundance of aquatic life. A unique species of salmon lives in these waters, as do two distinct types of pike-perch; caviar-yielding sturgeon make their home in the swamplands of the delta, and in former times, before the construction of the great hydro-dams on the lower course of the river, these fish would swim upstream as far as Vienna, where specimens of sturgeon more than thirty feet in length could be caught. In the past, the Danube's fierce current, deep valleys and dangerous rapids have also provided fertile spawning grounds for wild beasts of a more mythical provenance. Leigh Fermor was told about catfish that could and did consume geese, ducks, lambs, dogs and children, while an elderly count, living in a castle beside a lonely stretch of the river in Austria, swore blind to him that a catfish sporting glaring eyes, sharp teeth and cat-like whiskers had once had a whole, newly-swallowed poodle cut from its belly.

## SETTLERS AND STORYTELLERS: THE DANUBE IN ANCIENT TIMES

The Danube's length, and its age-old role as a routeway between Europe and Asia, meant that some of the continent's earliest settlers made their homes beside it. At Lepenski Vir in Serbia, evidence has been found of a community that thrived beside the Danube 8,000 years ago; its members fished in the river, domesticated animals and lived in stone dwellings; their settled agrarian culture is as old as any in Mesopotamia. In 1984 divers investigating a sunken ship off the coast of Turkey discovered that the vessel was laden with amber from the Baltic, which must have been brought downstream along the Danube to be traded with Greek colonies along the shores of the Black Sea. By the time that ship had slipped into its watery grave, around 1400 BC, the river was already a vital artery for trade in the classical world; but military leaders, too, had long recognized the possibilities afforded by this link from the Black Sea into the heart of the continent. The historian Herodotus (484-420 BC) described in his work *Historia* how Darius, the King of the Persians, had once commanded a fleet that sailed up the Danube for two days to facilitate the construction of a great bridge over the river; when the bridge was built, Darius crossed it with an army and engaged the Scythians in battle (his campaign, which struck deep into central Asia, was doomed to failure).

Yet other stories from classical times reveal a hazy knowledge of the river's geography—among them the legend of Jason and his quest for the Golden Fleece. This epic story has been worked and reworked by a number of poets and playwrights, some of whom could have done with a good map when spinning their tales. One version of the story tells how, after winning control of the fleece at Colchis, Jason and his fellow Argonauts supposedly sailed their boat out of the Black Sea and along the lower Danube—and, impossibly, finished up in the Adriatic. Some writers recorded that the Argonauts performed this feat by physically dragging their boat overland from the Danube to the sea, finding the time to lay the foundation stone of the Slovenian city of Ljubljana on the way; others maintain that the seafarers kept going upstream along the Danube until they were able to join the Rhône, which, according to a muddled understanding of the geography of Europe's rivers, supposedly diverged from the Danube's upper course to provide a direct link to the Mediterranean.

While these tales were being spun, musings on the river by the Greek historian and geographer Strabo and the Roman author Pliny were of a more academic nature: these writers wondered exactly where the Roman Danuvius (the name given to the upper course of the river) became the Ister (the Greek name for the lower course), and pondered the confusing notion that in their era, the first century AD, either name could be used to refer to the river's entire length.

## DIVISION AND DISUNITY

As empires expanded the Danube became a natural marker of territorial boundaries. Alexander the Great chose the Danube and another great river, the Indus, to mark the limits of his empire. Later on, the river formed part of the *Limes Romanus*, the ancient boundary line of the Roman Empire in Europe. Along most of the river's length, from southern Germany to the delta, Roman soldiers defended their empire against the barbarian tribes living beyond the *limes*. Fleets of ships ferried men and supplies between riverside camps; one of these ships was unearthed from the mud of a Danube tributary in Germany in the 1980s, while major riverside military encampments such as Carnuntum in Austria, Aquincum in Hungary and Novae in Bulgaria have survived as important archaeological sites.

For a short period, under Emperor Trajan, one of the barbarian tribes, the Dacians, was subdued, and the *Pax Romana* was extended to territory on the north bank of the river; but mostly the barbarian tribes proved a menace to the Romans, and the undoing of their empire began when mass barbarian incursions swept across the river in the fifth century AD. In the centuries that followed the Roman era, the lower course of the river marked the boundaries, at various times, of the Byzantine, Carolingian, Hungarian and Ottoman empires. And the Danube's role as a linguistic and political divide continues to this day. Currently the river forms international frontiers for around 600 miles of its length—principally around Romania, where it marks that country's borders with Bulgaria, Serbia and Ukraine. Upstream from here, Slovakia and Hungary are also separated by the river, and in recent decades the new boundary lines of an increasingly fractured continent have been drawn along its length, dividing in particular Serbia from Croatia after the violent break-up of the former Yugoslavia.

Yet through all this period of division, the river has continued to form a vital artery, principally for the movement of trade and armies. During the era of the First Crusade, in the eleventh century, Peter the Hermit and Godfrey of Bouillon led their armies along the Danube to Belgrade before cutting across the Balkans en route to Constantinople. During a later Crusade, the emperor Frederic Barbarossa left a trail of destruction behind him as he marched his army downstream along the Danube valley. In the centuries that followed the tables were decisively turned: Muslim armies from Turkey swept up the river from the Balkans to threaten Christian Europe just as the Franks had once travelled downstream to engage the Muslim states of the Levant in conflict.

As, in the sixteenth century, the Ottoman Empire expanded relentlessly towards Vienna, the Turks used the Danube to ferry supplies to their new military bases in Belgrade and Budapest. A string of great riverside fortresses, intended to provide a bulwark against the advancing Turks, was hastily constructed by the Habsburgs between the delta and Bratislava.

Many of the forts remain to this day, a legacy of hundreds of years of Turkish expansion in Europe that came to an end only in the nineteenth century. Until then, dealing with the Turkish threat formed the most important plank of Habsburg foreign policy. And the river played its part in the diplomacy as well as the battles. One of the most glorious boats ever to sail on the Danube was the one built in Vienna to ferry the Christian ambassador Johann Ludwig von Kufstein downstream so that he could make peace with the Turks in 1628. The hull of the boat was painted in an array of gaudy colours, while the leaded windows that punctured the sides were hung with plush curtains and the boat's interior design echoed that of a Habsburg palace. In the centuries that followed von Kufstein's diplomatic endeavours, as the Turks retreated further into the Balkans, the Habsburg Empire continued to maintain gunboats on the river, and Britain even maintained a small naval fleet on the Danube for a time, stationed in the delta.

The role of the Danube as an artery for armies continued well into the twentieth century. In the summer of 2003 a severe drought pushed the waters of the lower Danube to record lows, revealing rusting hulls of German ships from the Second World War lying high and dry on the river bed, close to the Serbian village of Kladovo. The ships had been sunk by their German crews to try to halt the advance of the Soviet Black Sea fleet along the river in 1944. On their re-appearance, the ships, with their gun turrets still intact, drew hundreds of sightseers; some resourceful locals even plundered the rusting vessels for still usable electric cables.

## TRADE AND COMMERCE: THE RIVER'S LIFEBLOOD

Trade, like military traffic, has been a feature of the river for thousands of years, and, while armies no longer use the river as a handy thoroughfare through the continent, industrial barges are still very much a feature of the Danube. During the grim centuries of European disunity, trade along the Danube tied the disparate parts of the continent together, albeit by a spindly, watery thread. The trade continues to this day. Almost every riverside town, from Regensburg in Germany to Galați in Romania, has a busy dockyard or a grimy harbour. Chemical works and steel mills spread out along the flat land beside the river and make use of the waterway for delivery of their raw materials. New canals at either end of the river—one in Germany linking the waterway with the Rhine and the other in Romania providing a short cut to the Black Sea—have been opened in the past thirty years specifically for barge traffic.

But these modern barges are merely the descendants of ships that have ferried goods along the river for hundreds of years. In the eighteenth century an English musicologist named Charles Burney, travelling along the German and Austrian reaches of the river, remarked on the wooden barges laden with produce that he saw being dragged upstream by teams of horses plodding along the banks; the same barges were floated back downstream by skilled bargemen who steered the craft in the swift current. Salt was a major commodity that was traded this way, and in the Middle Ages cities such as Linz and Passau grew into wealthy mercantile centres: "We met this morning a gang of boats, laden with salt, from Salzburg and Passau, dragged up the river by more than forty horses, a man on each," Burney recalled in his book about his travels. The "expense is so great," he went on, "as to enhance the price of that commodity above four hundred percent."

Other commodities that have long been traded are timber and stone. To this day, timber yards along the more forested stretches of the river load newly felled trees into waiting barges, and in the 1930s Patrick Leigh Fermor watched dozens of barges moving heavy cargoes of timber and rock along the great waterway in Austria. "These cargoes were quarried and felled from the banks," he wrote in *A Time of Gifts*. "Huge horseshoe-cavities were blasted out of the cliffs, and the mountains, from the water's edge to their summits, were a never-ending stand of timber... scattered with thousands of felled tree-trunks like the contents of spilled match boxes... From the riverside, every mile or so, came the zing of a circular saw and the echo of planks falling."

In recent centuries, as society has become more mobile, passenger traffic on the river has also grown steadily. By the sixteenth and seventeenth centuries Ulm Boxes, the wooden flat-bottomed boats built at Ulm in southern Germany, were accepting passengers for the ride from Ulm to Austria and beyond. In 1829 the first Danube steamship company that specifically operated passenger vessels was founded in Vienna by two British entrepreneurs, who had the first vessels built in kit form in England and then constructed on the water in Vienna. By 1900 the Donau-Dampf-schiff-fahrts-Gesellschaft (DDSG) maintained nearly 200 steam powered vessels and ran services along the entire length of the river. Slightly smaller was the Hungarian shipping company, Mahart, whose fleet of steamships on the Danube and Lake Balaton was originally owned and operated by Hungarian Railways.

Both companies exist today, albeit in a rump form. Mahart operates hydrofoils from Budapest to Vienna, and DDSG operates passenger services between Deggendorf in southern Germany and the Hungarian capital, via Passau, Linz, Vienna and Bratislava. (Both companies also operate separate freight services.) Upstream from Deggendorf and downstream from Budapest passenger services nowadays tend to be limited to tourist ships that run up and down scenic parts of the river, such the Iron Gates gorge, or the more adventurous cruise ships that give their passengers a glimpse of the Danube beyond the well-travelled reach between Passau and Budapest.

SPREADING THE WORD

The Danube has featured in literature since the days of Jason and the Argonauts and the musings of Pliny and Strabo. Poets, in particular, have been inspired by the great waterway for centuries. The most famous twentieth-century poem inspired by the river is probably "On the Danube", written by the Budapest-born poet Attila József. He describes the river as "turbulent, wise and great" in the poem, which develops into a lyrical paean to Hungary's forefathers after an opening in which the poet sits on the bottom step of a wharf in Budapest and watches a melon-rind float by on the current. An earlier and more ethereal poem, this time in German, was written by the romantic poet Friedrich Hölderlin (1770-1843) and is entitled "Der Ister". It describes the river banks as the home of gods whose existence was lost to those alienated by modern times. "It lives in beauty... I'm not surprised this distantly gleaming river made Hercules its guest," Hölderlin wrote. In 1942 the controversial German philosopher Martin Heidegger gave an entire lecture course on this comparatively short poem at Freiburg University, and in 2004 his lecture course became the inspiration for a remarkable documentary film entitled *The Ister*. This three-hour odyssey upstream along the river is a meditation on philosophy, archaeology, ecology, history, politics, war, time, poetry, engineering, myth—and the Holocaust. Turning a geographical journey into a philosophical one, *The Ister* must be not only the most extraordinary film ever made about the Danube, but also one of the few films ever to be inspired by a lecture course.

The river has inspired German artists and composers as well as writers. Strauss composed his *Blue Danube* waltz, Wagner adapted the *Song of the Nibelungs* as an opera cycle, and in the late Middle Ages the scenery along the upper course of the river inspired a whole school of painting known as the Danube School. But the Danube of Strauss, Wagner and Hölderlin is the Danube of *Mitteleuropa*, that hard-to-define heart of the European continent centred on former Habsburg cities such as Vienna, Budapest and Prague, and speaks of a rarefied and refined level of cultural mores. The Danube is not solely a river of *Mitteleuropa*; yet it is difficult to ascribe a precise cultural legacy to the waterway as it flows beyond Hungary and into the Balkans. In fact, until comparatively recently, the lower Danube has been associated with poverty and near-barbarism. Negley Farson, an American journalist who navigated a yawl down the Danube in the 1930s, wrote in his book *Sailing across Europe* that "for one thousand miles of its course the river flows through the most primitive part of the white man's world." With the same crass cultural superiority (racist to today's sensibilities), the English writer and critic Sacheverell Sitwell wrote in his book *Romanian Journey* (published at the same time as Farson's) that the river simply "passes out of civilisation into nothingness".

This somewhat schizoid cultural legacy makes it difficult to ascribe a personality to the river that acknowledges its passage through the backwaters of Bulgaria and Romania as well as sophisticated cities such as Budapest and Vienna. What exactly does the Danube stand for? The Nile, after all, is the great river of Egypt; the Thames is England's river; the Yangtze is China's; the Amazon drains the world's greatest rainforest; the Mississippi, the river of Tom Sawyer and Huck Finn, defines the American Midwest; the Congo is the river at the heart of Africa. But the Danube, with its multiple historical and linguistic associations, seems much harder to pin down.

But that is changing. If the Danube does have a unique and unifying culture, it is political and contemporary, rather than historical or cultural: for, after centuries of demarcating Europe's fracture lines—between the Ottoman and Habsburg empires, between communist and democratic Europe, and latterly between warring republics of the former Yugoslavia—the river now seems to be emblematic of a newly resurgent, united and dynamic continent. Cities along its length such as Bratislava and Budapest are the very embodiment of this spirit; many of the countries along the river, namely Germany, Slovakia, Croatia, Serbia, Ukraine and Moldova, have only existed in their current form for the past two decades or so; and even the political entities of Austria, Bulgaria, Romania and Hungary are creations of the twentieth century.

All the countries along the river are members of the European Union or aspire to being so. Meanwhile the divisions created by the Iron Curtain and the expansions of long-dead empires are quickly being forgotten. As central and eastern Europe confront the twenty-first century it looks as if the Danube, the old river of division and disharmony, might just be the thread that can pull the continent together.

*Part One*

# THE RISING RIVER

## FROM THE BLACK FOREST TO PASSAU

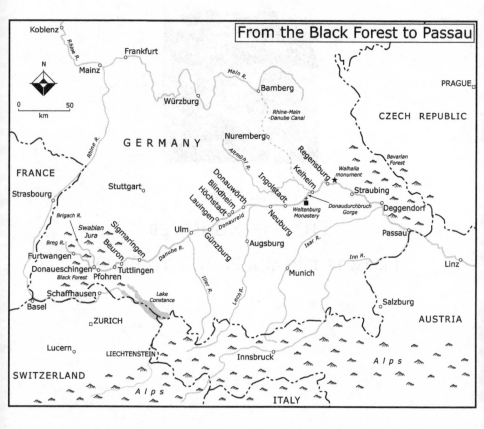
From the Black Forest to Passau

## Chapter One

# THROUGH THE BLACK FOREST AND SWABIA

### IN THE BEGINNING

Tucked away in the south-west corner of Germany is the small town of Donaueschingen. Everything here is as it is expected to be: pristine ochre-and-white churches, their squat towers capped by onion domes, overlook a fussy network of sloping streets and irregularly shaped squares. There is a *Rathaus* (town hall), a brewery and a pocket-sized palace built of grey stone, a reminder that Germany was once a patchwork of states ruled over by squabbling potentates who sprinkled the country with castles and palaces just like this one. Bubbling away beside the gardens of the palace is a channel that seems too big to be called a stream, but too narrow, too

tame to be called a river. This is the Brigach, whose name recalls the Briganti, the tribe that lived in southern Germany during Roman times.

The most useful task to which the waters of the Brigach are put seems to be in the brewing of the local beer, named Fürstenberg after the minor aristocratic dynasty that built the nearby palace. The dynasty has long-since gone and their former home is now the haunt of tour groups; but the brewery still produces a prodigious output, which is stacked in crates outside its pink-and-cream façade. East of the brewery and the palace the Brigach follows a straight course through a bland landscape that is half town, half country: one side is given over to riding paddocks and sports grounds, while on the other is a scruffy patch of woodland that fails to smother the grumble of traffic on a distant arterial road. It is a reach of waterway as unremarkable as it is possible to imagine. But then, some mile and a half from the centre of Donaueschingen, there is a brief stretch of water on which cartographers have heaped an almost monumental significance. At a spot overlooked by a small clump of trees, the Brigach is joined by another channel, the Breg—and at the precise point where the rivers merge, the Danube begins.

If an "official" starting point of the river is needed, then it is this muddy "V" of grassy soil where the Breg and the Brigach come together. A clutch of silver birches cling to the shallow bank, while some rusting and unidentifiable pieces of iron protrude from the water, washed by the merging torrents of water. The only suggestion that this might be a significant place is the presence of a sculpture of gleaming white marble that overlooks the grassy V: surmounting a rectangular plinth is the reclining figure of a woman with broad flowing skirts who watches benignly as an infant, tucked up against her lap, tips an urn on its side, letting loose a watery cascade. The small child is, of course, the Danube; the woman, rather less obviously, represents the Barr, the region of rolling hills and lush farming country that surrounds Donaueschingen. An inscription on the plinth indicates that this sculpture was placed here by a local couple, Max and Irma Egon, to celebrate their *Goldene Hochzeit* (Golden Wedding) on 18 June 1939. Their memorial is polished and cared for, but incongruous. Behind it is a private garden crammed with children's slides and swings; adjacent to this family home is a dog kennels that is the source of a continuous stream of bad-tempered barking and scrapping.

It is difficult to imagine a more ignominious starting point for a great

river than this. But it is definitely the start: on the bank opposite the marble statue is the first stone marker bearing the name *Donau*, the German name for the river. It takes the form of a chunky slab of grey stone smeared with moss, and indicates that the marker is 2,779 kilometres (1,726 miles) from the mouth of the river, and 610 metres above sea level. Just beyond the stone marker are two more "firsts" to tick off: a dribble of water in an artificial drainage gutter forms the Danube's first tributary, while the first bridge over the river is a low structure of poured concrete that carries Donaueschingen's bypass—as humdrum a structure as you would expect for an arterial road that skirts a fairly ordinary country town. Beyond the traffic lanes the river flows across a flat, spongy landscape of grazing land peppered with stands of trees and traversed by marching phalanxes of pylons.

Surely the Danube should have a more evocative beginning than this? Is the start of the river not announced by something more than a marble statue overlooked by a bypass? Well, the tapering "V" of land and the clutch of silver birches is one of three (or, at a pinch, four) places that lay claim to be the start of the Danube. Level-headed cartographers count this place as the river's beginning; but dreamers and romantics turn their back on the Breg-Brigach confluence and head back upstream along the Brigach for a mile and a half, to the gardens of the palace that the Fürstenberg family built for themselves in the sixteenth century. These gardens are as formal and symmetrical as the palace that flanks them. After shuffling dutifully past ornate tapestries and racks of eighteenth-century porcelain, visitors can make their way down to the banks of the Brigach through carefully tended lawns sprinkled with topiary bushes. Tucked into a corner of the gardens, overlooked by a wing of the palace and the twin onion domes of the neighbouring Johanniskirche, a circular enclosure surrounded by a stone wall shelters a deep pool that is known as the *Donauquelle*: the Danube spring. This is where the spirit of the Danube rises from the earth, like some watery deity—even if the place is not the actual start of a blue line drawn on a map that bears the river's name.

The spring is the palace's (and the town's) most remarkable feature. "Hier entspringt die Donau," announces an information board placed next to it, before informing readers that long before they came to this spot, their predecessors included the Emperor Tiberius (in 15 BC), the Holy Roman Emperor Maximilian (in 1499), and the last German Kaiser, Wilhelm II, who made a number of visits here in the years before 1913. But the scene must have changed since the days of Tiberius and Maximilian. The pool itself is deep and green, its bottom speckled with coins; bubbles burble from an unseen source deep within the pool, whose surface, devoid of weeds, sparkles when the sun shines. A grille at one end of the pool lets the water pass into a tunnel that leads under the palace gardens and empties into the Brigach.

The stone balustrade that the Fürstenbergs built around the pool is lined with plaques that announce that the spot is 678 metres above sea level and 2,840 kilometres (1,764 miles) from the Black Sea. (This second figure clearly conflicts with the figure on the marker post at the Breg-Brigach confluence; that is only two kilometres away, but the two figures suggest that it is 61 kilometres distant, a disparity that arises from the two different methods of measuring the Danube from its mouth to its source.) Overlooking the pool is another statue of "Mother" Barr: robed and earnest, her thrusting finger points eastwards towards the Black Sea; her other arm is draped around a semi-naked androgynous youth while a distracted infant at their feet blows a horn. *This* makes for a much more evocative start to the river than a muddy piece of land and a clutch of silver birches.

So does the Donauquelle mark the river's true beginning? The Fürstenbergs certainly claimed it did, and today the tour guides back them to the hilt, as they shepherd their groups from coach to palace to gardens and back again via the spring and its sparkling pool. But it is hard to ignore other claimants: officialdom cites the Breg-Brigach confluence as the start––and it is clear to all that these two rivers must start somewhere, too. Is not the true source of the Danube up in the hills somewhere, one wonders, where the Breg or the Brigach begins life as a gushing stream?

The main argument that is always mustered in favour of the Donauquelle being the true source of the Danube is that the spring here never dries up. In exceptionally rainless summers, both the Breg and the Brigach turn into muddy ditches—but water continues to gush from the pool in the Fürstenberg's gardens, come what may. Visiting Donaueschingen it is somewhat hard to believe this: the Breg and the Brigach are deep enough to make wading across them difficult, and to lob a stone from one bank to the other of either river would require a hefty throw. These are not rivers that look as if they are in the habit of drying up, even occasionally. The Fürstenbergs persevered with their claim and created, in popular imagination, an almost mystical devotion to their spring as the Danube's true source. Their success has outlasted them and is attested to by the myriad of plaques hanging on the stone wall that surrounds the circular pool, each one bearing a poem or aphorism that unites this spot with a country and a culture hundreds or thousands of miles downstream. One plaque carries an extract, in German and Hungarian, from Attila József's poem "On the Danube"; another, placed here in 1987 by the fourteenth Bulgarian League for *Menschenrechte* (Human Rights), celebrates this place as the "spring of the... glorious river that links Bulgaria to the heart of Europe." There are similar contributions from Slovakia and Romania. And all this in a location that until 1720 was little more than a collection of farm buildings spread over a boggy hollow with a useful fresh water source in their midst. It was in that year that Prince Joseph Wilhelm Ernst of Fürstenberg came down from his feudal castle in the hills to oversee the planning of his palace and princely capital on the banks of the Brigach. Now the town that he founded is typically south German; people go to bed early, even on Saturdays, and awake to a riot of church bells on Sunday morning.

Donaueschingen's fame as the source of the Danube ensures that the place has always been a cut above the rest of provincial Baden-Württemberg. Sophistication comes in the form of the Donauhalle, a concert venue that hosts a festival of contemporary music every October, where Hindemith, Boulez, Stockhausen and Stravinsky all had works premiered; a somewhat dowdier antidote to the high culture of the *Donaueschinge Musiktage* is provided by the souvenir shops lining the road opposite the Fürstenberg Palace, stacked high with fussy cuckoo clocks and Danube mugs and bookmarks.

Browsing among the souvenirs, dodging the curling lines of trippers filing from the buses, or relaxing in the sunshine with a glass of Fürstenberg beer in Donaueschingen's long and rather ordinary main square, it is hard not to be seduced by the town's claim to be somewhere rather special. But, truth to tell, Donaueschingen has for decades—if not centuries—been the subject of a whispering campaign orchestrated by the residents of the much smaller town of Furtwangen, some eighteen miles upstream along the River Breg. Furtwangen yaps away at Donaueschingen's heels like an overexcited sausage dog. It claims it, and not Donaueschingen, is truly the first town on the River Danube. Furtwangen's supporters point out that of the two rivers that merge just to the east of Donaueschingen, the Breg is the longer and has the highest source—and that the mountain hollow just above Furtwangen where the Breg begins life as a gushing spring is the highest place where the waters of the River Danube flow over open ground.

The claim is supported with vigour. Drivers who make the half-hour journey to Furtwangen from Donaueschingen are immediately signposted to the smaller town's rival Donauquelle, which is reached by a narrow road that winds up through hills and forests; snow covers the ground here until Easter and for much of the time access to the spring is only possible in a vehicle equipped with snow chains. Even before reaching it, this place seems like a more genuine beginning to a river. The road stops beside a busy Black Forest inn, the Kolmenhof, where rooftop solar panels peek out from behind traditional timber gables; inside, brusque ladies in floral-print aprons serve hikers and trippers with plates piled high with girth-expanding piles of gravy-smothered pork, potatoes and cabbage.

Adjacent to the entrance to the inn is an obelisk onto which a crude map of the Danube has been etched: a curvy blue streak whose beginning is clearly and proudly marked as being Furtwangen, not Donaueschingen. From the obelisk a slippery path leads to a fold in the hillside shrouded by trees, where a trickle of water emerges from behind a grey slab of stone. "Hier entspringt der Hauptquellfluß der Donau: die Breg," maintains a plaque nearby; "an Dieser Quelle beginnt die Geographischelängenmessung der Donau." We are 1,078 metres above sea level here, the plaque helpfully tells us, and 2,888 kilometres (1,794 miles) from the Black Sea. Beat that, Donaueschingen! Off the trickle of water flows, along the first of those 2,888 kilometres, along a shallow unspectacular valley sprinkled with farms and yet more pseudo-rustic inns. Claudio Magris, who discusses the sources of the Danube at length in his classic 1986 book *Danube*, writes that here in the Black Forest the water of the Breg "glitters in the grass... the spring flows quietly out, the green of the trees is good, and so is the smell. The traveller feels rather clumsy and small, aware of the superior objectivity in which he is framed. Is it possible that all those little trickles in a field are the Danube, the river of superlatives?" Magris contends that up here, seduced by the clear mountain air heavy with the scent of conifers, it is difficult not to believe in the veracity of the tireless campaign waged by a certain Dr. Ohrlein, the local land-owning bigwig: that it is this place, and not the distant upstart of Donaueschingen, that holds the true claim as the river's beginning.

A short stroll up the rise behind the spring is a ridge marking the watershed between the Rhine and the Danube, and so between the North Sea and the Black Sea. The crest of this major European hydrological divide is marked by a tiny chapel, the Martinskapelle, whose steep grey roof and whitewashed walls sit picturesquely framed against a thick stand of conifers. Yet another plaque here mentions a visit of the Roman Emperor Tiberius—although it is difficult to imagine him coming all the way up here just to look at a spring. But apart from the spring and the chapel and the inn, there is little to see here; no tour buses make it this far, and the place is given over to smaller groups of skiers and walkers—and those curious enough to seek out the "other" Danube spring that rivals the more popular one in Donaueschingen.

Five miles downstream from the spring, along the widening Breg, the small town of Furtwangen lies draped across low hills, its apartment blocks rising up slopes crowned by thick green forest: a true town of the German Schwarzwald. There is a clock museum, full of whirring cuckoo clocks (a Black Forest invention rather than a Swiss one) and a sense that the town is only a generation or so removed from being a true mountain settlement.

Donaueschingen, on the other hand, has a mainline railway station with direct trains to Frankfurt, Dortmund, Düsseldorf and Hamburg—an unconvincing sense of being in the thick of things for a place that claims to be the start of a great river. And by the time it reaches Donaueschingen, the Breg is wide enough to be counted as a river in its own right; it is surely the Danube in all but name, and Donaueschingen's claim to be the river's starting point begins to look more and more like the carefully crafted work of a self-promoting minor branch of aristocracy, or the pickiness of cartographers, rather than the genuine article.

Lastly—to complete this discussion of true beginnings—one final claimant deserves to be heard. The Breg's beginnings above Furtwangen are clearly revered, but what of those of the Brigach? In Donaueschingen, the Brigach is the wider of the two rivers; the Breg (or the Danube) is its tributary, rather than the other way around. But the Brigach is shorter than the Breg, and its source, an unnoticed and mercifully plaque-free patch of bogland some twelve miles from Donaueschingen, is much lower than the Breg's in terms of altitude. The Brigach has a champion in the form of a certain N. F. Breuninger, who wrote a treatise on the source of the Danube in 1718. He opted for the Brigach as the source only because he dipped his fingers in the channel and found its stream of water to be colder than that of the Breg. But he has garnered few supporters over the past three centuries, and his claims can safely be dismissed without too much fuss. The Brigach should not hold our attention any more—and nor should any more discussion over the Danube's true beginnings. It is time to return to the confluence of the Brigach with the Breg, to the marble statue and the *Donau* marker and the slew of pylons and the concrete bridge carrying the Donaueschingen bypass, and push on downstream along the first stretch of river that everyone agrees is called the Danube.

## CASTLES AND MONASTERIES IN THE SWABIAN JURA
One of the literary sensations of the 1860s in both Britain and America was a travel book entitled *A Thousand Miles in the Rob Roy Canoe*, the work of an Irishman named John MacGregor. Recounting the story of a journey

by canoe along the rivers of Europe, the title turned its author into a household name and inspired a bandwagon of similar books, such as Robert Louis Stevenson's *An Inland Voyage*. Those imitators have survived the test of time; MacGregor's book, these days, is barely in print. But his book has a special place among those titles that recount journeys along the Danube. Most authors, such as Patrick Leigh Fermor, who first saw the Danube at Ulm, or John Marriner, who followed the river from the Black Sea to Vienna, ignore the first reaches of the river; but MacGregor started his journey at Donaueschingen, taking a delight in seeing the river as it "toddled in zigzag turnings like a child" before it "roamed away... like free boyhood" deeper into southern Germany. No other book recounts the craggy scenery and the remote valleys of the Upper Danube as MacGregor's does, and his descriptions of hard-working farming folk and villages that seem to be scarcely removed from the Middle Ages have ensured him a unique status among Danube travellers.

MacGregor called his book the "log of a charming cruise in a small canoe". The vessel in question was built for him in 1865 by Searles of Lambeth (it is now in the National Maritime Museum in Greenwich). Although principally known as an author, MacGregor was something of a polymath, and over the course of his life he followed various careers as an explorer, a climber, a sharp shooter, a cartoonist for *Punch* magazine and a musicologist, specializing in traditional music from Egypt and Syria. Somehow he also found the time to paddle his canoe along the Jordan and around the Azores—and write books about those journeys too. In his later life he worked with impoverished children in Victorian London and lectured about his travels, often appearing with his canoe on stage and spicing up his talks with hammy theatricals; according to the writer Arthur Ransome, he possessed "a natural genius for publicity" by virtue of "his instinctive showmanship".

He was something of a showman on the water too: his kit was limited to a spirit stove, a wooden fork and spoon (carved at opposite ends of the same stem), a spare button and a change of clothes. In the canoe he wore a grey flannel Norfolk jacket, canvas wading shoes, blue spectacles and a straw boater. To break the ice when meeting people, he would show them his sketchbook or, more dramatically, set fire to a strip of magnesium ribbon and enjoy the reaction to the blinding glare. Sometimes, paddling low in the water, out of sight of workers toiling in the fields, he would break into a chorus of *Rule Britannia*, and then slip away before anyone could work out where the sound was coming from. He caused a stir in every town he came to; not surprisingly, his departure would often be greeted with gunfire and shouting, and a chorus of bells and whistles.

The first part of *A Thousand Miles in the Rob Roy Canoe* recounts John MacGregor's journey from London to Donaueschingen. In addition to canoeing along the Thames in London, and then the Rhine, the *Rob Roy* was also manhandled into railway wagons and on to oxcarts, to complete much of its journey overland. Donaueschingen itself, when MacGregor came to it, was in the midst of a great song festival being held in the Fürstenberg Palace. After enjoying the hospitality of the locals, MacGregor set out to investigate the conundrum of the river's true beginning, which was "by no means agreed upon any more than the source of the Nile". MacGregor quizzed the locals as to the Danube's true origins—in vain. He looked at the Danube Spring in the palace grounds and paddled the *Rob Roy* up the Brigach and the Breg until there was too little water to allow the vessel to float. Interestingly, he describes a romantic lake adjacent to the Breg-Brigach confluence, of which no trace remains nowadays. According to MacGregor, this lake came complete with a secluded island, a waterwheel and statues. Then, tiring of the fruitless quest to determine the exact place where the Danube begins, he set off from the Breg-Brigach confluence on 28 August 1865, "[shooting] off like an arrow on a river delightfully new".

The river curves through lush farmland, fertile but featureless, as it makes its first tentative steps eastwards from Donaueschingen. This region of southern Germany is known as Schwaben (Swabia to English speakers), once a medieval duchy but now obliterated from administrative maps and divided between the German *Länder* of Baden-Württemberg and Bavaria. MacGregor reckons that very soon after flowing out of Donaueschingen the river has acquired a width and a volume of water akin to that of the Thames at Henley. The course of the river here is followed by trains on the Donaubahn, a single-track railway line whose bumpy two-car diesel trains are as far removed from Deutsche Bahn's slick ICE intercity services as it is possible to imagine. The railway crisscrosses the river continuously, so that the channel is on the right, then the left, then on the right again, of the train.

From the train window the scenery remains rather drab, yet Mac-Gregor's description of the river gushes with the enthusiasm that accompanies the start of any journey. "It winds with serpentine smoothness," he writes, "with waving sedge on the banks and silken sleepy weeds in the water... pretty painted butterflies float on the sunbeams, and fierce-looking dragonflies shimmer in the air." At Pfohren, the first village through which the river passes, a stocky, pointy-roofed castle known as Entenburg rises from its banks, the first of dozens of castles built beside the river between here and the Black Sea. But this is no impenetrable rock-top fortress; those come further downstream. Instead, Entenburg is a hybrid between a castle and a country house, and, it turns out, another Fürstenberg foundation, built by a scion of the same family that built the palace beside the spring in Donaueschingen. Nowadays the walls are smothered by ivy and the place is given over to an art gallery and a sculpture park that are unfortunately as unremarkable as the countryside from which the building rises.

Beyond Pfohren the train bumps over a succession of steel girder bridges that span the frothing Danube, and every few minutes the carriages roll to a halt at yet another deserted country station. But soon the countryside closes in as the river begins to cut through a limestone plateau known as the Swabian Jura. One hundred and forty million years ago these rocks formed the floor of a broad sea; as the plateau rose, so the river sliced down into the thick grey limestone, creating a narrow winding gorge as it weaved from side to side. Nowadays the road, railway and river jostle for space on the narrow valley floor; above them, precipitous walls rise to toothy crags of pale grey rock. This area is known as the Bergland Junge Donau—the mountain country of the young Danube—and forms the first properly scenic area through which the river passes. "A grand panorama of river beauties," is how John MacGregor described it, complaining that the scenery was so dramatic that it disrupted his concentration on paddling the canoe along the dividing and often rocky channels into which the river sometimes split. "Few rivers I have seen surpass this upper Danube, and I have visited many pretty streams," he continued. "The wood is so thick, the rock is so quaint and high and varied, the water so clear, and the grass so green."

At Tuttlingen the river is swelled by its first proper tributary, the Elta. According to MacGregor, this place boasted "a good inn and a bad pavement, tall houses, all leaning here and there, big, clumsy, honest-looking men... very fat horses and pleasant-looking women, a bridge, and numerous schoolboys." The boys, for whom MacGregor's passing through their town must have seemed like the event of a lifetime, helped him find an inn to spend the night, and gathered on the river bank early the next morning eager to watch the canoe set off—only to find they could not because MacGregor did not depart until after the start of morning school.

Hikers begin filling the train beyond Tuttlingen. Indeed, they seem to be the only passengers getting on and off at the tiny country stations, their raingear flapping in the wet wind. In spring, it says in the hiking guide, you can walk in the Swabian Jura amid a blanket of snowdrops and narcissi that cover the slopes between the river and the crags; but a rainy day bestows the imposing cliffs with an aura as dour and as iron-grey as the sky, and it is tempting to think that the cliffs might close in on themselves at any moment and swallow whole the narrow valley with its little train and its villages and its twisting, foaming river.

These reaches of the river reminded MacGregor of the valley of the River Wye on the borders of England and Wales, particularly the "white rocks and dark trees, and caverns, crags and jutting peaks you meet near Tintern". In his own eccentric way he enjoyed the "magnificent crags that reached high up on both sides, and impenetrable forests that rung with echoes from the canoeist's shout in the glee of freedom and hardy exercise." Interestingly, another writer, Bernard Newman, who cycled the entire length of the Danube from Donaueschingen to the Black Sea in 1934, drew comparisons with exactly the same English river. "I might have been in the finer parts of the Wye Valley," he wrote in his book *Blue Danube*. "Little ravines, hidden in the beechwoods, beckoned to me to investigate their mysteries."

It is no wonder that, nearly one thousand years ago, the forbidding and secret valley of the Danube as it flows through the Swabian Jura provided an attractive location for the foundation of a monastery. The community of monks who came to Beuron in the year 1080 is still here today, their austere monastery perched on a low bluff that glowers over a spacious amphitheatre of cliffs formed by a sweeping curve of the river. The community here has had its ups and downs—for sixty years during the nineteenth century it was in fact dissolved—but since the refounding of the monastery in 1862 by two monks who gained the support and patronage of a widowed Hohenzollern princess, the monastery has been in robust health, and nowadays it supports twenty other monasteries and convents scattered across Europe.

The grimly imposing buildings at Beuron are spread over a large area, enclosing courtyards and private gardens just visible through gates and walls; the centrepiece of the complex is an airy baroque church with a cream-coloured nineteenth century façade and an onion-domed bell tower. A regular trickle of the faithful and the curious pass up the steps and through its doors throughout the day, making their way towards the Chapel of Grace, home to an exceptionally moving fifteenth-century *pietà* fashioned from limewood. This statue, depicting a seated Mary supporting the body of the crucified Christ on her lap, hangs above the altar at one end of the purpose-built chapel; every Whit Monday it becomes the object of veneration of thousands of pilgrims, thanks to the foresight of the Benedictines who reinstituted the pilgrimage here in 1863. The chapel in which the pietà is housed is built in Byzantine style, awash with swirling geometric designs, bold colours and broad curves designed to guide the eyes upwards to the central dome. During the pilgrimage the small town that clings to the skirts of the monastery must be swamped with people, and the tiny railway station with its bumping *Donaubahn* trains barely able to cope.

The rest of the year, however, Beuron slumbers quietly in the depths of its lush green valley, the only disturbance being the muffled froth and hiss of the Danube, and the sound of the almost continuously tolling monastery bell; those who manage to make it to a service here are treated to some of the best examples of Gregorian chant in the world—another tradition revived by the Benedictines in the nineteenth century.

Beyond Beuron the secret valley closes in on itself as the river twists and turns through the thick, 700-foot thick wedge of limestone that forms the heart of the Swabian Jura. On both sides of the Danube the cliffs culminate in craggy grey fangs of rock that poke up between the thick stands of conifers. Every so often a castle is glimpsed from the valley floor, occupying the most inaccessible of crags and reached by steep rambles up through the forest, along logging tracks that zigzag their way up the hillside. The whitewashed walls of Wildenstein Castle are visible from afar; in 1922 this fortress (yet another former Fürstenberg residence) was converted into a splendidly situated youth hostel, its battlements encompassing a view that takes in a whole swath of the Danube valley. On the opposite cliff, Werenwag Castle has been converted into a private and palatial residence, its steep red roofs and cream-coloured wings draped over a resistant knuckle of grey rock that millions of years of exposure to the ravages of wind and flowing water have failed to wear down. But Werenwag is the last of the craggy rock-top castles—at least for a while. Because just beyond it, the valley opens up, the scenery lowers, and suburbs and shopping centres suddenly can be seen from the train window rather than woods and cliffs. At last, the Donaubahn has drawn into somewhere substantial.

## SIGMARINGEN

In 1865, when John MacGregor made his epic journey along the Danube by canoe, Germany still consisted of a loose confederation of semi-independent and often quarrelsome states. Since the very early Middle Ages these motley dukedoms, kingdoms, princedoms and prince-bishoprics had been ruled over by aristocratic potentates who, from the time of Charlemagne to the era of Napoleon, were nominally under the political thumb of the Holy Roman Emperor. That title was abolished in 1806 by Napoleon, during the most vigorous phase of French expansionism. But Napoleon's winning spree was quickly over, and his defeat at Waterloo meant that his ambitious plans to redraw the political map of Germany never reached fruition. So, although the imperial title was gone, the German confederation was still limping along in MacGregor's day—but only just. When he paddled his way along the Danube, radical change was clearly just over the horizon: Prussia, the largest and most powerful German state, was throwing its political weight around, and within five years of the publication of his book it had swallowed up the other states one by one to create a new European super-state known as Germany. The new nation was born in January 1871 when the Prussian King Wilhelm I was made its first kaiser; Wilhelm's ambitious first minister, Otto von Bismarck, the orchestrator of unification, was appointed the country's first chancellor.

South Germany was always a more sluggish participant in the unification process than the north. Prussia and the Rhinelands had embraced the industrial revolution, and gradual economic union had heralded eventual political union; but the south remained resolutely agricultural, a land of peasant farmers toiling in conditions that were still virtually feudal, and Bismarck had to ignite a war with France to bring the obstinate southern states to heel. Centuries of political tradition in the south were overturned when a united Germany finally arose. Gone, now, were the independent

proto-states whose independence had been guarded so jealously through the centuries. Along the Danube, Donaueschingen had been in the hands of the Fürstenberg princes, whose castles are still scattered along the banks of the river's upper course. Further downstream, Passau was ruled by a powerful prince-bishop, and Bavarian riverside cities such as Ingolstadt were part of the Duchy (later Kingdom) of Bavaria.

Sigmaringen, the first sizeable town on the Danube, was ruled for 300 years by a Catholic family, the Hohenzollerns, major players in the politics of pre-unification Württemberg, and a junior branch of the more powerful (and avowedly Protestant) clan that had dominated Prussian politics since the late Middle Ages. By MacGregor's time, lands owned by the Sigmaringen Hohenzollerns extended as far as Canada, and members of the family had married into the ruling houses of Portugal and France, and provided the last dynastic line of Romanian kings.

The family seat had been at Sigmaringen since the family ousted their Habsburg rivals from the town in 1535; their magnificent castle, which they set about expanding over the centuries that followed, is still the town's most prominent feature. It overlooks the Danube from atop a rocky outcrop whose steep cliffs simply seem to sprout walls, turrets, towers and battlements as if they were leaves on a flowering plant, making the fortress look as if it is growing organically from the rock on which it is perched; an expression in brick and stone of the firm hold the Hohenzollerns once held over this part of Germany. Yet MacGregor was unimpressed. "Fancy a parish in London with a Prince all to themselves," he sneered after paddling through the town, admitting that he had "often laughed at this petty kingdom in geography books" (which, he admitted, nonetheless boasted "some of the most beautiful river scenery in the world"). Today, although aristocratic power has been consigned to the past, the castle and the pretty river views remain, and Sigmaringen is celebrated as being the most attractive small town along the entire course of the German Danube.

Although the Hohenzollerns originally conceived their castle as a redoubtable medieval fortress, the ravages of the Thirty Years War and a succession of disastrous fires have ensured that only small parts of the original building survive. In fact, with its steep red roofs and photogenic arrangement of fussy battlements, the place is more romantic folly than defensive fortress; its most recent rebuilding phase, in the late nineteenth century, took its inspiration from the multi-turreted fantasy castle of

Neuschwanstein built by "mad" King Ludwig in the Bavarian Alps. After unification, the Hohenzollerns went on living amid these fancy surroundings until the family was finally ousted by the Nazis in 1944; another castle, Wilflingen, was made available for them after its former occupant, Count von Stauffenberg, was executed for his part in a failed plot to kill Hitler. The new tenant at Sigmaringen was the government of Vichy France, which ruled the Nazi puppet state from this unlikely location (chosen as it was well out of the way of Allied bombing) for the last eight months of its existence.

After the war, the Hohenzollerns decided not to move back to their ancestral home; nowadays the surviving members of the clan live elsewhere in Sigmaringen and use their castle for private functions, keeping the place going by charging the hoi-polloi to shuffle around its courtyards and draughty corridors on the obligatory guided tour. The rooms are opulent and many offer tantalizing views of the river; the highpoint of the castle is a vast collection of armour and weaponry that borders on the fetishistic. The guided tour is unfortunately silent on how Marshal Pétain and his prime minister, Pierre Laval, lived during the Vichy era. Instead, the mechanically delivered commentary from the tour guide concentrates on the tapestries, the development of lavatory technology, the design of cutlery and the tale of how in 1893 a disastrous fire smouldered away in a forgotten corner of the castle for three days until someone noticed. A human bucket chain down to the Danube formed by loyal townsfolk was, however, no match for the spreading flames, and the fire was only extinguished when fire-fighting apparatus was brought to Sigmaringen from more than fifty miles away.

A few steps down from the entrance to the castle in Sigmaringen is a Renaissance-style building known as the Kunsthalle. It is another choice example of Hohenzollern whimsy. The high hammerbeam ceiling and creaky wooden floorboards certainly allow the place to exude an authentic Renaissance air; but in reality this is a pastiche of English Tudor architecture transplanted to the Danube valley, and dates wholly from the late nineteenth century. Elaborate gothic altarpieces and other ecclesiastical ephemera are displayed in the hall—plundered from churches all over Swabia—but more diverting are a group of paintings of the so-called Danube School, a tradition of landscape painting that evolved in southern Germany during the early years of the sixteenth century.

Work by artists of the Danube School can be seen all over Austria and Germany, in galleries and churches and museums. The paintings executed by members of the school are characterized by their depiction of verdant landscapes inspired by the scenery of the upper Danube. Many paintings on show in the Kunsthalle have a distinctive feature: they depict familiar biblical scenes transplanted from the arid landscapes of the Levant into the lushly forested countryside surrounding Sigmaringen. For instance, Michel Haider's *Dornenkrönung Christi* portrays a vivid scourging of Christ that takes place against a background of trees and forests and a genially snaking river that could easily be the Danube, while *Heimsuchung Mariae* shows Mary meeting her cousin Elizabeth amidst thick woodland with a churning river in the background that curls beneath grey limestone crags. Another painting in the Kunsthalle, by Hans Maler, portrays the appearance of the Angel Gabriel to Mary against a similar backdrop of river and forest, above which rises an unmistakably German town—steep red roofs clustering behind thick walls studded with round turrets.

Any pretence at a genuine biblical setting is abandoned in other ways, too. In *Dornenkrönung Christi,* the close-fitting hose, short tunics and pointed leather shoes worn by the scourgers turn them into unmistakably sixteenth-century, rather than first-century, torturers. And, like most paintings of the Danube School, the work juxtaposes scenes of earthy peasantry with those of Christian piety, something which Patrick Leigh Fermor comments on in *A Time of Gifts*. He writes of a painting by Wolf Huber, another artist of the Danube School, as featuring "Swabian peasant girls, bewildered gaffers with tangled beards, goodies with dumpling cheeks, crab-apple crones, marvelling ploughboys and puzzled woodmen—a cast of Danube rustics in fact, reinforced, in the wings, by a whole bumpkin throng." (Claudio Magris saw them in a different light, and was struck by the "bestial mobs, cruel snouts, obscene noses, [and] repulsive tongues" that fill the canvases: a "lacerating violence," he wrote, "plebeian and rudimentary.")

As Leigh Fermor also noted, Huber, Maler, Altdorfer and the other artists of the School executed their work in vivid colours—emerald greens, deep crimsons and peacock blues, the undimmed hues adding to the sense that the paintings are much more modern than they actually are. But in reality they date from the tail-end of the Middle Ages: the artists who made these works clearly wanted to create something radical and new, and their paintings still seem vibrant, striking and disturbing to this day. And at least one of the paintings in the Kunsthalle shocks in another way: the scourgers in *Dornenkrönung Christi* have absurdly hooked noses and wear an avid expression of mendacity and malice as they set about their grim task. Antisemitism of this nature has run like a poisoned thread through all aspects of German culture until comparatively recently, and seems brutally apparent in these extraordinary works of art in Sigmaringen.

## ULM: SPIRES AND BOXES

No journey along the Danube matches that of Patrick Leigh Fermor in terms of audacity and determination; and no written account of a Danube journey equals his in terms of literary style. In 1933, at the age of eighteen, Leigh Fermor abandoned his education at one of England's oldest public schools and set out to walk across Europe from the Hook of Holland to Constantinople. Much of his journey took him along the valley of the Danube: to Linz, Vienna and Bratislava, and then to Hungary and the great gorge known as the Iron Gates. In the opening section of *A Time of Gifts,* the first volume recounting his travels, he wrote that he wanted "to abandon London and England and set out across Europe like a tramp... I would travel on foot, sleep in hayricks in the summer, shelter in barns when it was raining or snowing and only consort with peasants or tramps." He saw his destination, the Black Sea, spreading "its mysterious and lopsided shape" on a map of Europe, at the "end of the windings of the Danube". Leigh Fermor lived on a pound a day, and not only did he spend many nights in barns and fields, he also slept in the houses of those whose curiosity about this wandering Englishman quickly turned to hospitality. His luggage consisted of little more than a change of clothes, and copies of the *Oxford Book of English Verse* and Volume One of Horace.

The rural Europe through which he travelled was, at that time, still home to a peasantry whose traditions had changed little in centuries. Remarkably, Leigh Fermor's travel memoirs were not published until decades after his journey. When it was published in 1977, *A Time of Gifts* was hailed as one of the greatest of contemporary travel books; readers had to wait another nine years for the publication of its sequel, *Between the Woods and the Water.* (A promised third volume, recounting the final part of the journey, is still yet to appear.) By the 1980s the Europe Leigh Fermor described had utterly vanished. But the long gap between his journey and the

books recounting it did nothing to dim Leigh Fermor's memory: in fact, it seems to enrich his prose, which is something akin to the literary equivalent of a cream-drenched plum pudding, bursting with vivid description and smothered in layers of anecdote and insight about everything from language to architecture.

Leigh Fermor first encountered the Danube at Ulm. It is an ancient city, located just over 25 miles downstream from Sigmaringen and situated at the point where the Iller, the Danube's first major tributary, joins the river after flowing north from the Bavarian Alps. Leigh Fermor recalls that the first sighting of the Danube was "a tremendous vision… It was a momentous encounter." He was here just after Christmas, when the river's central channel was close to being strangled by the ice slowly encroaching from both banks. He describes what remained of the liquid Danube as flowing "in the lee of battlements, dark under the tumbling flakes and already discoloured with silt." He goes on to admire the great medieval bridge over the river and the "roofs that retreated in confusion" behind the thick defensive walls. Rising over the cluster of roofs was the spire of the *Münster*, (minster) then and now the highest in the world, soaring 528 feet "into a moulting eiderdown of cloud". The next morning he did what every visitor to Ulm does: he climbed the spire and saw, on the distant horizon, the Swiss Alps—and in the foreground, moored along the river, the barges that for centuries had taken the goods in and out of Ulm and made the city rich.

At the time of Leigh Fermor's visit Ulm was the highest point of navigation on the Danube; since the early Middle Ages goods had been brought here from Vienna, Hungary and further afield, offloaded and sold—and Ulm's merchants took their cut, paid their taxes and made their city one of the wealthiest in Europe. It was they who provided the funds for the extraordinary Münster; they who endowed the place with one of the richest collections of medieval buildings in Europe; and they who jealously guarded Ulm's status as one of the "Free Cities" of the Holy Roman Empire, subservient only to the emperor and not some local potentate.

When Leigh Fermor came to Ulm he found it "suffused with a late medieval atmosphere" like nowhere else. Others have said the same: Bernard Newman likened it to "a city in a fairy story" and wrote of the "ancient houses" and "narrow and winding" streets of the old city. But then disaster struck: during a single air raid at the end of 1944, the medieval city was pulverized into dust. Nowadays Ulm is a mere shadow of its former self. The barges are gone, the river has been relegated to a tourist sideshow, and dreary rows of office blocks and department stores have risen where a glorious medieval city once stood.

No one arrives in Ulm by boat anymore. Most visitors come by rail: every few minutes another train rumbles over the Danube on a groaning steel girder bridge and pulls up in the city's bustling station. The plaza outside the station is a jumble of tramlines fringed by fast-food outlets and department stores, exuding the same sense of anodyne sterility that is common to many large German cities. The area immediately surrounding the Münster—the former Old Town—is no different. Miraculously, the Münster itself was spared the wartime firestorm, and its semi-transparent spire still bristles fussily with a hundred tiny spikes and turrets exactly as Leigh Fermor described it. In fact, the building was only completed in 1890; the spire was finished from plans that had been drawn up when building work first begun in 1377. Spectacular though it is, the church seems rather marooned nowadays, a gothic fancy adrift amid a sea of unremarkable redevelopment from the 1960s.

Things do not get much better a couple of hundred yards away, down at the river front. The Münster spire soars heavenwards behind a row of characteristic red-roofed houses lining the river bank. But the river is spanned by unremarkable modern bridges, the old city walls alongside the banks are crumbling and covered in graffiti, and the embankments themselves have been smothered by a network of mundane cycle tracks and jogging paths. In summer, a quay by the old city walls is the departure point for the tourist boats that chug up and down the Danube a little way, though in truth there is little to see, and in the end, wrecked by the bombs and abandoned by the barges, Ulm seems to turn its back on its river.

The city seems to take more pride in its famous offspring: Albert Einstein, for example, was born here in 1879, and Hans and Sophie Scholl, prominent figures in the anti-Nazi White Rose Resistance Movement before their executions in 1943, grew up in the city; a university is now named in their memory. Another famous Ulmer actually does have a connection with the river. In 1811 Albrecht Berblinger, the "Tailor of Ulm", constructed a pair of silk wings so that he could fly across the Danube. He failed, but a competition is still held every year for those who fancy that

they are blessed with better luck. A replica of Berblinger's flying machine is kept in the ground floor of the ornate town hall, which overlooks an attractive square between the Münster and the river bank.

Decoration on the exterior walls of the Rathaus gives an insight into Ulm's once close relationship with the river. One wall of the pastel building is adorned with an enormous piece of graffiti of a flat-bottomed wooden barge crammed with people, some of whom are steering the craft by means of oars dangling in the water, while others stand and watch the passing scenery—clearly, the vessel's passengers. In the centre of the craft is a makeshift wooden hut where the passengers would have sought shelter from rain and cold. This vessel is a trading and passenger boat known as an "Ulm box", and the city was once famous for them. The first boxes, intended solely for cargo, were built in 1572 by craftsmen who came here from Passau. They built the boats from spruce and pine, and made the vessels watertight by a method known as caulking: wooden chips and moss were stuffed into the gaps between each layer of timber, and then expanded in the water, making the structure watertight. These vessels (and others like them, named after other Danube towns, such as the Kelheimer boats from Kelheim) proved so popular that by the eighteenth century the vessels were also providing regular passenger services to Vienna, around eleven days away. The crafts were not propelled as such: they were simply steered by oarsmen, leaving the Danube's notoriously fast current to provide the pulling power. At the end of the journey the vessels were often broken up for timber; a different method of travel had to be sought by those who wanted to come back.

By all accounts a journey in an Ulm box was an uncomfortable one: "Very rudimental they are; huge in size, with flat bottoms... and a roofed house in the middle of their sprawling length" was how a nineteenth-century *Murray's Handbook* described them. "They are nothing better than wooden sheds floating in flat trays." One traveller who found out about Ulm boxes the hard way was an eighteenth-century English musicologist, Dr. Charles Burney, who travelled from Munich to Vienna along the Isar and the Danube in 1770 while he was researching his book *History of Music*; this became one of the most definitive books on the subject, but the actual account of Burney's journey in an Ulm box was published earlier under the title *Continental Travels*. "It was so cold [on the boat] that I could scarcely hold the pen," Burney complained. "My provisions grew short and stale, and there were none of any kind to be had [anywhere]".

In fact, the overall grimness of life on the box became a preoccupation for Burney: "I had now filled up the chinks of my cabin with splinters," he wrote,

> and with hay; got a button to the door, and reconciled myself to a filthy blanket... but alas! The essential failed: this was all external, and I wanted internal comfort! The last bit of my cold meat was fly-blown, to such a degree, that ravenous as I was, I threw it in the Danube.

He went on to describe the Germans as "barbarous and savage... except in the great trading towns, or where sovereign princes reside, the Germans seem very rude and uncultivated." His journey took a week, averaging 35 miles per day; the filthy conditions of the Ulm box must have made it seem much longer. (The editor of a volume of his journals, Cedric Howard Glover, indicates that Burney gave "no hint of his reason for selecting this unconventional method of reaching Vienna, and one can only conclude that his natural curiosity overcame his discretion or that he was the victim of bad advice, if not of a practical joke.")

Nowadays there is virtually no passenger traffic on any part of the German Danube, and no commercial barge traffic on its reaches until one reaches Kelheim, well over sixty miles downstream from Ulm. To get an idea of how Ulm looked in its trading heyday, it is necessary to cross the square from the Rathaus to the city's museum, which houses a reconstruction of Ulm in the year 1600. All along the waterfront logs are being cut and rafts are tied and tethered, while dozens of crafts are shown in various different phases of construction. The only houses shown in this imaginative reconstruction are situated where a district called the Fischerviertel can now be found. Today this is one of the oldest parts of Ulm, where half-timbered houses are crammed into an area of waterways, narrow lanes and tiny bridges around the branching channels of a small tributary, the Blau, which dribbles into the Danube here. Once this area was inhabited by tanners, millers and fishermen; now it is given over to chic galleries and smart waterside restaurants. The most distinctive building, the Schliefes Haus, is a heavily restored late medieval townhouse whose riverside frontage hangs picturesquely over the water on stilts; it is slowly sinking into the Danube mud, its beams and doors notably askew.

Heavily rebuilt and restored, the Fischerviertel is the only part of Ulm where the teeming medieval city that Patrick Leigh Fermor described can still be recalled. All the rest, the marketplaces and the ancient churches, the merchants' houses and the busy river traffic, are hinted at nowadays by dusty exhibits in the museum, or by the writings of travellers such as Leigh Fermor or John MacGregor. Interestingly, the canoeist saw a very different side to Ulm from that of Leigh Fermor; no lover of architecture or conventional tourist sites, MacGregor ignored the Münster but was entranced by the city's public wash houses built over the Danube, "each of them a large floating establishment with overhanging eaves, under which you can see, say, fifty women all in a row, half kneeling or leaning over the bulwarks, and all slapping your best shirts mercilessly," he wrote. Ulm was where his Danube journey ended. In some ways this was a pity.

Negley Farson, an American adventurer, who navigated a yawl down the Danube in the 1920s, wrote that the river seemed to him "a canoeist's paradise. It combines in the seventeen hundred miles between Ulm and the Black Sea everything dear to the heart of the paddler—swift water, rapids, whirlpools, wide, lonely lagoons, mountains, plains, forests and swamps". But Farson, from the security of his yawl, was ignoring one hindrance to canoeists—the barge traffic. And it was the barges that forced MacGregor off the river. He dragged his canoe up the river bank at Ulm and over to the railway station, and put it and himself on a train to Lake Constance. His trip from the start of the Danube had provided him with "a most pleasant week for scenery, weather, exercise, and adventure". By the time the river reached Ulm, it had turned into a "noble river, steady and swift, as if in the flower of age". But nonetheless MacGregor seemed happy to abandon the river, as did Leigh Fermor, who left the Danube valley here too, heading south-east to Augsburg rather than north-east along the river's course towards Ingolstadt.

# Chapter Two

# THROUGH BAVARIA

## FROM ULM TO INGOLSTADT: A LEAPING HORSE AND A DECISIVE BATTLE

The Danube at Ulm marks the boundary between the two *Länder* that make up southern Germany, namely Baden-Württemberg and Bavaria. But this political boundary is only two centuries old, and dates from the acquisition of eastern Swabia by the Kingdom of Bavaria in 1815. Those living downstream from Ulm in Bavarian Swabia consider themselves Schwob as much as Bavarian. Adjacent to Swabia is another ancient kingdom, Franconia, through which the Danube also flows, and it is not until Regensburg that the river can be said to be a truly Bavarian one. But this is an argument for cartographers, politicians and historians to pursue for as far as the map of modern Germany is concerned, the Danube flows into Bavaria immediately beyond Ulm, where it begins to cross a broad plain fringed by low and distant wooded hills. The plain is known as the Donauried. It is an area of fertile farming countryside, marshy in places, studded with ponds and lakes in others and crisscrossed over its entire width by a myriad of tributaries and artificial drainage channels.

The productiveness of the land ensures that settlements follow one another in quick succession. Günzburg, twelve miles downstream from Ulm, seems famous only for being the birthplace of Josef Mengele, the notorious Nazi doctor at Auschwitz. Further on, the town square at Lauingen is overlooked by a slender tower, one of whose panels depicts a leaping white horse against a blue background: this legendary steed, it appears, once jumped the river here in a single bound. After Lauingen the settlements become further apart, and most villages are sited several hundred yards away from the river, rather than beside it, because of the high incidence of flooding. But this allows the river to keep itself to itself, gliding silently through the open fields, its channel invisible until you are almost upon it, the distant villages identifiable by a whitewashed church steeple that rises from a blurred jumble of red roofs. One of these settlements—a mixture of farm buildings and commuter homes with carefully-mani-

cured gardens—is marked as Blindheim on maps, but is better known throughout the English-speaking world as Blenheim, the name it carried in the eighteenth century. It was here, a little over 300 years ago, that one of the most famous pitched battles of European history was fought, and where the balance of power in the continent was shaped for an entire century or more.

To English sensibilities at least, the name of Blenheim seems to be inseparable from that of the English commander at the battle, John Churchill, Duke of Marlborough, and the palace near Oxford that was his reward from Queen Anne following his decisive victory in Swabia. One of the most famous tapestries hanging at Blenheim Palace shows the battle in full flow: the flat plain of the Donauried is inundated with baying armies and engulfed by smoke from cannon fire, while in the background the blue ribbon of the Danube snakes past the village of Blenheim, with its familiar cluster of houses hugging the skirts of the steep-roofed church.

Marlborough and the English forces were in Bavaria because they were part of a Grand Alliance of European powers that had been galvanized into action three years previously, in 1701, when it looked as if the death of King Charles II of Spain would unify France and Spain under a single crown. Before his death Charles had nominated Philip, the grandson of King Louis XIV of France, as his successor. But England and Holland made it clear that they would not tolerate the rule of the newly-crowned Philip V. Quickly they became the leading partners in an anti-French alliance that soon included Austria, Prussia, most of the German states, and later on Portugal and Savoy. The alliance's rival candidate for the Spanish throne was Archduke Charles, the son of the Emperor Leopold I: and so the interminable War of the Spanish Succession began. The next thirteen years saw naval battles fought off the Iberian peninsula and land battles waged throughout France, Germany, Spain, Austria and the Low Countries.

Blenheim became a battle site because the Duke of Bavaria had come out in support of France. The French plan, in early 1704, was to send an army under Marshal Villars across southern Germany where it would link up with Bavarian forces for a combined attack on Vienna. The Duke of Marlborough, with an army of 60,000 English and Dutch troops, was determined not to let this happen—and to force the French out of Germany. In late July he marched into southern Germany and joined the English forces with those of Prince Eugene of Savoy and Prince Louis of Baden.

Discovering that the French were poised to cross the Danube, Marlborough marched his men towards their positions, which by then occupied a wide swath of land on the north bank of the river, in and around the villages of Blindheim and Höchstadt.

A night-time assault was ordered by Marlborough and after the engagement of well over 100,000 troops, victory for the Grand Alliance was declared on 13 August: half the French army was eliminated and, it is said, the River Danube ran red with the blood of French soldiers. The bedraggled remainder of the Sun King's supposedly invincible army staggered back to France, while Bavaria was occupied by Alliance forces. Despite this huge setback for France, the war dragged on for another nine years after Blenheim—finally ending in 1713, when Philip V was recognized as King of Spain but without formal unification of the Spanish crown with France. By then the English had lost interest in the war: their forces had pulled out so that they could concentrate on fighting colonial battles overseas. Europe, meanwhile, was left with a fatally weakened Spain but a voraciously ambitious Prussia and Austria: the seeds of German unification and Austro-Hungarian imperial power were arguably sown beside the Danube at Blenheim, and on the other decisive fields of battle of this pan-European war.

In common with many European battle sites, virtually no evidence remains of the fighting at Blenheim. As far as visitors are concerned, appreciation of what went on here only comes with imagination, aided by the various (and fairly low-key) memorials, information boards and museums scattered over a considerable part of this peaceful corner of Bavaria. At Blindheim itself there is virtually nothing to see, but just outside the village, next to a busy road and railway line, is a raised metal gantry that allows anyone curious to look over the grassy meadowland where, it says on a memorial stone, Marlborough's cavalry made a charge at four o'clock in the afternoon of that fateful August day. There is more to see at Höchstadt, four miles upstream along the Danube, where a sixteenth-century Schloss once owned by the family of Anne of Cleves has been converted into a museum. The Germans know the events of 1704 as the Battle of Höchstadt rather than Blenheim, and their take on the War of the Spanish Succession (as evinced by the tone of the museum) was that it sowed the seeds of a long, tortuous process of European co-operation that reached its culmination in the formation of the European Union. This view of history seems rather dubious, but at least it provides visitors with a whiff of controversy to ponder as they amble between all the illuminated battle plans and glass cases full of uniforms.

Beyond Höchstadt and Blindheim the river continues its leisurely journey across the Donauried. But at Donauwörth the hills finally encroach onto the plain. In early July 1704 this strategic crossing point on the river was the first Bavarian town captured by Marlborough as his forces marched to engage the French. Nowadays Donauwörth is a stop on the Romantic Road (the *Romantische Strasse*), the most famous of all Germany's long-distance tourist routes, which runs north-south through Bavaria from the baroque city of Würzburg to the Alps, and crosses the Danube here. Two million people, mostly foreigners, ply the route each year, ensuring many road signposts in English and Japanese, a steady throng of coaches and a good supply of tourist kitsch in towns along the route. But most Romantische Strasse tourists in Donauwörth ignore the Danube and head for the town's most striking landmark, the ochre Holy Cross Church, which occupies a commanding position on a high ledge overlooking the floodplain. The pious have been coming to this monastery church for centuries to venerate its famous relic, a chip of wood that is supposed to have come from the Cross.

Below the church, near the bottom end of the town's main street, a small tributary, the Wörnitz, drains into the Danube. A memorial to those who died in the Franco-Prussian war rises above the spit of land where the rivers join. But the Wörnitz is a mere trickle compared to the Lech, which joins the Danube a few miles beyond Donauwörth and almost doubles the river in size. This river, which has its origins in the beautiful Forggensee in the Bavarian Alps and flows into the Danube via the ancient city of Augsburg, is a major tributary, discharging as much water as the Iller at Ulm. The first settlement to occupy the banks of the newly-widened channel is Neuburg, some twelve miles beyond the confluence. In the days of the empire this town was the capital of the principality of Pfalz-Neuburg, whose rulers built a whitewashed Italianate palace known as the Residenzschloss on a low ledge overlooking the river. Within the irregular arcaded courtyards of this palace are Bavaria's oldest Protestant church and a grotto decorated with white shells from the river. Behind it, the Karlsplatz, where linden trees droop picturesquely in front of lines of historic buildings, is reputed to be the most beautiful town square in Germany.

Beyond Neuburg the river continues its course eastwards, along the south-ern fringes of the Altmühl Valley National Park, before flowing past the city walls of the former fortress city of Ingolstadt.

## INGOLSTADT

Ingolstadt's military heritage stretches back at least 2,000 years, to the reign of the Roman Emperor Augustus (27 BC-14 AD). It was Augustus who secured the Danube and the Rhine as his empire's European boundary. Beyond these rivers lay the territory of the violent and lawless Germanic tribes, who laid waste to three Roman legions that Augustus dared to send into Saxony's Teutoburg Forest in 9 AD. After that the Romans gave up on ever subduing the Goths. Instead, Augustus created a string of forts and garrison towns along the entire south bank of the Danube, from southern Germany to the Black Sea, to defend the empire from the tribes across the river. This defensive line became known as the *Limes Romanus*. One of the most significant Roman finds ever unearthed in Germany are those of two river ships that were discovered in 1986 at Oberstimm, the site of a fort very close to Ingolstadt. The ships were raised from the Danube mud eight years later. The vessels took the form of a hollow shell with places for ten rowers on each side and a tall sail, and were probably used for the transportation of men and supplies between the various Danube encampments.

Despite the dense network of fortifications, Roman provinces along the south bank of the Danube suffered raids and invasions from Germanic tribes from the fourth century onwards, and camps such as Oberstimm were abandoned one by one under the onslaught. In the centuries that followed the collapse of Roman rule in central Europe Ingolstadt remained a strategic crossing point on the river. Its defensive role was fully revived in 1392, when the city became the capital of the Duchy of Bavaria-Ingolstadt, a proto-state of the Holy Roman Empire. In 1418 the splendidly-named Duke Ludwig the Bearded laid the foundation for a formidable riverside castle, the Neues Schloss, which has survived to this day in the centre of this wealthy Bavarian town, an uneven jumble of box-like defensive towers and steeply pitching roofs whose whitewashed walls gleam brightly in the sunshine. Nowadays the castle is given over to a military museum stuffed to the brim with weaponry and uniforms.

Still more fortifications, from a much later era, line the banks of the Danube opposite the castle. In 1828 King Ludwig of Bavaria decided that Ingolstadt should serve as his kingdom's state fortress, and a slew of fortifications and bastions fashioned from red brick and creamy limestone was constructed over the course of twenty years, largely to provide a refuge for the Bavarian royal family in time of crisis. During the First World War, Charles de Gaulle and the Russian Marshal Tukhachevsky were imprisoned behind these solid, virtually windowless walls. Today the bastions are scrupulously preserved but entirely useless; they form an attractive backdrop to carefully tended riverside gardens, the harsh stonework softened by the presence of fountains and flowering plants. One of the bastions is home to yet another armaments museum, this one named after the great military commander General Tilly, who led the Imperial forces during the Thirty Years War, and who, in 1632, successfully repelled an attack on Ingolstadt led by the Swedish King Gustavus Adolphus. The whole defensive complex is named after Ludwig's architect, Leo von Klenz, and what he and King Ludwig would make of the place now is anyone's guess. In 1992 the whole site was given over to an expansive Garden Festival, and where a tiny tributary enters the river below the bastions, a set of horse-shoe steps has been built for quietly contemplative angling.

Modern buildings, including a new art gallery and a gunmetal grey theatre, line the river bank opposite the bastions. They have risen from the wasteland left by wartime bombing, which spared the Neues Schloss and Ludwig's bastions, but put paid to a sturdy medieval bridge that spanned the river. This structure is shown in the woodcut map of Ingolstadt prepared by the sixteenth-century printer, astronomer and cartographer Philipp Apian, and is on display in the city museum. Between debating the movement of the stars and planets with the Emperor Charles V, Appian travelled all over Bavaria and produced the first map of the state, presented on 24 woodcuts. One of his maps forms the oldest remaining record of Ingolstadt's medieval townscape and shows that once it came close to rivalling that of Ulm. But now much of this has gone, and in place of the old bridge across the Danube is a new structure named after Konrad Adenauer, the first chancellor of post-war Germany.

Away from the city centre gardens and medieval walls, Ingolstadt shows another, very different face: for this is the first industrial city on the Danube. The eastern fringe of the city is home to a vast, smouldering oil refinery, linked to Trieste on the Adriatic by one of Europe's major oil pipelines, while to the north is the main production centre for Audi cars. Yet neither is dependent on the river: the Audi plant is well away from the Danube, and though the Esso and Bayernoil refineries loom closer to the river, the only use they make of its water is for cooling their plant and equipment. No barge traffic can reach Ingolstadt and industry does not truly embrace the river until further downstream. Instead of docks and cranes and warehouses, much of the Danube waterfront in Ingolstadt is in fact put to recreational use, in the form of the Donautherme Waterpark, a clutch of bathing pools and tennis courts that cling to the river's forested banks in the west of the city: a huge expanse of green on the town map, cut through by the blue slice of the Danube.

## INGOLSTADT TO REGENSBURG: A NAVIGABLE RIVER FOR THE FIRST TIME

Beyond Ingolstadt, the Danube weaves its course across a wide, thick layer of gravel that once, in geological eras long past, formed the bed of a shallow sea. The main channel shifts its position continuously; in times of heavy flow gravel bars can form, and then disappear completely, within the course of a single day. There is hence no way to create a navigable path for ships along this reach, as it is barely possible to mark the channel here, still less to control it. And it would not even be possible to canalize the river: the gravel is hundreds of feet thick in places, rendering impossible the construction of retaining walls. For this reason the Danube immediately below Ingolstadt remains free of commercial shipping, and only the smallest of pleasure craft ply its waters as the river flows under the Munich-Nuremberg autobahn and then eastwards across featureless farmland.

After the small town of Neustadt, however, the scenery suddenly changes. Instead of skirting the fringes of the upland area of the Altmühl National Park, as it has done since Donauwörth, the river actually gouges a canyon right through it, named the Donaudurchbruch Gorge. Here the river narrows to a width of some 250 feet, with no river bank to speak of: the craggy faces of the gorge rise precipitously from the water's edge. The writer Bernard Newman, cycling along the road above the gorge, saw "iron grips protruding from the rock [that] are used by local boatmen, who sometimes find it difficult to make headway against the forceful current." Tens of millions of years ago, during the tertiary era, this channel belonged to another river entirely—a tributary of the Danube, whose course at that time ran well to the north of here. But after the gorge was cut by the smaller river, the Danube somehow commandeered it as a shortcut, and shifted its course southwards to claim the channel as its own.

The Benedictine monastery of Weltenburg commands the western entrance to the gorge. It occupies a low-lying wedge of land just as the cliffs start to close in, and happens to be the oldest religious house in Bavaria, its foundation dating to the early seventh century, while the monastery's brewery, which to this day brews a dark and invigorating concoction, is the oldest of its type in the world. A dazzling altarpiece depicting St. George fighting the dragon takes centre stage in the monastery church; the carved figures seem to shimmer against a painted backdrop of the Immaculate Conception. And when visitors to the church turn their eyes to their right, they are alarmed to see the prow of a boat almost bursting through the stone wall into the nave: it is a vivid fresco, depicting the Virgin Mary at the helm of a vessel packed with Benedictines coming to christianize the New World, and its design was surely prompted by the fact that access to the monastery is principally by a launch on the Danube. But the river here is the monastery's foe as well as its friend. It can be treacherous and unforgiving as it forces its way through the narrow gap between the pale cliffs, as indicated by marks on an exterior wall of the monastery that indicate the height reached by various floods. The inundation of 1845 rose to twice the height of a man, while that of August 2005 reached a head taller even than that.

At the eastern end of the gorge the river breathes a sigh of relief as it breaks out onto flatter ground. Here the Danube is overlooked by an extraordinary monument, the Befreiungshalle (Liberation Hall), which takes the form of a giant ochre rotunda sitting atop a planed-off pinnacle of land, surrounded by thick stands of trees. Bernard Newman was very sniffy about the monument. "It is not the fault of the architect that the general effect is that of a giant gasometer," he wrote in *The Blue Danube*. This monument, an early expression of German nationalism, was raised by King Ludwig of Bavaria to celebrate the liberation of Germany from the dominion of Napoleon. Its architect was Leo von Krenz, who had earlier overseen the construction of Ludwig's grandiose fortifications upstream in Ingolstadt. Pompous, posturing and graceless, the exterior of this overbearing structure consists of 18 sides crowned by figures that are supposed

to represent the 18 German races that defeated Napoleon (and the fact that the major victories, at Leipzig and Waterloo, both came on the eighteenth of the month).

Inside, the circular pantheon, echoing and shiny, is overlooked by 34 statues of Victory, one for each of the states that made up the pre-unification German Federation, and looking, according to Newman, "for all the world like angels about to play ring-a-ring of roses". At the time of the monument's construction, of course, Germany was still only semi-formed: but within fifty years its constituent states had come together to create a new nation. Ironically, for all Ludwig's pan-Germanic sensibilities, Bavaria was an unenthusiastic partner in the unification process. In fact, it was the madness of Ludwig's grandson, King Ludwig II, the builder of the fantasy castle at Neuschwanstein, which caused the Bavarian political establishment of the day to finally abandon its monarch and to shift its political allegiance towards the new national government in Berlin.

For all its grandiosity, it is the view from the exterior balconies of the Befreiungshalle, rather than the structure itself, that provides its most alluring feature. From the gallery below the dome it is clear that the Befreiungshalle sits on a rocky wedge of land that separates two very different waterways. To the right is the free-flowing Danube; to the left is a thinner, arrow-straight channel supported by concrete banks and divided by lock gates. This is the canalized River Altmühl, forming here the last stretch of the Rhine-Main-Danube canal; the canal links up with the Danube just beyond Kelheim, the small town that spreads itself between and beyond the banks of the two waterways.

The Rhine-Main-Danube canal is one of the great artificial waterways of Europe; *the* greatest, perhaps, as it provides a route across Europe's principal watershed, and thus forms the sole inland link between the North Sea and the Black Sea. The idea of such an important waterway link has been around since early times. It was considered by the Romans, but their plans were abandoned because they had no way of raising a canal up and over the Franconian Jura, the low ridge of hills forming the crest of the watershed. In 793 Charlemagne's engineers began work on a canal known as the Fossa Carolina, which was to link the Altmühl with the Pegnitz, a tributary of the Main (itself a tributary of the Rhine). This project was also abandoned, because parts of the route were too marshy. (Some of the earthworks of this early venture are still visible at Weissenburg, near

Nuremberg.) The failure of the Fossa Carolina put paid to any more attempts at the construction of a canal for an entire millennium.

The instigator of the next attempt at a canal was King Ludwig. Ever keener to forge closer ties between the German states, he made his engineers survey a route for a new canal from Bamberg, on the Main, to Kelheim, via Nuremberg. Construction work began soon after and the canal, named the Ludwig Canal, opened in 1846 after eight years of work. It provided ships with a 35-feet wide channel over a distance of some 107 miles; at long last, it was possible to transport goods by water from Amsterdam and Cologne to Vienna and Central Europe. The journey, however, was slow going: on average there was a lock to pass through for every one of the canal's 107 miles. As a rail network was constructed across Germany the canal's usefulness began to decline. In 1905 the writer Donald Maxwell brought his boat *Walrus* through the canal, on a journey from Holland to the Black Sea. He reported that in places the draught beneath boats was less than three feet. "The *Walrus* did not see ten craft in action during the whole one hundred and seven miles of the canal, and until nearly half way through did not observe one," he wrote in *A Cruise across Europe*, his book recording the journey. (Maxwell only got his boat through the more difficult stretches of the canal by walking along the towpath and pulling it with a rope.)

By 1925, when Negley Farson travelled in his yawl from Amsterdam to the Black Sea, the waterway could be used by small vessels such as his, but not by large commercial barges. Farson recounted the trials he and his boat *Flame* faced on the canal and other European waterways in a series of articles dispatched to the *Chicago Daily News*. Later he published an account of the trip in a book entitled *Sailing across Europe*. He describes the Ludwig Canal as "probably the most unknown and least-used waterway in the world" and complains that the German consulate in London had never heard of it. "This obscurity perturbed us," he wrote as he pressed on down the Rhine. "What if the canal had disappeared?" Every time he sought information about the canal he received a different answer as to whether or not it was still operational. At Bamberg an official finally confirmed the existence of the canal, charged Farson 150 marks for using it, and told him that whole years had passed without a single boat using the route. When, at last, Farson's yawl set off from Bamberg, through a lock barely fifteen feet wide, the entry of a ship into the canal caused something of a stir. According to Farson, his departure was accompanied by "a loud cheer from the bank! Waving of hats! An event had transpired in Bamberg. Another ship had entered the Ludwig's Canal!"

By that time the canal had suffered decades of neglect and was in a dreadful state. "In some places the weeds were so thick that the surface of the canal looked like dry land," Farson wrote in *Sailing across Europe*. "They fouled the propeller like rope. In the old days the weeds were cut… But now the canal is almost deserted. A veritable inland Sargasso Sea—it will soon pass into history." He was right: a few years later the canal was little more than a muddy waterless ditch. But by then a new canal was under construction. In 1921, four years before Farson took his trip along the Ludwig Canal, work had begun on a new, wider, straighter canal, which was to follow the route of the old waterway for large parts of its length.

Work on this new canal was perused enthusiastically by the Nazis, but by the end of the Second World War it was far from complete. In the decades following the war the government of the Federal Republic dragged its heels over finishing the project, fearing that the opening of the canal would lead to their inland waterway network being dominated by cut-price barges from Eastern Europe that would price West German boat operators out of the market. By the time of German unification in 1991 the canal was still not open—after exactly seventy years of dithering and on-off construction work.

This lack of a waterway through Europe proved immensely frustrating to freight operators—and to some adventurers who followed in Negley Farson's wake. In 1985 the sailor and writer Tristan Jones decided to embark on an ambitious (verging on the foolhardy) journey through Europe from London to the Black Sea on an ocean-going trimaran named *Outward Leg*, largely following the same route as taken by Farson. But Jones had no canal to get him over the Franconian Jura. At Nuremberg he walked up a grassy bank to investigate the state of the new Rhine-Main-Danube canal—but found that its concrete bed was empty of water, with the sign "Eintracht Verboten" ("entry forbidden") pinned up on a set of lock gates that would have given access to it. Determined not to abandon his journey because of the unfinished canal, Jones and his boat soon became a *cause célèbre* in Germany.

The wrangling about how to get the boat from Nuremberg to the Danube dragged on for three months, which happened to coincide with one of the fiercest European winters on record—not the best time to spend hanging around in Nuremberg docks, as Jones and his crew soon discovered. Eventually, as the weather thawed, Jones managed to persuade a haulage company to transport the boat by road to Ingolstadt, where it was gently lowered into the Danube. When the waters of the Danube were finally lapping against the hull of *Outward Leg*, Tristan Jones could claim that his was the first ocean-going vessel ever to traverse the upper course of the river.

If Jones had made his journey just a few years later this mammoth road haulage feat would have been unnecessary. German unification provided the final impetus to the completion of the Rhine-Main-Danube canal, and the first ships finally made use of the waterway in 1993. Four years later, Bill and Laurel Cooper, two boating enthusiasts and writers who had journeyed all over the world by a variety of forms of water-borne craft, undertook yet another journey similar to that of Tristan Jones and Negley Farson—and they were able to make use of the new canal. Their voyage from Calais to Istanbul was by barge, the *Hosanna,* and they recounted their experiences in an engaging travel book entitled *Back Door to Byzantium.* Some of the most memorable descriptions in this book are of the monster-sized locks along the Rhine-Main-Danube canal, which the Coopers described as being something akin to a "concrete cathedral… roofed with a vault of blue, patched with wispy cloud."

One experience common to all these adventurers—and noted as soon as they steered their crafts into the Danube—is the river's legendarily fast-flowing current, whose virulence and unpredictability is a running theme in all accounts of journeys along the river. (It is also a part of Danube mythology: legend tells of Noeck, a hybrid of Old Man and giant fish, who lives in a palace on the bottom of the river and entices travellers with promises of jewels and gold, only to drown his prospective guests in the swift flow of the current.) Though Noeck may be a creature of myth, the myriad accounts by mariners of the river's powerful surge gives a clue to his origins. The Coopers found out about the Danube's current the hard way. As they edged their vessel out of the canal and into the Danube at Kelheim they realized that

far from being the Blue Danube this swirling river was mud-brown with silt, laden with large debris and travelling at twenty kilometres an hour… it was a shock, after the comparative peace of the River Altmühl, to find ourselves in a raging torrent with ambitions to become a water-fall… we were riding a runaway horse, and the torrent bucked and kicked and tossed its mane in a shower of spray.

Sixty years previously Negley Farson had encountered problems with the same vicious current at Kelheim, where the old Ludwig Canal also joined the Danube. He describes the Danube as an "icy-grey flood rushing out from the gorge above Kelheim", and recalls that "with a 'here goes' sort of zest we sent *Flame* out of the Altmühl and were whirled away like a leaf." As for Tristan Jones, his difficulties were far from over as his boat was lowered into the water in Ingolstadt. "No sooner had we reached the exit from the basin than some monstrous *thing* grabbed *Outward Leg*, as if she were a child's toy boat, and flung her, beam on, downstream into the nearest gravel bank, which she hit with a shock," he wrote in *The Improbable Voyage*. "We knew this was the upper Danube all right, and that his current was a vicious, violent, unforgiving torrent… we were knocked sideways and grounded in less than five seconds." In the end a German army launch had to be commandeered to help the craft safely on its way to Kelheim and beyond.

The confluence of the canalized Altmühl with the Danube is located just east of the medieval centre of Kelheim. The exact spot is awash with offloading cranes and is overlooked by a cluster of smoking chimneys—the highest riverside industrial facilities on the Danube. Swelled by the waters of the Altmühl and controlled by locks and barrages, the Danube is now properly navigable for the first time as it curves through sombre wooded countryside towards the city of Regensburg. Immediately before it flows through this city, a bankside statue of St. Nicholas, the patron saint of mariners, marks the exact spot where the river reaches it most northerly latitude; up until now, its course has been a north-easterly one, but under the statue's watchful gaze it curves and re-orientates itself south-eastwards, towards Regensburg, Passau and Austria.

## REGENSBURG: SAUSAGES AND SPIRES

Unlike Ingolstadt and Ulm, Regensburg escaped unscathed from wartime bombing, and its medieval heart is gloriously intact. Like so many Danube settlements Regensburg was founded as a Roman garrison town, known as Ratisbona, which is why the city is known to English speakers as Ratisbon. In the sixth century the city became the capital of Bavaria and in 1245 it was declared an Imperial Free City, placing it, like Ulm, under the direct control of the emperor. Three hundred years later, Emperor Maximilian I described the city as "the most flourishing of the rich and famous cities of our German nation... it surpasses any German city with its vast and beautiful buildings." And this is still the case: the *Dom* (cathedral) and the Rathaus and the narrow, cobbled lanes that link them with the Danube endow the city centre with a medieval flavour shared by no other city on the German Danube. Not surprisingly, many travellers through the ages have been impressed by the place. In *A Time of Gifts* Patrick Leigh Fermor wrote that "its battlements and steeples, wrapped in myth, dominate one of the most complete and convincing medieval cities of the world."

Spanning the river itself is the city's most noted landmark, the twelfth-century Steinerne Brücke, a stone bridge consisting of fifteen arches that become higher and broader towards the centre, giving the bridge its dis-

tinctive middle hump. "A bridge that rivals all the great bridges of the Middle Ages," is how Leigh Fermor describes this graceful structure, whose stonework glows the colour of honey when the sun shines. At the time of its construction it was the only fortified bridge on the entire length of the Danube; nowadays it is merely the most beautiful.

The hump in the centre makes it look as if a giant finger has come down from the sky and pulled the bridge upwards, out of the river; and a legend associated with the bridge, and with the *Dom*, which is built on a high ledge of land less than two hundred yards from the river bank, suggests this too. The story goes that the bridge builder and the master mason of the cathedral had a bet as to who would finish their structure first. The bridge builder then made a secret pact with the devil: if Satan offered to help with the completion of the bridge, then the first three souls that crossed the finished bridge would be cast into hell. Eleven years later the bridge was completed, and with the cathedral consisting of not much more than foundation walls, the devil looked forward to claiming the souls of the first three men to cross: a local merchant, the Duke of Bavaria and the Bishop of Regensburg. But at the last moment the bridge builder pushed a cockerel, a dog and a hen across the bridge in front of them, and the devil had to take their souls rather than those of the three dignitaries. In a rage, the devil tried to uproot the central arch, thus giving the bridge its characteristic profile.

The famous Danube current means that the water rockets underneath the central arch in a raging torrent, foaming white and churning as if escaping from a waterfall. This is the famous *Donaustrudel*, which translates as "Danube whirlpool". In former times the *Strudel* under the bridge provided navigators with a terrifying watery roller-coaster that often claimed lives. In *A Cruise across Europe*, Donald Maxwell described it as "a mass of racing waters, white with foam and flying spray... a foaming wave was piled up against each pier of the bridge. The roar was incessant." Negley Farson, navigating his yawl under the bridge in 1925, wrote that it was difficult "when carried along by the swift current, to straighten out in time to hit the hole of the arch. I got a fleeting glance of Ratisboners hanging over the bridge with their mouths open as the arch opened its black mouth before us... the exhilaration was a great deal like strong drink, and [just] as treacherous." Nowadays no ships travel beneath the bridge: they use a bypass canal that skirts the northern part of Regensburg's Old Town. The bridge is closed to cars, but buses still trundle over the cobbles, scattering the camera-clicking crowds over to the parapets as they pass.

Tourists gather on the bridge because it offers one of the most satisfying urban panoramas in Germany: steep-roofed houses coloured mint green, mustard yellow and dark orange line the river, while a myriad of spires and square towers rise above them, most prominent of which are the twin towers of the cathedral. The town end of the bridge is marked by a formidable defensive tower, the Brückturm, and by a less formidable adjacent hut, the Wurstküche, which serves *Wurst* from dawn to dusk and claims to be the oldest sausage stall in Germany. A roaring trade is assured because of the lush aromas that drift from the cooking pans along the river bank; it is said that nine centuries ago the *Wurstküche's* sausages kept the builders of the bridge contented between bouts of building work on the bridge.

Like many cities on the Danube Regensburg grew wealthy through its trade. Adjacent to the Brückturm, and overshadowing the sausage eaters, is an enormous building that was in former times a salt warehouse, while lining the banks of the river are the elegant three-storey town houses once home to the city's merchants who controlled the coming and going of all the salt. One of these buildings, with dark oak beams and creaking floors, was the house where the seventeenth-century astronomer Johannes Kepler lived and died. Not surprisingly, it has been turned into a museum celebrating his work. Kepler's contribution to astronomy consisted of three ground-breaking scientific laws, the most noted of which was that the orbits of planets described an ellipse, not a circle, around the sun. This and Kepler's other theories appeared in his most famous work, *Tabulae Rudolphinae*, which was published in Ulm in 1626. When Kepler died in this riverside house in Regensburg four years later, he was in dire poverty and had come to complain to Emperor Ferdinand II that his salary had not been paid. But the emperor did not have time to respond to his complaint: Kepler died and was buried in Regensburg's Protestant cemetery, in those days situated outside the city but nowadays adjacent to the railway station.

Another figure associated with Regensburg's glorious heyday was the artist Albrecht Altdorfer, the leading exponent of the Danube School. Altdorfer was also a prominent politician and architect as well as an artist. In 1519 he was instrumental in the expulsion of the Jews from Regensburg, and he made etchings of the town's principal synagogue just before it was destroyed. Altdorfer's paintings heralded the beginnings of the tradition of landscape painting in European art. Rejecting the bold, stylized nature of the gothic tradition, Altdorfer favoured moody and expressive swirls of colour and an appreciation of light and nature, making his style seem more in keeping with eighteenth-century Romantic artists than with the traditions of the Renaissance. The scenery he painted was that of the Danube valley, with its craggy cliffs smothered in thick stands of firs and larches, as the river (often painted wider than it actually is in southern Germany) curls away into the background. Patrick Leigh Fermor was enthusiastic about this artist's work, and discusses it in considerable depth in *A Time of Gifts*. "Altdorfer outshines his fellow Danubians like a lyre-bird among carrion-crows," he concludes. "How faithfully his landscape echoes the actual Danube."

Many of Altdorfer's paintings now hang in the Alte Pinakothek in Munich. One of these is his *Danube Landscape near Regensburg* (1522-25), which, it is claimed, is the first purely landscape painting executed since antiquity; no humans or man-made structures appear in the scene, allowing the viewer to concentrate on the extraordinarily vivid patterns in the sky, the lush forest and the distant peaked hills sloping down to the wide river. In the same gallery is the *Alexanderschlacht*, a dramatic depiction of the victory of Alexander the Great over the Persian King Darius III at the Battle of Issus in 333 BC. This extraordinary painting presents a bird's eye view of armies of ant-like soldiers clashing beneath a distinctive conical hill on which sits a very medieval-looking castle. In the background a river that could be the Danube swirls and loops beside a typical German city from the Middle Ages, and curls away into a distant mountain range under a sky exploding in a celestial starburst of colours. The battle was actually fought across the arid semi-desert of Asia Minor (now south-eastern Turkey), but, this being a painting of the Danube School, the events are relocated to the verdant Danube landscape of the sixteenth century. Leigh Fermor writes of the "apocalyptic flash [that] revealed [to him] that the painted stretch of water in the picture was no Asian river... It was the valley of the Danube." And it is true: the castle, with its squat towers and solid walls, and the town, with its cluster of spires rising from amidst the tightly-packed red roofs, are both clear representations of those found along the reaches of the Danube further downstream in Bavaria and Austria.

All of Altdorfer's most famous works have been removed from his home town, but in Regensburg itself visitors can at least feast their eyes on *The Two St. Johns*, which hangs in the city's Historisches Museum; the saints are depicted speaking with each other against a familiarly luxuriant landscape of river and forest, while the Virgin Mary watches them from on high.

By the turn of the nineteenth century Regensburg's reputation as a trading centre for goods was complemented by its role as a passenger terminal. In the Brückturm museum a poster dating from 1838 indicates that passengers could be taken from Regensburg to Linz for 15 florins in first class, or ten florins in second. Downstream from the Brückturm, the shipping theme is continued in the form of a restored paddle-wheeled tug named *Ruthof*. This ship was constructed in the Regensburg shipyards in the early 1920s; the Mississippi riverboat-style paddlewheels were considered better than propellers as they could cope with the shallow waters that prevail in the upper Danube. The *Ruthof* worked in Hungary until June 1944 when it hit an RAF mine and sank. Twelve years later, the Hungarian state shipping company Mahart raised the vessel from the Danube mud and renamed it *Ersekcsanad* after the closest town to its former watery grave. The ship resumed its working life in Hungary until the 1970s, when it was purchased by the local authority in Regensburg and turned into a museum ship. Nowadays the ship goes nowhere—its stationary wheels are clogged up with debris, jammed in by the fast flow of the current—but the piston room has the authentic smell of engine grease and the living areas for the crew are complete with teapots and working sinks. Most of its rooms below decks are crammed with models of various forms of Danube transport, from medieval barges and Ulm boxes to the modern cruise ships that often call in at Regensburg.

## Regensburg to Passau: Myths and Legends in Upper Bavaria

Downstream of Regensburg the city's docks spread out on the south side of the river. Phalanxes of cranes are kept busy hauling cargoes of grain, fertilizer and steel from barges, and loading them onto the railway wagons or articulated trucks waiting on the quayside. The port facilities seem slick and modern rather than grimy and decrepit. In an age given over to rapid transport by road or rail or air, the river still forms a vital transport link

through Europe, and the barges lined up against the wharfs bear the names of ports far downstream—Budapest, Belgrade, Galaţi in Romania, or even Sulina on the Black Sea; the names painted on the bows of some of the ships are written in Bulgarian, Serbian or Russian Cyrillic. Not much barge traffic continues upriver from here to Kelheim and the canal, and it is at the docks of Regensburg, for the first time, that the sense of the Danube forming a bridge between two halves of Europe—old and new, east and west—becomes apparent.

A few miles beyond the docks a whitewashed version of the Parthenon pokes incongruously above the trees on the summit of a hillside that rises steeply from the north bank of the river. This is the Walhalla, an extraordinary, almost vulgar monument from the early nineteenth century, taking its architectural influence from Greece and its name from the fabled resting place of Nordic warriors. It is yet another whimsical folly dreamed up by King Ludwig of Bavaria to celebrate his dream of a united Germany: an unidentical twin for Ludwig's other shameless architectural indulgence, the Befreiungshalle above Kelheim. With its heavy whitewashed columns and grandiose flights of steps leading up from the river, the Walhalla is a curious but eye-catching structure that has drawn comments, mostly negative, from a succession of travel writers through the ages. Negley Farson, sailing past it in his yawl, looked up and saw a "stray bit of Greece [that looms] ghostly and unreal against the tempestuous sky." Bill and Laurel Cooper, who skippered their barge in the Aegean before navigating it down the Danube, thought the place looked "incredibly wrong without the wash of Greek sunshine… cold, white and plastic, lost in this northern forest". Nowadays the Walhalla has been commandeered as a popular excursion from Regensburg. On busy days tourist boats disgorge their passengers every hour or so onto the landing stage at the bottom of the steps below the Walhalla, while the laden barges drift past them in the main channel, trailing their wake behind them.

When Ludwig built the Walhalla he honoured within its walls 118 artists, composers, sculptors, writers and politicians whom he considered guardians of the German soul. Now the number of busts and plinths lining the marble-lined interior of the main hall has increased to 161—and every so often this tally increases by one more. The latest bust to have been added is that of Sophie Scholl, the celebrated leader of the White Rose Resistance Movement; she was just 22 when her passive opposition to the Nazis led her and her brother Hans to their executions in Munich in 1943. The bust of Sophie depicts the face of a thoughtful young woman with hair curled into a distinctive 1940s bob. The caption underneath reads: "Im Gedenken an Alle, die gegen Unrecht, Gewalt und Terror des Dritten Reiches mutig Widerstand leisteten" (In memory of all those who courageously resisted injustice, violence and terror in the Third Reich.)

The other, older personalities whose busts and memorial plaques line the echo-beaten walls of the Walhalla are a motley collection: Kant and Schiller rub shoulders with one another along one row, while along another are a bewigged Bach and a chin-thrusting Wagner. Close by are bearded Kepler and moustachioed Bismarck; a fleshy-faced Konrad Adenauer is positioned alongside an equally jowly Brahms, while above them is the skeletal, aged and distinguished visage of the scientist Wilhelm Gottfried Leibniz. Somewhat alarmingly, Ludwig's definition of "German" is a broad one including those who would normally be thought of as Austrian, Dutch, Swiss or English—a form of cultural appropriation that has an unfortunate, distant progeny in the form of Hitler's *Lebensraum*: so the three men of Rütli Meadow, who founded modern Switzerland, and

Horsa, the leader of the Saxon tribes who settled in Kent, and Egbert, "Erster Koenig von England" (first King of England), and William of Orange, and Rubens, and Mozart, line the walls of the hall enjoying the same veneration as Beethoven, Mahler, Goethe and the other giants of German culture and history that you would rightly expect to find here.

Straubing, the next major settlement along the river, is a small agricultural town set in the heart of an area called the Gäuboden—the granary of Bavaria. It seems best known for its drinking fair, a smaller version of Munich's Oktoberfest. It is also the birthplace of Mozart's principal librettist Emanuel Schickaneder. In October 1950 some of the most important Roman finds in Germany were unearthed from former forts near here, and a fine museum in the town is crammed with iron and bronze tools, richly ornate ornamental statues and finely crafted and outstandingly preserved masks once used by soldiers and horses in parades. Languishing beside the Danube is a castle dating from the fourteenth century, when Straubing was united with the Dutch provinces of Holland and Zeeland. Nowadays the courtyards of the *Schloss* are whitewashed and silent and the corner towers guard nothing; its rooms are given over to a museum and offices of the local council.

A more appealing diversion lies half a mile away along the river bank, in the form of St. Peter's Church, an austere Romanesque basilica built on the site of a former riverside Roman fort. The twin towers of the church overlook a cramped but peaceful graveyard that contains three individual chapels rising between the trees—and one of those chapels has a tragic tale to tell, possibly the saddest of any story associated with the entire length of the German Danube.

When the House of Straubing-Holland was dissolved, the town passed into the hands of a Bavarian dynasty and became the residence of a minor nobleman named Albrecht. In 1432 young Albrecht took part in a jousting tournament in Augsburg and while there he fell in love with a woman named Agnes Bernauer, the daughter of one of the city's barbers. The couple married in secret and Agnes bore a daughter. But Albrecht's father, Duke Ernest, found out about his son's secret marriage and, believing he should marry a member of the aristocracy, ordered Agnes to be drowned in the Danube on grounds of witchcraft. One legend surrounding her execution recounts how Agnes was thrown into the Danube with her legs tied together; but she escaped and swam to the shore, whereupon the executioner held her head under the water until she was dead. Later on, in a fit of remorse, the duke had the chapel beside St. Peter's Church erected in memory of Agnes, and to this day she is depicted on a marble epitaph with a rosary in her hands and two dogs at her feet—a symbol of conjugal fidelity. Albrecht, meanwhile, did the decent thing and married the daughter of an aristocrat—and in time became Duke Albrecht III of Bavaria.

Beyond Straubing the Danube skirts the fringes of the gloomy and deserted Bayerischer Wald (the Bavarian Forest), a region of dark hills and lonely valleys. The summits of the rounded peaks form the Czech-German border, and together with the Bohemian Forest on the Czech side, the area forms the largest continuous woodland in central Europe. At Deggendorf, the main town at the foot of the hills on the German side, the Danube is joined by a major tributary, the Isar—the river that flows through Munich. A legend associated with Deggendorf recounts that in the Middle Ages its inhabitants behaved so sinfully that Satan thought he faced competition— and decided to drop a rock on the town's citizens. But he was disturbed by the sound of church bells from the town and ended up dropping the rock too early: now a rocky outcrop bearing the name "Devil's Rock" towers above the river as it flows into the town. Despite the attraction of this minor legend Deggendorf does not feature in the pages of many guidebooks. The same cannot be said for the city of Passau, 25 miles further downstream, which has claimed its crown as one of the most visited cities in the whole of Germany.

## THE SONG OF THE NIBELUNGS

The tourist hordes that descend on Passau every summer are there to see one of the prettiest and best-preserved medieval towns in central Europe. The city's architectural splendour is the legacy of its medieval rulers, the prince-bishops, and it was probably for the entertainment of their extravagant court that the most famous piece of ancient literature associated with the Danube was composed. This is the epic German poem *Das Nibelungenlied (The Song of the Nibelungs)* written some time around the year 1200 by an anonymous poet who is believed to have come from the Danube region. (Only three manuscripts of the *Nibelungenlied* survive from this era; one is held in the former library of the Fürstenberg princes in Donaueschingen.) The author of the *Nibelungenlied* packed his work full of incident and excitement, as would have been expected by his courtly patrons in Passau. In the poem, which would have been recited in front of an audience over the course of several days, tragedy and romance mix with tales of battles, heroism and treasure, a heady narrative mix with origins both in history and in oral tradition; the early English epic *Beowulf* features some of the same characters, and ancient Icelandic sagas recount some of the same tales. But the *Nibelungenlied* is not a mere re-telling of these stories: it is an original work, and is deliberately set during the time when it was written rather than in some distant land of long ago and far away.

The poem's narrative universe is vast. Over the course of over 2,000 lines of metred verse, a cast of characters including dwarves, dukes, queens, knights, bishops, counts and princes crisscross Europe by boat and on horseback from Iceland to Austria and from the Netherlands to Denmark. The first part of the story takes place largely in the Rhinelands, along the banks of the river known as the *Schicksalsfluss* or "river of destiny", and tells the story of Siegfried, a prince from the Netherlands, who according to the *Völsungasaga* of Iceland has managed to capture a vast hoard of treasure from the King of the Nibelungs. But the *Nibelungenlied* provides only a brief summary of Siegfried's treasure hunting and says nothing about his slaying of the dragon that guards the Nibelung hoard. Instead, the poem recounts how the heroic prince falls in love with a Burgundian princess, Kriemhild, whose brother Gunther is in turn in thrall to an Icelandic queen, Brunhild. Siegfried dons an invisibility cloak and helps Gunther trick Brunhild into marriage. Gunther then gives his blessing for Siegfried to marry Kriemhild. But the subsequent cycle of trickery and betrayal leads to murder, culminating in Siegfried's death at the hands of Gunther's henchman Hagen.

In the second part of the story the action moves to the Danube valley, where Kriemhild takes revenge on Gunther and Hagen for their murder of Siegfried. First she takes King Etzel (a character based on the fifth-century warrior-king Attila the Hun) as her second husband and marries him in Vienna, gaining strength from the union. Then she invites Gunther and Hagen to her husband's castle beside the river at Pöchlarn, whereupon mayhem and carnage ensue: Kriemhild arranges for Gunther to be murdered before she slays Hagen herself, with Siegfried's own sword.

The tale in its form told in medieval Passau gradually seeped into German consciousness over the ensuing centuries and was retold in many subsequent versions. In the nineteenth century the dramatist Friedrich

Hebbel wrote a play based on the poem, but the most famous version of the story was the *Ring* cycle of operas composed by Richard Wagner and presented in their entirety for the first time at Bayreuth in 1876. Wagner, however, drew more from the Nordic version of the legends rather than from the Germanic *Nibelungenlied*. In the following century, partly to provide a counterbalance to Wagner's rendering of the stories, the poem was made into a two-part silent film by the great German director Fritz Lang, who took the story back to its original roots. Later, the legendary exploits of the characters of the poem were clumsily incorporated into the skewed version of Germany's mythical history propagated by the Nazis, and indirectly the poem also inspired the writings of J. R. R. Tolkien, who borrowed themes and motifs from medieval epics such as *Beowulf* and the *Nibelungenlied* to create his own wonder-filled tales of mythical heroes and battles that were played out on a similarly epic scale.

A number of towns along the upper Danube between Passau and

Vienna feature prominently in the second part of the *Nibelungenlied*. However, one stretch of narrative—one of the bloodiest in the whole poem—is set upstream of Passau in an unidentified region of Swabia. In this part of the poem, King Gunther and his henchman Hagen are travelling from Burgundy to Kriemhild's castle in Austria, accompanied by thousands of warriors. When the party reaches the Danube they find no way of crossing the river. "Hagen tied his horse to the trunk of a tree," the poem recalls, "and stood on the sand, watching the river flowing along, its waters rising high on the banks. Where were the ships? The Rhineland warriors sat on their horses, wondering if they'd get themselves across such gleaming wide water."

They realize that the Danube is in spate, and its floodwaters rising rapidly. So Gunther tells Hagen to go and find a boat. Off Hagen sets along the bank, his helmet and his chainmail gleaming in the sun and his double-bladed sword "honed to such a fearsome sharpness it could kill at a stroke". Hagen does not find a boat, but he does come across two water nymphs having a swim, and one of them offers him a prophecy: she tells him that all the Burgundians will die in Austria—with the exception of King Gunther's personal priest. Hagen ignores the prophecy, and demands that the nymphs tell him how to cross the river. They tell him of a ferryman living on a hill nearby who is "terribly fierce". Hagen finds the ferryman and bellows at him across the river, pretending to be the man's brother. The ferryman crosses on his boat and finds that Hagen has lied about his identity, so he begins battering Hagen with an oar. Hagen's response is to cut the man's head off with a single blow of his sword. After the deed is done Hagen throws the head in the river and rows the ferryboat to the waiting Rhinelanders, who wonder why so much blood is sloshing around in the vessel. Hagen offers no explanation for the blood, maintaining that he simply found the boat tied up under some willow branches. Then he uses the boat to ferry 9,000 soldiers, and their animals and supplies, across the river.

The last to be brought across is King Gunther's priest. Hagen remembers the prophetic uttering of the water nymph and is determined to prove her wrong. This he must do by killing the priest to ensure that the man does not return to Burgundy alive. "Wasting no time, he threw the priest out of the boat... Hagen refused to show the slightest mercy, pushing the priest's clutching hands back off... fiercely he pushed him down into the water... The priest splashed and churned until God's hand reached down and, still alive, he was back on land." But the priest has splashed his way to the wrong bank: he must return to Worms, and thus Hagen realizes that the prophecy of the water nymph will come true, and that the Burgundians now face certain death at the hands of Kriemhild. Hagen, however, chooses to keep this knowledge to himself. As the party prepares to set off southwards towards Austria, he "smashed the boat and scattered its boards on the water," claiming that no cowards could use it to turn back and return, for if they did they would suffer "death by bitter drowning, which cowards deserve".

Safely across the river, the Burgundian army pushes on into Bavaria, whose ruler Gelpfrat is killed by Hagen's brother Dancwort. They soon arrive in Passau, where they are welcomed by Kriemhild's uncle, Bishop Pilgrim, who "felt intensely happy, seeing his nephew and many Rhineland men riding through his own Bavarian lands... The roads to Passau were fairly lined with welcoming friends. The town itself did not have room enough for guests in such number. They had to cross the river and camp in fields, where they set up their pavilions and tents, and where they could truly sleep. And there they remained for only a single day and a night. But Passau's people managed to work out ways of treating them well!"

Yet further downstream the prophecies of the water nymphs unfold in an orgiastic bloodbath reminiscent of a Quentin Tarantino film. Beyond Passau, in the castle beside the Danube at Bechlaren (now Pöchlarn in Austria), Hagen, King Gunther and the rest of the Burgundians meet a violent death at the hands of the Huns. Kriemhild herself is killed by Hildebrand, a master swordsman, and her death is recounted in the very last stanzas of the poem: "The old man sprang at the queen, fiercely angry, and began striking at her with savage strokes of his sword. Her hands were unable to hold him off, she screamed in utter terror... And so the entire doomed but noble Burgundy band was dead."

## PASSAU: "IN ALL OF GERMANY I NEVER SAW A TOWN SO BEAUTIFUL"

The prince-bishops of Passau, who commissioned the *Nibelungenlied*, bestowed their city with an architectural legacy as rich as its literary one. Passau's tourist board dubs the city the "Venice of Bavaria", or the *Drei-Flüss-Stadt* (the three rivers town); and Passau is indeed beautiful, dominated by water so completely that on occasions the city appears to be floating. Passau's Old Town is built on a tapering peninsula whose final "V" marks the confluence of the Danube with the Inn, one of its major tributaries. As the Inn joins the Danube from the south, a smaller tributary, the Ilz, emerges from a gorge from the north, at a spot overlooked by two picturesque castles whose turrets and walls are draped over a forested crag. Rows of houses in sweetshop colours—chocolate brown, mustard yellow, peppermint green and sky blue—are built along the banks of all three rivers. Above them rises a vista of onion-dome spires and square towers crowned by steeply sloping roofs. In his book *Danube* Claudio Magris describes the city as being a "prevalence of rotundities, of curves, of spheres... the elusiveness and lightness of the water give an airy levity to the palaces and churches, which appear far-off and mysterious, as unreal as a castle in the evening air."

The heart of the peninsula, reached by a maze of streets climbing steeply from the banks of the Inn and the Danube, is occupied by the cream-coloured St. Stephen's Cathedral, whose stucco decoration seems as edible as icing on a wedding cake. No wonder that Napoleon was moved to remark of Passau that "In all of Germany I never saw a town more beautiful."

In former times the peninsula between the Inn and the Danube provided a draw for defenders and settlers. A fortified Celtic settlement was well established there by 500 BC, its inhabitants conducting a brisk trade in salt and other commodities up and down both the Danube and the Inn. In the first century AD the fort was replaced by a Roman camp, Castra Batava, from which the modern name of Passau is derived. When this camp was destroyed by the Alemani tribe from across the river in the second half of the third century, the Romans established another settlement nearby. This was Boitortro, on the banks of the River Inn, half a mile from its confluence with the Danube. Foundations and masonry from this camp still survive, scattered around a grassy courtyard of a museum dedicated to Roman finds. But in time Boitortro too was abandoned, as the empire slowly crumpled under the onslaught of Germanic tribes.

In the Christian era the city was reborn and emerged as an important bishopric. In the ninth century missionaries headed downriver from here to convert the heathen tribes of Pannonia (modern-day Hungary) and Austria. In 1217 the incumbent bishop, Ulrich, was invested by Emperor

Frederick II with the title of imperial prince and Passau became a prince-bishopric, its ecclesiastical rulers exerting secular power over territory stretching along the Danube to Vienna and beyond. It was Ulrich who began construction of the Veste Oberhaus, the citadel that glowers over the confluence of the Ilz and the Danube from atop a wooded hill. The rule of the prince-bishops was not popular with townsfolk; in the fourteenth century the citizens of Passau, unhappy at the rule of one of Ulrich's successors, laid siege to this redoubtable fortress, but without success. Since then the Veste Oberhaus has been expanded, re-fortified and prettified, and nowadays it takes the form of a clutch of turrets, walls, towers and royal residences that nestle picturesquely among the trees. It can be reached by climbing a flight of 200 steps that rise up through the woods from the Danube river bank.

While the prince-bishops held court in the Veste Oberhaus, and paid their court poet to compose and recite the *Nibelungenlied*, the merchants and townsfolk who lived beneath the citadel on the peninsula used the proceeds of trade to endow their town with a rich architectural legacy. It is thought that the first product traded along the Danube was flint. Boats loaded with this valuable building stone were probably plying the river as early as 4000 BC. By Roman times salt, from the mines at Hallein near Salzburg, was traded through Passau along the Salzach and Inn rivers, and in the Middle Ages other commodities such as ceramics, wine and grain also filled the city's riverside warehouses. Passau was the place where these commodities were offloaded and taken overland by pack animals into Bohemia. Back the other way to be loaded onto boats came grain, malt, hops, spirits, animal hides and wool. Beside the confluence of the Ilz and the Danube, immediately below the Veste Oberhaus, a small fort whose defensive walls rise straight out of the water was built to protect the trade and extract customs duties from merchants. Known as the Veste Nieder-haus, this fort with its solid square towers is now in private hands, forming a rather desirable riverside residence.

Meanwhile the merchants ensured that their Rathaus was one of the most splendid civic buildings on the German Danube. Dating from the late thirteenth century, the pinky-orange façade of the town hall lines one side of an expansive square whose open side, across from the building's entrance, comprises the river bank: in this way, Passau seems to embrace the river and to acknowledge it as the source of its wealth and prestige even more so than Regensburg or Ulm. Inside the building, the grand assembly hall with its heavy columns and stained-glass windows provides more testimony to the wealth of Passau during the high Middle Ages. A florid nineteenth-century painting covering the ceiling of the hall depicts a scene from the opening of the second book of the *Nibelungenlied*: Kriemhild arrives in Passau by boat, on the arm of her uncle, Bishop Pilgrim, who is about to offer her as a bride to King Etzel. (This is an altogether happier occasion than the second time Passau features in the poem, when Gunther and Hagen and the Burgundian horde are on their way to destruction at the hands of King Etzel.)

On the earlier occasion, as depicted in the painting, the arrival of Kriemhild caused something of a stir in the city: "All who lived in the Bishop's Palace and every house in the town had given themselves the pleasure of rushing to greet the visitors," the poet recalls. "The bishop was riding next to his niece. And when the merchants of Passau learned that this was Kriemhild, no matter how rich or hard, close-fisted they were, they warmly welcomed the highborn prelate's royal guest." The painting also depicts the Danube water nymphs warning Hagen that the expedition of the Burgundians to Austria is doomed.

At Passau, the Danube becomes a mature river. It has lost the zest of its youth: the rapids and the whirlpools, the tight curves through the steep gorges, are behind it now. The simultaneous joining of the Ilz and the Inn create a new river twice the width of the old one. In fact, the river's conjoining with the Inn (though not the Ilz) creates headaches among hydrologists and geographers: for the Inn is clearly the wider of the two rivers, and carries more water, and has travelled further to get here. Surely the Danube is in fact a tributary of the Inn? Well, strictly speaking it is, but it has never been considered thus, partly because of the angle of the join, which seems to suggest that, on a map at least, the Inn flows into the Danube and not the other way round. And from the high vantage point of the former Bishop's Palace another noteworthy characteristic of the three rivers is apparent—they are all different colours. The water in the Ilz is dark, almost black in hue, the Danube is blue-brown but the Inn is much lighter in colour, almost tending to silvery-grey. This is because of the glacial discharge carried by the Inn from its source near St. Moritz in the Swiss Alps: the load of the river consists of tiny particles of pale dust scoured from high mountainsides by moving ice.

The Inn's Alpine origins also result in the river's high propensity to flood. In 1954 snowmelt in the Alps swelled the river to such an extent that its floodwaters broke right across the low part of the peninsula in Passau, draining into the Danube and turning the cathedral into an island. Marks on the wall of the Rathaus indicate the heights of the various floods: only the floods of 1501 and 1595 exceeded those of 1954 (the marker showing the height of the most recent floods, of 2002, is lower, but still reaches a head taller than a man). But the flooding can not dim Passau's beauty, and cannot stop the tide of tourists either. Dozens of cruise ships, with wide sundecks, well-stocked bars and glassed-in restaurants, berth along the quayside outside the town hall and disgorge their passengers. It is not just the rivers and the boats that draw comparisons with Venice: it is the crowds too, who on warm days in summer can seem so overwhelming as to inundate the city in a flood of people rather than water.

The place where the Inn and the Danube actually merge is marked by a shady patch of grass and flower beds. The view, east along the widened river as it drifts between distant hills, and west towards the spires of the Old Town, makes this one of the most romantic places on the Danube. An anchor is set on a plinth just above the confluence, shaded by trees. A plaque affixed to the plinth bears the words "Den Opfern der Donau; errichtet von den Freunden der Flüsse und Meere." It offers a surprising note of caution and melancholy: "To the victims of the Danube, erected by the friends of rivers and seas." And it is with this knowledge, that the Danube is a waterway to be reckoned with, that the traveller along the river leaves Passau and heads east into Austria.

*Part Two*

# THE BLUE DANUBE

## PASSAU TO BRATISLAVA

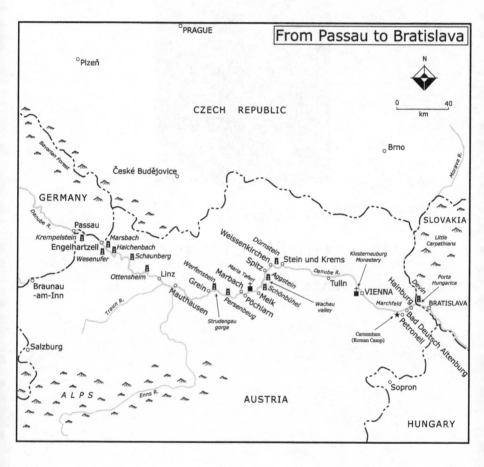

*Chapter Three*

# THROUGH LINZ AND UPPER AUSTRIA

## INTO AUSTRIA

Less than three miles downstream from its confluence with the Inn, the Danube takes on its first incarnation as an international frontier. This is a foretaste of things to come: for around a third of its length the river is a marker of political boundaries. Further downstream Slovakia and Hungary are separated by its waters, as are Romania and Serbia and, for more than 250 miles, Romania and Bulgaria. But these are all linguistic and cultural frontiers, where in former times the river was wide enough to halt the advance of a tribe or provide a permanent defensive shield at the boundary of a kingdom.

The border between Germany and Austria is neither linguistic nor cultural; in fact, for a decade during the twentieth century, when Austria was incorporated into the Third Reich, the border ceased to exist at all, and in these days of European integration it is now barely noticeable as one. But the presence on maps of a dashed line drawn midstream along the river for some twelve miles downstream from Passau, and the different colour schemes used by cartographers to represent the separate countries the line divides, provides a secure recognition of the river's long-standing

role as a frontier. Moreover, the presence of a border here is a reminder of the historic role played by the river when, for over three centuries, it marked the eastern and northern limits of Roman rule in central Europe, separating civilization from barbarianism all the way from the German heartlands to the shores of the Black Sea.

Nowadays there are no formalities for those crossing from Germany into Austria. In fact, crossing the river on the small car ferry at Obernzell, six miles downstream from Passau, you would be hard pressed to find any sort of acknowledgement that you had actually crossed out of one country and into another. The villas that hide amid the trees on one side of the river look no different to those on the opposite bank, and the same can be said for the motor yachts bobbing at the water's edge, tethered to private jetties. But it was not always so, and for centuries Passau was a customs station for those passing along this stretch of the Danube. In 1925 Negley Farson, navigating his yawl from Weimar Germany into the newly-proclaimed Austrian Republic, put aside a bottle of schnapps to bribe the customs officials who checked over his boat at Passau, hoping it would ease along the formalities. But in the end it was not needed: the customs men gave his boat only a cursory glance and signed him off for free transit along the Austrian Danube, leaving Farson to drink the schnapps himself. Sixty years later, Tristan Jones was astonished when a customs official at Passau did the complete reverse, and actually brought him and his crew a bottle of the same liquor as they waited to gain clearance into Austria. "This was the first time in 33 years of passing through customs in a small craft that a customs officer ever brought me a drink," Jones recalled in *The Improbable Voyage*. "Those officers usually expect the boot to be on the other foot, and often demand that it should be."

Some fifteen miles downstream from Passau, at a spot marked by its confluence with a small tributary called the Dantelbach, the Danube becomes a wholly Austrian river. Austria embraces the Danube in a way that Germany has never done. In Germany the Danube is a trickling sideshow flowing through the country's rural backwaters. It is the Rhine that is Germany's freight artery, its industrial heart, its *Schicksalsfluss* or "river of destiny" as the *Nibelungenlied* would have it. But Austria is defined by the Danube to a greater degree than any other country along the river (with the possible exception of Hungary). Even the name of the country echoes its riparian status: *Ister* was the name by which the Greeks and Byzantines knew the Danube, and the people who lived along its banks were the *Histerichi*, whose country gradually became known as Österreich, the German name for Austria. (A rival claim to the derivation of the country's name is less beguiling: it was simply Charlemagne's eastern Reich, his *Öster Reich*, which formed a distant province of that ruler's great Franco-German Empire.)

Four centuries before the rule of Charlemagne the river was still the boundary of the crumbling Roman Empire, its riverside garrisons kept going by supply ships and by a road that ran the entire length of the southern bank. Some of the former garrison towns later evolved into medieval settlements that depended on the river: for instance, a thousand years after its foundation as a Roman camp, Engelhartzell, the first village on the entirely Austrian Danube, was the site of a customs and toll station controlled by the Bishops of Passau, and its merchants staged busy trade fairs to sell their wares (the town was also endowed with a Cistercian abbey which prospered for five centuries until its dissolution by Emperor Joseph II). The summits of the craggy granite hilltops rising above these riverside towns were used by the Romans as hilltop forts and lookout stations; as the Romans departed, their forts were abandoned to the ravages of nature, only to rise again in the medieval era as baronial castles.

Nowadays virtually every crag between Passau and Linz has a fortress hiding away shyly in the trees or staring moodily from a bluff. Some are in ruins, with trees growing from their foundations and moss covering their walls, some are privately occupied, while others have been turned into fancy restaurants which offer their clients dinner with a view. Whatever their state, the castles provide an imposing backdrop to a journey along this wooded and hilly stretch of the river. On his bleak midwinter trudge through this part of Austria in 1938, Patrick Leigh Fermor noted that

> Castles were seldom out of sight. Clustering on the edge of country towns, recumbent with sleepy baroque grace on wooded ledges or beetling above the tree tops, they loomed from afar. One is aware of their presence all the time... Who lived in those stone-flagged rooms where the sun never came? Immured in those six-foot-thick walls, overgrown outside with the conquering ivy and within by genealogical trees all moulting with mildew? My thoughts flew at once to solitary figures...

a widowed descendant of a lady-in-waiting at the court of Charlemagne, alone with the Sacred Heart and her beads, or a family of wax-pale barons, recklessly inbred, [or] bachelors with walrus moustaches, bent double with rheumatism.

And each riverside castle has its own story to tell. Krempelstein Castle, four miles downstream from Passau on the Austrian side of the river, is known as the Tailor's Castle because of the story of a dead goat that was flung into the river by a tailor but became caught in the man's clothing, dragging him in too. In the seventeenth century the castle at Wesenufer doubled as a hostelry. Here, in 1626, a detachment of a thousand soldiers was brought in to put down a revolt by local peasants. But the men got drunk and were slaughtered by the very peasants whose rebellion they had come to quell. Nowadays a stone tower hidden amid trees is the only indication that a castle stands here. Further on, Marsbach Castle provided a lair for a robber-baron named Othmar Oberheimer, whose private mercenaries preyed on passing cargo ships. Oberheimer was beheaded in 1520 and his castle was requisitioned by the Duke of Bavaria. It is now a plush hotel.

One of the tales associated with Haichenbach Castle, a little further on still, concerns one of its former occupants, who, languishing in the castle dungeons after being condemned to death, spat some cherry stones over the wall from his cell, whereupon a forest of cherry trees sprouted. Years later his son returned to the castle to seek revenge for his father's death, gaining access to the fortress by climbing the cherry trees outside the walls and dropping down from the branches into the courtyard. The square tower of the castle is now almost choked by trees; it perches high up on the banks as the river churns and froths far below. Further downstream at Aschach, Schaunberg Castle has been in the hands of the same family, the Starhembergs, ever since the sixteenth century.

Beyond Aschach the river at last has Linz in its sights. It straightens out for the final push, passing a cream-coloured castle at Ottensheim, whose square tower and pointed turret make it look like a child's toy. A ferry takes cars across the river here, little more than a floating platform with a diesel engine and a propeller attached. A high wire suspended across the river, to which the boats are loosely tethered with cables, prevents the fearsome current dragging the vessels downstream as they make the crossing.

## LINZ AND MAUTHAUSEN: AUSTRIA'S NAZI LEGACY

Austria entered the decade of the 1920s as an embittered rump of the once-sprawling Habsburg Empire. The Treaty of St.-Germain, signed in 1919 by the victorious allied powers of the First World War, reduced the country to a tiny remnant of its former self, with seven million inhabitants compared to the 54 million souls who had been ruled over by the Habsburgs. Facing severe social and economic problems, and wracked by resentment over its lost territory and politically revised borders, popular opinion in Austria began to favour union with Germany, while the political leadership doggedly clung to the ideal of Austrian independence. A tense stand-off, which often flared up into Nazi-aggravated violence in key Austrian cities, smouldered away during the 1920s and 1930s as the Austrian leadership staked its survival on garnering support from Italy and other anti-Nazi powers in Europe.

But by the middle of the 1930s dark storm clouds were brewing. Hitler was by then convinced that Austria should unite with Germany, believing that this would further one of the Nazis' most cherished ideological dreams. The first point of Hitler's 1920 programme for the German Nazi Party had demanded "the merger of all Germans in a greater Germany" and on the first page of *Mein Kampf* the future *Führer* had maintained that "one blood demands one Reich." On a more practical level Austria was rich in iron ore deposits vital for the German steel and armaments industry. In February 1938 Hitler saw that the time had come to act decisively. He arranged a meeting with the Austrian chancellor Kurt Schuschnigg at the Berghof, his mountain retreat in the Bavarian Alps.

There Hitler confronted Schuschnigg with a series of demands: that Austria should take steps towards economic union with Germany, that prominent Austrian Nazis should be given key government posts in Vienna, and that convicted Nazis should be released from Austrian jails. Hitler threatened a military invasion of Austria if his demands were not met. But once he was back in Vienna, the wily Schuschnigg staged a wholly unexpected delaying tactic: he proposed a referendum in Austria to see whether union with Germany met with popular support. Furious, Hitler at once instructed that plans for an invasion of Austria be drawn up. Schuschnigg turned to the British government for support but was informed bluntly that it would not be forthcoming. He was left with no other option than to resign.

On 11 March Arthur Seyss-Inquart, one of the country's most prominent Nazis, assumed the Austrian chancellorship. His very first action was
to send a telegram to Berlin inviting the German army into Austria on the
pretext of restoring order in the country. The telegram had actually been
dictated to him by Hitler from Berlin. And it was irrelevant: German
forces were marching into Austria 25 minutes before the telegram was even
sent. A few days later, on 15 March, in the wake of his advancing armies,
Hitler appeared on the balcony of the Hofburg Palace in Vienna in front
of thousands of ecstatic supporters. The following month more than 99 per
cent of Austrians voted for unification with Germany. But the plebiscite
was a farce: by then tens of thousands of prominent anti-Nazis had been
arrested and incarcerated, and a fifth of the population was made ineligi-
ble to vote by virtue of their race or political opinions. The resulting *Anschluss* or union saw Austria's name wiped off this map: it was simply
incorporated into Germany and renamed the Danube and Alpine
Provinces of the Reich.

Echoes of the Nazi era chime louder in the city of Linz and the area
surrounding it than almost anywhere else in Austria. Yet until the 1930s
the capital of Upper Austria had led a fairly unremarkable existence. In
fact, the city's earliest history is similar to that of dozens of other settlements along the Danube. Linz was a Roman garrison town reborn as a
trading and mercantile centre in the Middle Ages. The Romans knew the
place as Lentia; part of the old Roman wall is now visible in the structure
of the Martinskirche, Austria's oldest church, which dates from the time
of Charlemagne and sits on a high ledge above the south bank of the river.
The merchants who prospered in Linz during the Middle Ages, largely
through the trade in salt, paid their dues to the Bishops of Passau and then
later on to the Babenbergs, the powerful family who ruled Upper Austria
from 976 until 1273, the year when the Habsburgs first appeared on the
political scene. Linz had a brief moment in the sun in the 1490s when the
Habsburg Emperor Frederick III made the city the imperial capital following a Hungarian attack on Vienna. (Frederick's heart is buried in one
of the city's churches; the rest of him is in Vienna.) It was Frederick who
endowed Linz with a dour, fortress-like Schloss that rises above the
Danube as the river enters the town. The building has served as a hospital, a prison and an army barracks, and is now a museum and art gallery.
Frederick also built a bridge across the Danube during his brief sojourn

here (he died of gout in the castle in 1497). In Renaissance times this was the only fixed river crossing between Passau and Vienna, but no trace of it now survives.

Centuries of successful trading made Linz rich. As in Passau and Regensburg, the merchants ensured that their city was bequeathed with fine civic buildings and glorious churches. Patrick Leigh Fermor wrote of the "buoyant cupolas and globes" of Linz's skyline, forming "a vision of domes and belfries... pargeted facades rose up, painted chocolate, green, purple, cream and blue. They were adorned with medallions in high relief and the stone and plaster scroll-work gave them a feeling of motion and flow... a town built for pleasure and splendour. Beauty, space and amenity lay all about." (In fact the only sour note was provided by the "fierce keep on the rock".) The merchants were also inspired by their colleagues upstream in Regensburg to provide patronage for leading musicians, scientists and artists. The astronomer Johannes Kepler worked here and taught at the university, Mozart paid a brief visit and composed the *Linzer Symphonie* in 1783, and in the following century Anton Bruckner was appointed organist and choirmaster in the cathedral.

Industry also made an appearance. In 1832 the first horse-drawn railway in continental Europe was constructed from Linz to the Bohemian city of České Budejovice, now in the Czech Republic, and by 1900 Linz was the busiest railway junction in the Austro-Hungarian Empire. But the city faced decline in the aftermath of Austria's defeat in the First World War. Negley Farson, sailing through the city in 1925, found it to be "sad and shabby, and in the pale spindly-legged children who stared, so curiously silent, at our boat, we saw the blow which the hand of war had dealt Austria." He was advised not to leave the boat unattended in case "desperate men on the river front... might cut it adrift—and rob it below— on the islands." It was amid this economic and social malaise that Nazism was allowed to flourish, just as it had in Germany.

Adolf Hitler was born in the small town of Braunau-am-Inn, 45 miles west of Linz, but lived as a child in Leonding, a village just outside the city into which he travelled every day to attend his school, the Realschule. For this reason Hitler always thought of Linz as his *Heimatstadt,* his home town, and in time he came to regard Linz as one of the spiritual centres of the Reich, along with Berlin, Munich and Nuremberg. After leaving school at the age of fifteen, Hitler spent a further two years in Linz, daydream-

ing, sketching and attending performances in the local opera house, before setting off for Vienna, where his political ideas began to take shape. He only made one further visit to Linz, in 1938, when he arrived in the city in an open-top Mercedes just days after the Nazi annexation of Austria. He addressed the adoring crowds from the balcony of the Old Town Hall, barely two hundred yards from the river bank, before continuing his triumphal progress to Vienna.

But Hitler had special plans for his old home town. He instructed Hermann Göring, overseer of Nazi economic policy, to establish a huge steelworks in the city, its location chosen partly because of the transport links afforded by the Danube, and partly because it was in the heart of central Europe and so in theory out of reach of Allied attack. Raw material for the works came from the rich seams of iron ore found in southern Austria. Sixty years later, the steelworks is still there, and remains the major steel production centre in Austria, although it no longer carries Göring's name.

Along with the new industry, Hitler wanted to transform Linz into a riverside city whose architectural glories would rival those of Budapest. A giant statue of the *Nibelungenlied* hero Siegfried was planned for the summit of the Freinberg hill, just outside the city, where Hitler also wanted to build his retirement home. In the city centre itself, the main town square, with its eighteenth-century Trinity column and attractive civic buildings, was to remain untouched, but the riverfront was to be wholly transformed. The designer of the grand new urban landscape was to be the architect Hermann Giesler, who accepted Hitler's commission to rebuild Linz in the autumn of 1940.

Giesler's plans for the Linz waterfront called for buildings of pharaonic proportions to be constructed on both banks of the Danube. Included in the blueprints were a concert hall, an opera house, parks, boulevards, fancy new bridges and a university. In Urfahr, on the north bank of the river, a tower soaring 525 feet was to house a carillon that would chime out the theme from Bruckner's Fourth Symphony, and a crypt at its highest part where Hitler would be eventually be buried. In the event, the only building constructed was a new bridge over the Danube known as the Nibelungen Brücke, over which trams and traffic rumble to this day. As for the rest of the grandiose plans, they were realized only in the form of a giant model, constructed by Giesler, that Hitler spent hours brooding over in the basement of the Reich Chancellery building in Berlin. Hitler was keen for the model to be constructed even as the Reich caved in around him. In January 1945, as the Ardennes offensive crumbled and the Red Army had Berlin in its sights, Hitler's adjutants, including Martin Bormann, were instructed to keep telephoning Giesler to ask when the model would be ready. When at last the Führer was presented with the finished model, on 9 February, he spent hours inspecting it, lost in a grotesque fantasy world that would never materialize. Less than three months later he was dead.

Linz gets a bad press in contemporary Austria. It tends to be seen as both heavily industrial and deeply provincial; its visitors are business travellers rather than tourists. Like most of Austria, it is both visibly prosperous (some would say smug) and crushingly orderly (some would say boring). Sleek trams glide calmly along streets lined with expensive shops, while the chemical works belches and churns beside Winter Harbour and the steel plant hums and clanks beyond the city's northern limits. The setting of the city is a fine one. An exhilarating array of Alpine peaks rises on the southern horizon, while to the north and west are closer, less animated hills. But much of Linz itself is dispiriting. The area around the main square of the Old Town is attractive, yet does not seem deserving of the praise heaped upon it by Patrick Leigh Fermor.

Most disappointing is the river front itself. The Danube is wide and curls away from the city towards low, wooded hills, but a bland collection of buildings line its banks, with dull apartment blocks and civic buildings rising up behind an unenthusiastic stretch of greenery. Cruise ship passengers disembark from floating pontoons, but it is difficult to know what they make of the place; it is hardly Vienna, or Passau, or the Wachau, the glorious stretch of the Danube that lies further downstream. Only the new art gallery, Kunstmuseum Linz, opened in 2002 and stretching along the river's south bank, adds a distinctive touch to the scene. It is a steel and glass monster taking the form of a squat, stretched out letter n, but unfortunately the hard edges and sea of dark, opaque glass panels that adorn the exterior do little to elevate one of the dreariest city riverfronts on the entire length of the Danube.

Travelling downriver from the centre of Linz brings little improvement in the scenery. The south bank is occupied by the Winter Harbour, the busiest port in Austria, which handles five million tonnes of goods each year. Adjacent to its docks and cranes is a huge riverside chemical works, tall thin chimneys slicing the sky and steel pipelines curling their way through a landscape of concrete towers and gushing boilers. Some of the heaps of coal languishing on the quaysides are so old that they have developed a covering of soil and grass. Only the orange and blue shipping containers, painted in the liveries of the different freight companies, add a splash of colour to a scene that seems to fester cheerlessly in various shades of sooty grey. The riverside docks and industrial facilities in Germany, in Kelheim and Regensburg, are a pale echo of this smoke-belching leviathan languishing beside the river in Linz. This is the first fully-fledged industrial city on the river, and the giant chemical works provides a foretaste of the heavy industry that gravitates towards the Danube in distant Hungary and Romania.

When the sprawl of industry peters out, the countryside begins, and the river is joined from the south by a tributary, the Traun, along which salt was once transported, using chutes and rollers to move the cargo over the steep parts further upstream. A little further on is the village of Mauthausen, a former toll station where ships paid dues to ensure safe passage along this stretch of water. (Passing travellers were not always happy to hand over their fees: in 1198 the town was burned to cinders by the forces of the Emperor Frederick Barbarossa after money was demanded from his army of crusaders.) In 1933 Mauthausen provided a charming riverside halt for Patrick Leigh Fermor on his journey from Linz to Vienna; he crossed into the town "by a massive and ancient bridge" and met his friends Hans and Frieda on the quayside, realizing "as we waved to each other from afar, that another cheerful evening lay ahead." Since 1945, however, Mauthausen has been indelibly identified with the Nazi era in Austria, for hidden in a fold of the hills above this apparently innocuous holiday village is the country's most notorious former concentration camp.

Mauthausen was never an extermination camp along the lines of Birkenau or Treblinka, which were set up with the specific purpose of murdering millions of Jews. But the place was no less terrible for that. It served primarily as a slave labour camp where enemies of the Nazi state, among them Jews, Gypsies, Spanish Republicans and Russian prisoners of war, were forced to live on starvation diets while they were worked to death in granite quarries that occupy a narrow cleft in the rock adjacent to the river and the camp. Conditions in Mauthausen were terrible: around 130,000 prisoners died here between 1938 and 1945, through disease, maltreatment, overwork and exhaustion. One of the most famous prisoners incarcerated here was Simon Wiesenthal, who survived the war to become one of the world's most formidable hunters of former Nazis who had escaped prosecution (Linz-born Adolf Eichmann, the architect of the Final Solution, was for many years his principal quarry). Wiesenthal recalled that during his time in the camp he lived on 200 calories a day and his weight sunk to 100lbs. "Sometimes we thought we were the last men alive on earth," he recalled later in his memoirs of that time. "We had lost touch with reality. We didn't know whether anyone else was still alive."

Many more testimonies of the horrors of Mauthausen are chronicled in Martin Gilbert's book *The Holocaust*. Gilbert recounts how, in February 1941, 360 Dutch Jews were sent to Mauthausen as a reprisal for the accidental killing of some Amsterdam SS officers. The Jews were whipped and beaten as they climbed the 148 steps of the *Todestiege*, the "stairway of death" that linked the quarry with the camp, and were then machine-gunned at random by the camp's sadistic guards. On the fourth day after their arrival at Mauthausen ten of the Jews linked hands and jumped to their deaths over the edge of the quarry, and were referred to thereafter as "parachutists" by the guards. The remaining Dutch prisoners were placed under the care of two of the most sadistic guards, and within a few months they were all dead.

Gilbert also recalls the testimony of Albert Gurisse, a British agent who was Belgian but went under the false name of Lieutenant Pat O'Leary, who after the war told of the fate of seven other Jewish prisoners. "With no purpose other than brutal destruction the SS had said that all seven must die by Christmas," Guerisse told Gilbert. "The emaciated skeletons were still dragged out every morning to work in the stone quarries. Silent, drooping they set off, some with tears in their eyes, some talking to themselves, some with the furtive look of hunted animals… while seven skeletons struggled to move stones weighing more than they themselves did, with heavy snow soaking their thin garments and tongues sucking the snow to quench their thirsts, the Kapo [overseer] leapt on one man, dragged him down, and as his screams echoed round the quarry, beat out his brains with a pick-axe." One by one, in that cold winter, the other prisoners died, including an elderly father and his teenage son who threw themselves against the perimeter wall and were instantly killed by machine-gun fire of the guards.

Even as the Nazi war machine crumbled in Europe, Mauthausen continued its murderous regime. On 10 March 1944 the camp was the venue

for a meeting chaired by Adolf Eichmann which organized a deportation plan for the 750,000 Jews of Hungary; nine days later 200 Budapest Jews whose names had been taken at random from a telephone directory arrived in the camp. By the early months of 1945, as other camps were being overrun by the advancing Allied armies, many Jews were moved from those camps to Mauthausen, whose central location in Europe ensured that it kept operating even as other camps were abandoned by the Nazis.

Simon Wiesenthal was moved here from Buchenwald in February 1945 on a "death march" that saw 800 out of 3,000 prisoners die. When the Americans liberated the camp on 4 May of the same year, four days after Hitler's death in Berlin, cannibalism was rife among the remaining prisoners. The Americans found 10,000 bodies in a communal grave and 110,000 survivors living in the most squalid conditions imaginable. Wiesenthal recalls staggering out into the parade ground for roll-call on the morning of liberation to find no one there; then, a few hours later, the first grey American tanks rumbled through the main gate. Many well-meaning American soldiers gave the starving inmates jam and chocolate and canned lard and corned beef, which killed the former prisoners as this rich food could not be digested by stomachs so unused to it. Three thousand Mauthausen inmates died in the weeks following the American liberation.

Nowadays the former camp is a memorial to those who died and suffered here. Coaches are lined up in the car park and there is a sleek new visitors' centre with lecture rooms, a bookshop and a café. Documentary films about the camp are shown in multi-lingual cinemas. The fortress-like exterior walls of the camp, made from quarried granite and punctured by squat lookout towers, survive, as do some of the wooden barracks within their walls, their interiors crammed with photos, documents and testimonies. Private memorials, dripping with photos and flowers and erected by relatives of victims, line the walls of many of the rooms. A flight of stairs leading down from the former sick bay give access to a warren of dank concrete cellars: the gas chambers disguised as showers, the crematorium with its stack of soot-encrusted ovens, the execution chamber with its gallows and its central metal roof beam, have all been preserved. Outside the perimeter wall of the camp, on the hillside overlooking the quarry, are the various memorials erected by different nations whose citizens perished here. For the most part they are modernist structures of sombre concrete, their brutal outlines softened by wreaths of flowers at their bases and, more distantly, by trees and by the distant views of rolling hills. The most prominent of all is a striking representation of the Jewish ceremonial candelabra known as a menorah, standing four times the height of a man, whose seven twisted branches fashioned from dark iron overlook the former quarry itself.

Another tributary, the Enns, joins the Danube at Mauthausen, marking the border between the provinces of Lower and Upper Austria. It was along the Enns that most of Austria's iron ore deposits were carried, from mines in the Erzberg mountains near Graz. A grimy array of docks and warehouses mark the confluence of the two rivers, but the straggle of industry is invisible to the villagers and holidaymakers of Mauthausen on the opposite banks, thanks to a fortuitously thick stand of trees. According to the *Nibelungenlied*, it was on the banks of the Danube here that the Austrian Count Rudiger treated Kriemhild and her party to a wonderful feast, as the queen travelled to Vienna to marry King Etzel. "She crossed the River Traun to open fields along the Enns, and saw men setting up pavilions and tents where guests would sleep that night," the poem recounts. "Knights of the worthiest kind came riding happily from both directions. The fields were filled with warriors, who began to play at battle games."

Eight hundred years later, the events of the Second World War that were played out over this rather nondescript countryside were deadly serious, rather than mere battle games. Victory in that war only came when the American and Russian armies finally linked up with each other east of Linz, completing the Allied encirclement of Germany. When victory was secured, the American General Patton and his Russian counterpart Marshal Tolbuchin celebrated together in the riverside castle at Wallsee, twelve miles downstream from Mauthausen. For the eleven years that followed, the River Enns was to mark the border between the American and Russian zones in occupied Austria. Today, some sixty years after the departure of Allied armies, the inexorable ebb and flow of the river has not entirely removed the legacy of the Nazi era along this stretch of the Danube, despite the best efforts of the tourist boards.

*Chapter Four*

# THROUGH VIENNA AND LOWER
# AUSTRIA

## "A FIERCE, IMPATIENT AND UNKINDLY FLOOD": THE
## STRUDENGAU RAPIDS

There is one matter on which every mariner who navigates a vessel along the upper reaches of the Danube seems to agree: that the current is one of the fiercest and most dangerous of any river in the world. "From Regensburg down to Vienna… the Danube is largely a mountain torrent in character," wrote John Marriner, whose book *Black Sea, Blue River* describes a Danube journey by motor yacht in the mid-1960s. "The frequent narrow channels and turbulent rapids, not to mention dangerous sandbanks which change so often, make it a really difficult piece of navigation… it is not until after Komárom, well into Hungary, that the great river quietens, breathes slowly again and runs, more like a lake than a river, gently over the Hungarian plain." Negley Farson, heading downstream from Kelheim to the Black Sea forty years earlier, was another voyager for whom the strong current was a perpetual source of worry. "This was no Mississippi, or Thames or Hudson," he wrote in *Sailing across Europe*, "but a fierce, impatient and unkindly flood that seems to feel it has a long way to go—and a short time to get there."

In former times the river's current was a nightmare for boatmen but a boon for corn millers. The German word *Mühl*, meaning mill, appears frequently on maps of these reaches of the river: towns named Obermühl and Untermühl hug the banks, while tributaries such as the Mühl and the Kleine Mühl swell the channel still further. Sometimes the medieval mills were not even fixed to the banks; it was common practice along the Austrian reaches of the Danube for mills to be housed in boats anchored midstream. One boat would contain living quarters and a storeroom, while the other boat supported the millwheel and its axel. In modern times the mills have been replaced by grandiose hydroelectric schemes. Between Passau and Vienna eight barrages hold the river back, water cascading from sluices in the dams as ships negotiate the deep, long concrete locks beside them.

Passage through the locks comes with a distinct aural accompaniment: the rush of water, the metallic groans and creaks as the gates open and shut with aching slowness, and the constant hum of machinery from somewhere under all the concrete. The grey concrete barrages are not exactly pretty structures; in fact, their monumental size, their array of glaring floodlights and the high military-style control towers lend them a faintly sinister air. But the barrages provide a significant proportion of Austria's power needs, and their presence has made the difficulties faced by boats along this stretch of the river a thing of the past.

The most notorious rapids were those of the Strudengau Gorge, a steeply wooded valley whose very name once struck fear into the hearts of even the most experienced of mariners. It was the succession of churning whirlpools along the narrow gorge that proved the greatest threat, as any ship caught up in them would be thrown by the raging torrent against the steep grey cliffs to face total destruction. The river enters the gorge at Grein, eighteen miles downstream from Mauthausen, where boats heading downstream would stop so that their crews could say Mass in the village church and then take on an experienced pilot to see them safely through the gorge. Vessels would often be lashed together and steadied by hawsers from the shore as they set off on their perilous journey downstream. The perils of the journey made the sailors who plied this route superstitious: trips were commenced with the words "In the name of God", a picture of a saint was fixed to the bows, and any sailors that fell overboard were simply left to drown, a sacrifice to the river gods. Whistling was strictly forbidden as it was supposed to summon storms.

And it was not only the foaming current that provided a threat: small craft faced dangers from pirates as well. Werfenstein Castle, perched above the Hausstein rapids, the third whirlpool along the gorge, was the lair of gangs that regularly wrecked and plundered passing ships. (One military convoy proved too much for even the Werfenstein brigands. In *A Time of Gifts* Patrick Leigh Fermor describes how Barbarossa's army of thirteenth-century crusaders was simply too large to be attacked, and "the castle-dwellers gazed through the arrow-slits and gnawed their knuckles with frustration as the crusaders trudged downstream.") The castle was also meant to be the home of a ghostly Black Monk who dwelled among the towers, and whose sighting by medieval mariners was supposed to foretell imminent death amidst the foaming waters.

Today, even with the current tamed by the barrages, the reaches of water below Werfenstein can still provide a challenge to smaller craft, as Bill and Laurel Cooper found when they navigated their barge *Hosanna* through the Strudengau in 1997: "Any idiot casting his eyes up the cliff for Black Monks when they should have been steering through rapids deserves disaster and death," they wrote in *Back Door to Byzantium*. "The gorge may be a fraction of the terror it once was, but it is still a beast when the river wills, and we experienced a little beastliness that day."

The taming of the Strudengau rapids was begun in the eighteenth century. The instigator of the work was Empress Maria Theresa, whose reformist and enlightened rule marked the creation of the modern state of Austria. Not only did she improve navigation along the Danube, but she also ended torture of prisoners and abolished capital punishment, and created a state education system throughout Austria controlled by a modern government bureaucracy in Vienna. In the 1740s she instructed her architect, Johann Bernhard Fischer von Erlach, to remove the cliff above the Schwallweck rapids by blasting away at the projecting rock bit by bit, thus calming forever the ferocious whirlpools that swirled and churned in the most dangerous section of the Strudengau. Maria Theresa's son, Emperor Joseph II, continued his mother's work, authorizing the use

of tons of explosives to blast away underwater rocks along the length of the gorge, and to straighten out the tortuously twisting channel.

Continuous initiatives made over the following two centuries culminated in the hydroelectric barrages constructed before and after the Second World War. They make the reach of the river between Passau and Vienna one of the most controlled stretches of water anywhere in the world. The last barrier to be completed, in 1959, was the one at Ybbs-Persenbeug that dams the eastern end of the Strudengau. A frieze showing events from the *Nibelungenlied* has been painted along the concrete walls of the adjacent lock, leavening somewhat the stark greyness of the imposing structure. Overlooking this barrage, in fact perched right above the concrete chasm that provides the lock for barges, is Persenbeug Castle, where one of Maria Theresa's descendants, Emperor Karl I, was born in 1887. Karl was destined to be the last Habsburg ruler of the Austro-Hungarian Empire, and in fact his last-ditch attempt to reclaim Hungary for the Habsburgs was played out beside the Danube in Baja, 360 miles downstream from here, in 1921 (see page 174). To this day the smart cream-hued castle, its central tower capped by an onion dome, remains in the hands of the Habsburg family. It provides a potent reminder, in brick and stone beside Austria's great river, of the dynasty that dominated the country's politics for more than 800 years.

## MARIA TAFERL, PÖCHLARN AND MELK

Beyond the Ybbs-Persenbeug barrage the countryside opens out and the river becomes less threatening. Very soon one of the most distinctive landmarks along the Austrian Danube hoves into view—the pilgrimage Church of Maria Taferl, perched magnificently atop a wooded hillside, floating like a cloud above the pretty riverside village of Marbach. The church's onion-domed twin towerÖÖös overlook the river and are visible for miles around. Once, according to legend, a venerable oak tree stood on this spot. Hanging from the broad trunk of the tree was a wooden board (*Taferl*) onto which was fixed a crucifix. In 1633 a local farmer tried to chop the tree down; but he found that his axe suddenly developed a mind of its own, and he ended up hacking his own legs off. Then the confused farmer spotted the crucifix, and immediately prayed for forgiveness—whereupon his legs were miraculously healed. Pilgrims immediately began to besiege this previously unremarkable spot, and many reported seeing visions of the Virgin Mary. Eventually, in 1660, the foundation stone of a basilica was laid; today it attracts pilgrims by the busload.

The interior of the church is as ostentatious as its setting: the wedding-cake decoration is smothered with gold and drips with trompe-l'oeil masonry, while a *pietà*, fashioned from the wood of the original oak tree that the farmer tried to cut down, provides the focus for pilgrims. In 1770 Dr. Charles Burney, passing this way to research his *General History of Music*, saw a group of women approaching the church, and was struck by the beautiful plainsong he heard them chanting. "The sound was carried several miles, by the stream and wind, down the river, upon whose smooth surface it passed without interruption," he wrote in his memoir of that journey.

Three miles further on, the riverside village of Pöchlarn has its origins in Roman times and features on two separate occasions in the *Nibelungenlied*. According to the poem, Bechlaren (as it was then known) was home to the magnificent palace of a wealthy nobleman, the Margrave Rüdiger. Right at the end of the poem the castle serves as the setting for the final bloody showdown between the Huns and the Burgundians, which climaxes with the death of Kriemhild at the hands of the master swordsman, Hildebrand. Earlier in the poem, however, the mood is much happier: the Burgundians are treated to a four-day feast at Bechlaren, to celebrate Kriemhild's betrothal to King Etzel. The poem recalls that, after an exchange of lavish gifts, the margrave's wife and daughter took Kriemhild "by the hand and led her into the massive palace, where everything was handsomely arranged. The stately Danube flowed underneath the castle. They sat in the open air, and were nicely entertained." But despite the warm welcome, Kriemhild's knights started to complain that they had stayed too long at the castle, and begged to resume their journey towards Vienna, where the wedding was scheduled to take place. After yet more gift-giving—the poet recalls how "almost all the strangers left Bechlaren with fine bright jewels or brand new clothes"—the party finally departed, only to face a similarly warm welcome as they passed through Medelik, the next village downstream along the river, where "people came to the road, bearing gifts of wine in gleaming cups of gold, which they handed up to the guests."

The author of the *Nibelungenlied* does not mention the famous monastery of Medelik. But he could have done, as the monastery was founded in 1089, and in the high Middle Ages, when the *Nibelungenlied* was written, the Benedictine foundation would have dominated the small village beside the Danube just as it does now. At the time of the monastery's foundation Medelik was under the control of the Babenbergs, who established a castle later handed over to the Benedictines for the founding of the monastery. Centuries of burnings, sackings and rebuilding followed. The last major sacking, in 1683 by the Turks, left the place completely ruined, but the new monastery that rose from the ashes was to take the form of a resplendent mustard-yellow baroque palace that to this day occupies a wide rocky bluff above the river. Over time the name Medelik became Melk, and nowadays the monastery is one of the most opulent in Austria, a working religious foundation that sees over half a million tourists pass through its gates every year.

Owing to its setting high above the Danube, which here flows across a broad plain, the monastery, like the Church of Maria Taferl, can be seen from afar—and is a splendid sight. Not surprisingly, Patrick Leigh Fermor was struck by his first glimpse of the monastery as he approached Melk on foot from Pöchlarn. "High on a limestone bluff, beneath two baroque towers and a taller central dome, tiers of uncountable windows streamed away into the sky," he recalls. "It was Melk at long last, a long conventual

palace cruising above the roofs and the trees, a quinquereme among abbeys."

In addition to its appearance in many accounts by travellers, the monastery has also made at least one appearance in fiction, providing the setting for the opening of Umberto Eco's medieval whodunnit *The Name of the Rose*. Eco's 1986 novel, a book introduced by its author as being "shrouded in many shadowy mysteries", purports to be a transcription of a fourteenth-century manuscript written by Adso (or Adson), a monk "confined now with my heavy, ailing body in this cell in the dear monastery of Melk". The bulk of the novel, as recounted by Adso, tells of the time when, as a young Benedictine novice, he travelled to a monastery in northern Italy where he witnessed the deaths of a number of monks in mysterious and suspicious circumstances. Travelling to Melk by boat from Vienna to try to uncover Adso's original manuscript, the narrator of the novel is, like Leigh Fermor, struck by his first view of the monastery, "perched over a bend in the river", but he finds no trace of Adso's purported manuscript in the foundation's enormous library.

The library forms just one part of the grandiose vision of Melk that was conceived by Abbot Berthold Dietmayer, who was responsible for the monastery's rebuilding after the destruction wrought by the Turks. In fact, his vision was so grandiose that when he first presented his plans, Dietmayer faced a rebellion by his own monks who saw such a florid building as an affront to their asceticism. But Dietmayer persisted, and along with his architect Jakob Prandtauer created an extraordinary building that is as overwhelming as any of the Habsburg palaces in Vienna. The library, with its shelves of aspen, walnut and oak heaving with books and ancient manuscripts from floor to lofty ceiling, is one of the highlights of the building for visitors, along with the red and grey Marble Hall, with its ceiling fresco depicting allegorical scenes. A curving exterior terrace linking the two rooms allows for superlative views over the Danube.

The heart of the monastery, the Stiftskirche, was finished in 1738, and its interior seems to drip with gold. Its beauty inspired some of Leigh Fermor's most evocative descriptive writing: "Concave and convex uncoil and pursue each other across the pilasters in ferny arabesques," he wrote in *A Time of Gifts*, "liquid notions ripple, waterfalls running silver and blue drop to lintels and hang frozen there in curtains of artificial icicles. Ideas go feathering up in mock fountains and float away through the colonnades in procession of cumulus and cirrus." He did not remark on the side chapels, however, which present a grisly view, for they house glass coffins whose occupants are skeletons dressed in faded garments studded with glitter and jewels. The body of the Irish missionary St. Koloman, known when he was alive for his powers of healing, seems to be housed with rather more reverence: it lies in a stone sarcophagus, although one of Koloman's teeth is housed in a separate reliquary and is brought out for reverential gazing by the faithful once a year on the saint's feast day, 13 October. Also paraded on that day is the Melker Kreuz, a fourteenth-century cross studded with pearls and gems surrounding a chip of wood from the Cross of Christ. A legend recalls that in the Middle Ages the Melker Kreuz was stolen and found its way back to Melk from Vienna by floating upstream along the Danube, against the natural current of the river.

The village of Melk, hemmed in beside the Danube and beneath the monastery, cannot hope to compete with the building that dominates it so completely. There is a monastic school, which educates 700 children, and narrow streets lined with townhouses sporting painted shutters, and an Altes Posthaus (old post office) replete with stuccoed eagles above its front door. Tourists jam the streets all day long in summer; in former times the monastery provided luxurious rooms for passing members of the aristocracy to stay in, but nowadays the clientele has swelled in number, and today's visitors have to make do with one of the timber-framed hotels that front the village's pretty main square. Around the square, bikes are hired, guidebooks are consulted and vast quantities of strudels drenched with cream are consumed in the open-air cafés. Meanwhile, a few yards away, hidden behind a thick stand of trees, the Danube continues its relentless course eastwards, through countryside that once again begins to close in to form a deep, winding valley.

### The Wachau: Heartland of the Austrian Danube
It is "an unspeakably beautiful valley", according to Patrick Leigh Fermor, overlooked by castles "perched on dizzy spurs, dramatic with decay and cobwebbed with fable." This is the Wachau, the most beautiful stretch of the Austrian Danube, where the river flows through an almost impossibly romantic landscape of castles, forests and sleepy villages that languish amid vineyards and apricot groves. "If any landscape is the meeting place of chivalrous romance and fairy tales, it is this," Leigh Fermor went on. "The

stream winds into distances where Camelot or Avalon might lie."

The Wachau derives its name either from the word *wacta*, meaning a watch-tower, or from *vahen*, meaning to catch (as in fish). Its vineyards date from the time of the Celts; its apricot orchards might be even older, and for centuries have been the source of a fiery brandy known as Marillenbrand. In former times, the fruit growers of the Wachau sent their produce to Vienna by boat. They would leave towns such as Spitz at around ten in the evening and would arrive in Vienna before dawn, ready to sell the produce in the busy markets. Boats had no cabins and limited steering, and were at the mercy of the wind and the weather. The Wachau posed other dangers too. The area was a byword for danger and disease; the river was once again threatening to mariners, the castles were the lairs of pirates and vagabonds, and in 1338 the entire fruit harvest was wrecked by a plague of locusts. But nowadays the villages are thronged with tourists rather than brigands, while the river is lively with sleek pleasure cruisers heaving with day trippers from Vienna. On a warm day in summer, the sunlight glints sharply on the river and bathes the countryside in richly luminescent colours: lush greens smother the hillsides, while splashes of terracotta identify the roofs of a slumbering riverside village and a silvery-grey streak marks the stonework of a castle that rides the roll and swell of the countryside as if its turrets and towers had been cast adrift on a wave.

The dramatic castles and peaceful riverside settlements follow in dazzling succession. Schönbühel, a mere three miles downstream from Melk, is a ninth-century fortress perched on a smooth rocky mound almost entirely surrounded by water; its immensely tall white tower is crowned by a red onion cupola. Ruined Aggstein, a little further on, is very different: suspended precariously a thousand feet above the river, its grey walls almost seem to grow from the rock itself, and on a misty day its towers and battlements create a trap for unsuspecting wisps of cloud drifting along the forested valley. Like many castles in this part of Austria, Aggstein was a Babenberg foundation that eventually fell into the hands of the Habsburgs. One of its lords was Jörg Scheck vom Wald, known as the *Schreckenwald*, the Terror of the Forest, who murdered his prisoners by abandoning them on rocky ledge and giving them the choice of either starving or jumping to their death into the void of the Danube valley. He also amused lady friends by taking them to the grating of the dungeon after dinner where they could see his starving prisoners. Now the castle is a decently priced restaurant, serving hearty meals in the open courtyards, while guides in medieval garb show visitors round the ruins.

Just beyond Aggstein is the village of Willendorf, the site of one of Austria's most distinctive archaeological finds, known as the Willendorf Venus. This stout limestone figure with drooping breasts is only a few inches high, but its enormous antiquity—it was carved more than 25,000 years ago—makes this fertility symbol fashioned by a long-forgotten Danube culture an object of enormous veneration. After being pulled from the mud of the Danube valley the figure was given a newer and cleaner home, in the Naturhistoriches Museum in Vienna.

Three miles further on, Spitz an der Donau is a small town that, like many settlements in this part of Austria, quietly oozes the prosperity that comes with being situated within easy commuting distance of Vienna. The old rustic dwellings have been smartened up by urbanites, and every other house proclaims *Zimmer frei* (room to let); visitors busy themselves by shuffling round the former Habsburg castle, or by visiting the Schiffahrt-museum, an exhibition of Danube shipping and trading, housed in a baroque mansion once owned by a wine-producing order of monks. Then tourists press on to Weissenkirchen, a few miles further on, where red-roofed houses jostle for space around a tiny cobbled square, while the narrow winding streets that emanate from it untangle themselves amidst extensive vineyards. The *Pfaarkirche* (parish church) here is enclosed, like many other village churches in the Wachau, by stout defensive walls, a reminder of the time when settlements had to be fortified against marauding bands of sixteenth-century Turkish raiders.

Nowhere in the Wachau pulls in the crowds like Dürnstein. The village sits on a ledge on the north bank of the river just beyond Weissenkirchen, hemmed in between the water and a forested knuckle of pale rock. Clustered on top of the hill are, inevitably, the ruins of an ancient castle. But this is no ordinary Danube castle. The Kuenringerburg, built by the Lord of Kuenring in the twelfth century and later a Habsburg property, was where Richard the Lionheart, England's crusader king, was imprisoned and held for ransom, and it is Richard's connections with Dürnstein that gives it such allure. Richard, chivalrous and courageous, a lover of poetry and music, humorous and wise, and endowed with a mane of flowing blond hair, was every inch the medieval soldier-monarch of popular legend. But other aspects of his character spoil the romantic image: he was a heavy drinker, and possessed a sharp and often violent temper that led him to commit acts of cruelty. One story from the Crusades tells how Richard marched 2,000 Muslim prisoners out of his camp and murdered them one by one in front of Saladin and the remainder of the Muslim army. This, Richard thought, was just punishment meted out to Saladin, who had reneged on a treaty. Later, in 1192, Richard's army captured the port city of Acre, in present-day Israel, fighting alongside the armies commanded by the French King Philip II and by Leopold, the Babenberg Duke of Austria. But this victory was to sow the seeds for Richard's later imprisonment in Dürnstein.

After the battle, Leopold raised his standard above the captured city—undeservedly, the incensed Richard thought, as Leopold had played only a minor role in the battle. Richard instructed his knights to take down the standard and trample it in a ditch. Leopold never forgave the insult. Soon afterwards, Philip and Leopold left the Holy Land, and Richard was moved to follow them, concerned over reports he had received that England was being poorly governed by his brother John. He left Acre in October 1192, hoping to travel all the way back to England by sea. But a shipwreck in the Adriatic changed his plans and he ended up travelling through continental Europe in disguise. He grew a beard and adopted a false name, but in a tavern near Vienna he was spotted, allegedly because of his vibrant good looks and the opulence of his clothes. Richard fell into the hands of his nemesis, the Babenberg Duke Leopold, whose standard his troops had so wantonly trampled into the Levantine dust. Leopold duly passed him over to his suzerain, Henry VI Hohenstaufen, the son of the great crusader general, Frederick Barbarossa. And that was how Richard came to spend two years incarcerated in the castle at Dürnstein, which was in Henry's hands at the time.

Accounts of Richard's stay in Dürnstein are rich in legend. It was here, according to one such myth, that Richard earned his famous sobriquet of "Lionheart". The castle jailer kept a lion, and was also father to a beloved daughter. One day Richard succeeded in seducing the jailer's daughter; the furious jailer's response was to push the lion into Richard's prison cell. Richard showed no remorse or fear, promptly killing the lion by thrusting his hand down the beast's throat and wrenching out its beating heart. Then he simply ate it. Another legend concerns Richard's eventual discovery in the castle by Blondel, his loyal French minstrel. Blondel travelled from castle to castle in Europe in a desperate search for his master. Outside each one he sang a particular song that was known to both of them. When Blondel burst into song outside Dürnstein, he was surprised and overjoyed when Richard joined in, singing from the window of the high room in which he had been imprisoned. Blondel took the news of Richard's imprisonment back to England (where Richard's death had already been announced by his brother) and two knights were duly dispatched to Austria to pay a ransom and bring Richard safely back home.

The castle in which Richard had been imprisoned was eventually destroyed in 1646 during the Thirty Years War. Over time its romantic ruins, with their expansive views along a lovely stretch of the Danube, became a place of pilgrimage for English visitors to Austria. In the 1830s Frances Trollope, the mother of the novelist Anthony Trollope, visited the castle and wrote that she believed this place had been chosen as the place of Richard's incarceration "in the hope that the unequalled desolation of the scene might appall the Lion's heart, even while his imprisoned body was suffered to live." Nowadays it is hard to describe the scenery around Dürnstein as desolate; beautiful and beguiling would be more suitable adjectives to describe the views from the castle. And even if visitors to Dürnstein do not make it up the hill to take in the wonderful view, the town beneath the castle is attractive in itself. The most famous landmark is the church bell tower that hovers right over the river. Bristling with statues and crowned with a gold cross, the bell tower is a rich wedding-cake concoction whose juxtaposed pastel blue and gleaming white plasterwork gives it the appearance of being made from icing sugar. Surrounding the bell tower are pastel pink and orange monastery buildings, while the church itself features a richly decorated chancel, and yet more clothed skeletons, similar to those in Melk, languishing grimly in glass coffins lying in niches along the nave.

## Approaching Vienna: Stein und Krems and Tulln

Beyond Dürnstein the countryside flattens as the river winds its way out of the Wachau. The small town of Stein is the next settlement downstream. It is joined to another settlement named Krems—the production centre for Kremser wines—to form Stein und Krems. Krems still has many beautifully preserved buildings left from the time when it was an important customs town, the finest among them being the Renaissance Rathaus. In 1153 the great Arab geographer and cartographer Al-Idrisi thought the place more splendid than Vienna, and over nine centuries later Claudio Magris was struck by its "townscape of alleyways climbing emptily upwards, tiny balconies jutting out into small, slumbering squares, [and] hidden flights of steps giving out onto forests of rooftops." But Magris came here in winter, when the hotels were shuttered up and the streets deserted. "All is silent, miniscule and dead," he observed. "All one hears in the courtyards is the rain, discreet and soft."

Stein, like so many towns along this reach of the river, was also associated with the mercantile traffic that passed along it. On the waterfront, where a succession of tiny cobbled squares open out onto the river, some former salt barns, the *Salzstadel*, have been preserved, near the modern landing dock for cruise ships.

This reach of the valley is rich in associations with the *Song of the Nibelungs*. The village of Mautern, opposite Krems, is mentioned in the poem as the place where Kriemhild "received a royal welcome and won much favour." But her party did not linger long: they were anxious to reach Tulln, the next major settlement downstream, where Kriemhild would at last meet her husband-to-be, Attila. "There is a town along the Danube, in Austria, called Tulln," recounts the poem, where "Kriemhild encountered customs new and strange, things she'd never seen before." Those customs new and strange belonged to Attila and his band of warriors known as the Huns. They met with Kriemhild's party amidst scenes of great pomp, witnessed by men who had travelled here from all the corners of Europe: Russia, Greece, Romania, Poland, Denmark and Turkey. "A splendid band came riding into Tulln," the poet relates, "enthusiastic proud and merry men" who watched as "noble Kriemhild greeted her new husband with a kiss... she lifted the veil of her headdress, and her white skin shone against the gold of her hair." A bout of jousting, feasting and merriment followed, before the celebrants took to their boats and headed downstream to Vienna.

The wedding celebrations there dragged on for seventeen days. When at last the parties and the formalities were over, it was time for the Burgundians to return home. They left Kriemhild behind with her new husband, and made once again for the river. The poem tells how "The travellers boarded ships. So many horses and so many men covered the river that wherever anyone looked they thought they were seeing dry earth… they lashed together numbers of excellent, strong-bottomed ships so accidents wouldn't happen and none of the boats could go down. Tents were stretched across the decks. It was almost as if they were not floating along on water but grass and solid ground."

In Roman times, centuries before the time of the composition of the *Song of the Nibelungs*, Tulln was known as Comagenis, and was the base for an important Danube flotilla. A Roman bastion from the time of the Emperor Diocletian still survives, overlooking the river among a stretch of unprepossessing civic buildings that form Tulln's waterfront. Later the building was used to store salt, and to this day it is known as the *Salzturm*. But the attractions of Tulln go far beyond a simple tower. Barely a hundred yards along the river bank from the Salzturm is a former prison that now serves as a gallery displaying the works of the avant-garde artist Egon Schiele. Schiele was born in 1890 above the town's railway station, where his father Adolf was the stationmaster. But it is appropriate that his works are displayed in a prison, as Schiele himself spent time incarcerated, in Neulengbach, west of Vienna, after being found guilty of displaying his erotic drawings in a room that was open to children (he also faced charges of conducting a sexual liaison with a girl under the age of consent, but these were eventually dropped).

His paintings and drawings are arresting and immediately distinctive, full of contorted faces, intense gazes and twisted and grotesque nude bodies drawn with expressive lines. Some of his work is disturbing and explicit. Not surprisingly, conservative Viennese society was shocked; at his trial in 1912 the judge burned one of his drawings in court, over a candle flame. Intellectuals, however, saw Schiele as a major figurative painter of the early twentieth century, and the radical artist became strongly associated with the Austrian Art Nouveau movement known as *Jugendstil*. Towards the end of his life Schiele was judged famous enough to be given a solo show of his work at a gallery in Paris. He died in 1918, at the age of 28, a victim of the strain of Spanish 'flu that claimed twenty million victims throughout Europe that year. Although the majority of Schiele's work now hangs in a gallery in Vienna, originals and reproductions cram the walls of the museum beside the Danube in Tulln. They include sketches of nudes and oil paintings of places such as Trieste that Schiele visited using cheap tickets available to children of railway workers.

## KLOSTERNEUBURG: THE MONASTERY ABANDONED BY THE DANUBE

Beyond Tulln comes the definite sensation of an approaching city. Chimneys belch smoke from sprawling riverside factories, while ships load and offload at neighbouring jetties. The horizon seems to hint at suburbs and apartment blocks hidden just beyond its arrow-straight edge. And the river is intensively managed. First comes the Altenberg barrage, the last of the eight great dams that control the river between Passau and Vienna. Then the channel splits in two, the main branch curving east, taking the river away from the next settlement downstream, the monastery town of Klosterneuburg. Once, the monastery here directly overlooked the river; an engraving from the seventeenth century shows the twin towers of the great monastic abbey rising above a wide river channel choked by ever-shifting shoals and islands. Now all the monks can see from the windows of their rooms is a muddy trickle in a broad gutter, with the main arm of the river relegated to a position several hundred yards away behind thick stands of trees. The channel was moved in the late nineteenth century to ease navigation and improve flood control: worthy reasons, of course, but ones that deprive the palatial abbey of its former riverside setting.

The town of Klosterneuburg is, of course, the site of yet another former Roman garrison. In 1106 the rocky mound that supported the old Roman fort was commandeered as a royal palace by the Babenbergs, and seven years later the adjacent monastery was founded. The foundation stone of the abbey was laid by the Babenberg margrave Leopold III, reputedly on the site where he found his wife's veil hanging in the branches of a tree. The veil had been snatched from his wife's head by a sudden gust of wind nine years previously; Leopold eventually came across it on a hunting trip. When he reached up to take the veil from the branches, a vision of the Virgin Mary materialized and ordered him to build a monastery on the spot in her honour. Leopold did so, and his monastery is now the richest in Austria, built over several spacious courtyards and, like Melk, controlling a school (where Egon Schiele was once a pupil). It is also the last of the great chain of religious houses that line the banks of the upper and middle Danube, stretching from here all the way upstream to Beuron in Swabia, by way of Melk, Engelhartzell, Niederalteich, Wiblingen and Obermarchtal.

As with many of these foundations, the original medieval buildings of

Klosterneuburg were given a baroque facelift in the eighteenth century. But when it was rebuilt, Klosterneuburg was endowed with an additional architectural twist: a grandiose palace, or at least the wing of one, constructed right beside the monastery abbey. The instigator of the palace was Emperor Karl VI, who lost control of Habsburg territory in Spain to the Bourbon kings. To compensate for his loss, Karl decided that he wanted to create a palace in Austria that would imitate—and rival—the Escorial, the "Spanish Versailles" built outside Madrid at the behest of the Spanish Habsburg Philip II. Karl's vision was extraordinarily grandiose: the original monastery would be surrounded by a cream-coloured palace, built around four courtyards, bristling with spires and domes and turrets and sitting among luxurious gardens reached from the palace by sweeping staircases curving between ornate balustrades. Each of the domes was to be capped by a representation of one of the Habsburg crowns. But the vision was never realized, as the money quickly ran out, and building work stopped when Karl died. His daughter and successor, Empress Maria Theresa, showed no interest in continuing the project. In the nineteenth century work was begun again, but the completed buildings still amount to less than a quarter of those that Karl envisioned.

Ostentatious to the point of vulgarity, the palace drips with technicolour frescoes, vast tapestries, stuccoed ceilings that look as if they are made from icing, marble fireplaces and extravagant rugs and carpets. Here, as much as in the opulent but bland palaces in Vienna, is the innate tastelessness of the Habsburgs laid bare: dull interiors that boast of wealth rather than suggesting harmony. This was a dynasty that claimed the grandiose title of Holy Roman Emperor almost as a right for over five centuries, a power that considered half of Europe as its own private estate. But at Klosterneuburg, the would-be palace is coated with melancholy as thick as cake icing. The whole place is a vainglorious memorial in marble and stone to dreams that were never fulfilled, and to the hurt and shame of the loss of territory and power. The Danube itself seems to acknowledge this. It stays hidden away in its new channel behind the trees, avoiding the awkward prospect of a face-to-face meeting with its old friend. And even in its truncated state, the colossal scale of the palace threatens to overwhelm the church and the monastery next to which it stands. The monks must have heaved a collective sigh of relief when the building work was finally abandoned.

The abbey church of Klosterneuburg is a far more restrained affair than the adjacent palace. The church is extravagantly decorated with frescoes, including one depicting the Christian armies ejecting the Turks from the town, with the shimmering Danube curling away in one corner as turbaned warriors are trampled under the hoofs of rampaging horses. The medieval cloisters allow access to a baroque chapel in which Margrave Leopold is buried; he was canonized in 1485, and is the patron saint of Austria, so his tomb receives a steady stream of pilgrims. A stunning twelfth-century altar, known as the Verdun altar after its designer Nicholas of Verdun, once decorated the grave, and is now housed in the abbey museum. The astonishingly beautiful altarpiece consists of fifty gilded enamel plaques illustrated with Biblical scenes drawn with almost mystical intensity, crammed with flowing colours, geometric designs and moons, stars and animals. One panel shows twelve cows, arranged in a circle, carrying a large basin into the courtyard of King Solomon. The scene is painted from above, and the cows almost seem to be revolving around the circular basin as if it was a Catherine wheel; the colours in the basin swirl and shimmer in a miasma of blues, greens, yellows and golds before deepening to the most vivid hue of aquamarine in the very centre.

## Vienna: City of the Blue Danube

It is one of the most instantly recognizable pieces of music ever composed. In fact the *Blue Danube Waltz* is one of those pieces that seem so familiar that the listener is tempted to switch off after hearing just the first few notes. Those who force themselves to listen are treated to a musical slice of Vienna itself: as rich as a gooey Viennese cream cake, as dramatic as its imperial architecture, as florid as the decoration in a rococo church, as refined as the city's nineteenth-century reputation for social and intellectual *hauteur*. But the piece is just as rich in irony as it is in melody; firstly, the poet who coined the phrase "Blue Danube" was referring not to the river as it passes through Vienna, but to a reach of the Danube hundreds of miles downstream, in deepest Hungary; secondly, the Austrian capital turns its back on its supposedly fabled river, splitting it into four separate channels and relegating all of them to outlying districts rather than taking them to its heart; and thirdly, the Danube is far from blue. "The Danube in its course is green, grey, brown, a mixture of all three, or just plain muddy, but never blue," Bernard Newman wrote in the introduction to his

1935 book *The Blue Danube*, before apologizing to readers for the falsity of his chosen title. "Nor does the Danube ever suggest a waltz. There is no river in Europe less suggestive of a ballroom. Sometimes it is wild and majestic, sometimes broad and pastoral, but its changes are too erratic ever to make a good dancing partner." Newman's views chime with those of Negley Farson. "Strauss did this noble river a great deal of harm when he wrote *The Blue Danube*", Farson wrote in *Sailing across Europe*. "It is not blue, it is a wild, spreading, sullen yellow flood."

Vienna's association with the Danube, and the Danube's association with the colour blue, is solely due to an incident of accidental public relations on the part of Johann Strauss the Younger, the waltz's composer. He never expected the piece to be as successful as it was—and indeed, its first performance suggested it was destined to be a flop. But later performances caught the imagination of the public, and with its catchy rhythm and lilting melody, the piece was adopted as a sort of unofficial anthem of Vienna, of Austria and of the Danube itself. The waltz is played at the annual New Year's Concert in Vienna, where it always receives an encore, and the most famous bars provide the aural signature of Radio Austria International, the country's equivalent of the BBC World Service or Voice of America. The piece also provides the aural wallpaper churned out by the tannoy systems on the pleasure cruisers that, in summer, steam up and down the Danube from Vienna westwards to Linz and Passau, and eastwards to Budapest and Bratislava. (Apparently this is an ages-old practice. When he was travelling by boat along the Romanian reach of the Danube in 1933, Patrick Leigh Fermor watched a steamer from Vienna saunter past, playing *Tales from the Vienna Woods* and *The Blue Danube Waltz* over a loudspeaker linked to a record player.)

Johann Strauss the Younger was 42 years old when he composed his most celebrated work. By that time he was already the most popular composer in Vienna and an unofficial court composer to the Habsburg monarchs. He was known, in particular, for his waltzes and his patriotic marches (although his famous operetta, *Die Fledermaus*, was yet to flow from his compositional pen). On the evening of 9 February 1867, he lifted his conductor's baton in a Viennese concert venue known as the Dianabad-Saal, and the classic opening refrain of the *Blue Danube Waltz* was heard by an audience for the very first time. The official title of the work was *An der Schönen blauen Donau* ("On the Beautiful Blue Danube"), a phrase taken from a poem by Karl Beck, a German speaker who lived in the town of Baja, which lies beside the Danube on the Great Plain of southern Hungary.

The piece was commissioned by the Wiener Männergesangsverein, the Vienna Men's Choral Association. They clearly wanted to be a part of the performance, and Strauss obliged by writing vocal parts for their choir of tenors and basses. The text he used for that first performance in the Dianabad-Saal was written not by Karl Beck but by another poet, Josef Weyl. In this original form the piece met with a muted, rather ho-hum approval. But later that year Strauss reworked the piece for a performance at the World's Fair in Paris. This time he abandoned the vocal text and turned the piece into a work solely for instruments. The piece was greeted with instant success and rapturous admiration. It is this reworked orchestral version, first heard in Paris, which is most commonly performed today.

However, to complicate matters, another text, this time by Franz von Gernerth, was later written to accompany the reworked music, and this is the text now used in any sung performances the work receives. But this second attempt at providing a vocal accompaniment yielded a text so stodgy and sickly-sweet that it is hard not to draw yet more analogies with Viennese cream cakes. Von Gernerth's version opens with the words "Donau so blau, so schön und blau" ("Danube so blue, so bright and blue") and continues: "Through vale and field, you flow so calm, our Vienna greets you, your silver stream... Far from the Black Forest you hurry to the sea, giving your blessing to everything." Mermaids, castles, mountains, blue skies and the glorious city of Vienna itself, with its "full chest... of heartfelt German wishes... flown away on your waters", complete a bucolic, lyrical, quasi-mythical picture of the river as it flows through the heart of Austria. Weyl's original words, sung at the first performance, were, in contrast, bawdy and satirical rather than sentimental, and were written in the wake of the defeat of the Austrians by the Prussians at the 1866 Battle of Königgrätz, one of the worst military disasters ever to befall Habsburg Austria.

The Dianabad-Saal concert venue (the name translates as "Diana Baths"), the scene of that first ever performance of the most famous piece of music associated with the Danube, no longer exists. In its place rears the modern glass façade of a multi-storey office block that serves as the Austrian headquarters of the computer multinational IBM. Claudio Magris actually saw a connection between Strauss and the multinational: both, he maintained, were "the heart of a business world... [Strauss, like IBM] was a hive of industry turning out consumer goods for the mass market."

But although the concert venue has gone, the Danube is still there— or, more specifically, the arm of the river known as the Donaukanal, which lies across the road from the IBM building. It is this arm of the Danube that penetrates furthest into the centre of Vienna. Although nowadays no wider than a main road, the Donaukanal was once a much more stately affair, for it was the original channel of the Danube as it flowed past the ancient city. The waterway forms the north-eastern boundary of the *Innere Stadt*, literally the "inner city", the oldest district of Vienna, which is bounded on its other sides by the *Ringstrasse*, a line of broad avenues and showpiece boulevards marking the positions of the city's former walls. The *Innere Stadt* was the site of the Roman fortress of Vindobona, where in 108 AD Marcus Aurelius met his death while defending the Roman province of Pannonia from attacking tribes of Slavs and Teutons.

At the centre of the district, a good 700 yards from the Donaukanal, is the Stephansdom, Vienna's gothic cathedral with its distinctive roof of gaudily coloured tiles. The adjacent Stephansplatz, with its vibrant street

life and expensive cafés, is always busy with tourists; few if any will make it to the Donaukanal, only one stop away on the metro, but in a part of the city that the Viennese have claimed back from the tourist crowds. Here, the citizens of Vienna jog or stroll or cycle on the tree-lined banks of the canal by tall rows of dour nineteenth-century apartment buildings that peep over the crowns of the trees. But the din of the traffic pounding along the roads lining each side of the canal, and the bump and roll of trams over the bridges, mean that the canalside is not a place to linger.

Leigh Fermor dismissed the canal as "a dismal scene of sad buildings and dirty snow under a cloudy sky" after he walked beside it, and to this day it seems a rather forgotten part of the city's ancient heart. And what is more, it is not a canal: the current in the Donaukanal is as rapid as on any other stretch of the Austrian Danube, presenting a challenge for the occasional small craft that ventures along it. Most Danube voyagers simply ignore the canal and navigate their vessels along the main channel, which lies several hundred yards to the east. But in 1986, Tristan Jones was given special permission to moor in the waterway. "We were honoured indeed to have the privilege of being the first ocean vessel ever, in the two-thousand-year history of that great city, to reach her heart," he wrote in *An Improbable Voyage*. Once moored, Jones and his crew were treated like mini-celebrities. They welcomed a constant stream of well-wishers and visitors onto their boat, including the professor of art at Vienna University, and the entire chirruping horde of the Vienna Boys Choir, who came for a look round and then invited Jones to one of their concerts.

Vienna was a Celtic settlement long before the Romans established their *limes* settlement of Vindobona. For centuries, before, during and after the Roman occupation, the place was a crossroads of river and overland trade routes. Salt came downstream from Passau, spices were brought in by merchants via the overland treks stretching eastwards towards Asia and Russia, and amber came to the city from trading routes that snaked across north-eastern Europe towards the Baltic. In the Middle Ages political patronage from the Babenbergs, and then the Habsburgs, transformed Vienna into a powerful military stronghold. But this was to render the city a tempting prize. In 1529, and then again in 1683, Turkish armies laid siege to Vienna, but were successfully sent packing both times, even though defending Austrian forces were vastly outnumbered on both occasions. The second Turkish defeat marked the beginning of Vienna's role as the *Kaiserstadt*, the Imperial City of the Habsburgs, a role it was to retain until the end of the Habsburg era in 1918.

Until the second Turkish defeat Vienna had been just one gathering place of the peripatetic Habsburg court. But the final routing of the Turks and the promise of political stability encouraged the Habsburg court to stay. Nobles and grandees followed, and soon Vienna's famed and glorious baroque appearance began to take shape. The Hofburg, until the seventeenth century a fortress, became an extravagant residential palace, and it was soon surrounded by yet more palaces constructed by obsequious noblemen, anxious to be associated with the most glorious royal court in continental Europe.

The end of Ottoman expansion into Balkan Europe also established a second tradition in Vienna—one which, unlike the Habsburgs, still survives: it is the city's obsession with coffee. The story goes that an enterprising Hungarian who had a nose for profit as well as coffee discovered some beans that had been left behind by the retreating Turkish troops in 1683. He opened the city's first coffee house soon after the final Turkish legions were heading off back down the Danube. Two hundred years later, the coffee houses provided the meeting points for the Vienna's vibrant communities of intellectuals and artists; nowadays they are mostly patronized by tourists. But no *Kaffeehaus* in Vienna has ever offered its patrons a view of the Danube. That is because the river seems so separate from the rest of the city, hidden away "out the back" like the rubbish bins in a Viennese apartment building or the servants' quarters in the Hofburg. In fact it would be perfectly possible to visit Vienna and not actually realize the river is even there.

The Danube is kept at a distance from the city centre for a very good reason. Before the late nineteenth century, any buildings close to the river were liable to spend much of their time half-submerged in sludgy brown floodwater. As the Hofburg rose in the western part of the *Innere Stadt*, a good mile and a half west of the Danube Canal (and even further removed from the current principal channel of the Danube), the area to the east of the city was abandoned to the water, an ever-shifting quagmire of muddy islands and swampy lagoons. When Dr. Charles Burney approached the city by boat in 1770 he indicated that "the approach to Vienna from the river is not unlike that of Venice... forty or fifty towers and spires may be seen from the water." Boat was the principal method of transport, and agricultural produce from the rich farmland beyond was bought and sold at floating market stalls. Poverty was rife, as was disease, spread by the stagnant water that sloshed around in the muddy ponds and pools. The foul air and regular inundations by dirty water ensured that the district, named Leopoldstadt, was the poorest in the city. No wonder the Habsburg monarchs kept their shiny new palaces well away from the place. Solace did not come until the 1870s, when the area was drained and the Danube was confined to two principal channels and two smaller ones (of which the westernmost one was the Donaukanal). Control of the river put an end to the flooding and eradicated the poverty and disease. The slums were cleared and the area finally became incorporated into the life of the city after centuries as a watery, neglected adjunct.

The most obvious result of the drainage work was the creation of a large island dividing the main channels of the Danube from the Danube Canal. This island, part of which was once a Habsburg hunting ground, now became a wooded playground for the Viennese, a place where the inhabitants of this notoriously cramped city could venture into something approaching countryside, and breathe fresh air. Soon after the drainage work was complete the island gained its most famous feature, the *Riesenrad* (ferris wheel), which was designed by a British engineer, Walter Bassett, and opened in 1898 to huge acclaim. It is still there to this day, clanking round and round day in day out, giving those in its swinging wooden cabins a bird's-eye view over the entire city as it completes its rotation. Of course, the wheel became an iconic feature of the city after its appearance in a scene of the 1947 film *The Third Man*. It is popular with tourists, who are surprised to find that the venerable wheel is marooned within a tacky funfair known as the Volksprater, which sports a tawdry assortment of rollercoasters, miniature railways and fairground stalls. Beyond the funfair the island is divided between gloomily silent residential districts and an extensive area of trees and parkland known as the Prater (named by the Habsburgs from the Spanish *prado*), where wealthy Viennese come to spend time with their over-dressed, perfectly behaved cohorts of dogs and children.

The two main channels of the Danube run east of the Prater. They form cuts across one corner of the tourist maps of Vienna. In fact, on maps the parallel blue channels take on the appearance of a wide blue highway, built to whisk river traffic through the city's inner suburbs and away from the busy centre, forming a sort of watery version of London's north circular road. Between the two channels (the easterly one is slightly wider) is a long, slender island of grass and trees, the Donauinsel, which stretches over twelve miles, from Klosterneuburg in the north to Vienna's extensive river port in the southern outskirts of the city. For their entire length the banks of the twin channels are occupied by fast arterial roads, railway lines, marshalling yards, scruffy public parks, boathouses, housing estates and low-key yachting marinas. In the south the fast roads and weed-infested suburban railway tracks give way to commercial harbours, with their familiar assortment of cranes and warehouses and loading wharfs. The scene is not particularly ugly, but it is dreary and bleak, particularly on grey days in winter when a biting wind from Russia or Poland whips up the surface of the water and chills to the bones those hardy cyclists and pedestrians braving a crossing of one of the wide bridges. On days like these the baroque palaces and grand avenues seem a world away from the Danube waterfront. But it is along the Danube in Vienna that the modern city is split open at the seams, to reveal its inner workings.

The most distinctive buildings beside the Danube in Vienna are located on a small island created by the river's fourth channel. This thin, sinuous waterway, known as the Alte Donau, curves eastwards from the twin channels like a cupped hand, cradling a lozenge-shaped island in its gentle grip. The island is known as the Donaustadt and the clutch of tall, faceless, glass-fronted concrete leviathans that rise from its centre are collectively known as the Vienna International Centre. Vienna is not a city of tall buildings and the giant vertical slabs of the VIC form a dominant feature on the city's skyline. The curving office towers book ended by solid walls of concrete, the squat cylinder of a conference hall and the windswept concrete walkways that run between them all rose from the muddy flood deposits of the Danube in the 1970s at the suggestion of the Austrian prime minister of the day, Bruno Kreisky; their designer was the noted Austrian architect Johann Staber.

The most prominent tenants of the complex are the United Nations, which is why the place is colloquially known as "UNO City". The UN presence here means the place has special "extraterritorial" designation: it belongs to no one state of the world, and to all of them. And the UN's presence is also a reflection of the shifts in historical fortune that have buffeted Vienna over the past hundred years or so. In the nineteenth century, this was an imperial city, where military officers from Hungary, Jewish

traders from Poland, sailors from Trieste and artists from Bohemia would rub shoulders in the streets and coffeehouses. Then came the scourge of antisemitism in the decades leading up to the Second World War, the *Anschluss* with Germany, the division of Vienna between the armies of the four victorious Allies after the war and finally an unwanted role for the city on the frontline of the Iron Curtain that divided Europe for nearly fifty years. The decision to site an important hub of the UN here acknowledges these turbulent counter-currents of history; in these austere buildings Vienna atones for the sins of the 1930s and 1940s, and at the same time celebrates its history as a city with an international reputation for art, culture and intellectual radicalism.

When the UN offices were established in Vienna, during the frostiest era of the Cold War, the Danube seemed like a watery thread that could draw eastern and western Europe towards one another; so it seemed right to site the UN buildings here, right beside the river, and so tall that from the uppermost floors you can see as far as Hungary. The Cold War is over now, of course, and Vienna lies at the heart of a united Europe rather than at the fracture-point of a divided one, but its official position alongside Geneva and Nairobi as a second-rank centre of the United Nations (below New York) seems secure. At present, the UN bodies that make their home here include the International Atomic Energy Authority and offices dealing with drugs, crime, industrial development and outer space.

One last building beside the Danube in Vienna merits a mention. The Donauturm is a 820-foot tall tower whose slender concrete stalk takes root in a small park close to the United Nations buildings. The bulbous-headed tower was opened in 1964 as the centrepiece of the Viennese International Horticultural Exhibition, whose temporary flower beds and fancy arboreta formed the undergrowth around its base. It is the tallest free-standing structure in Austria and, apparently, the 66th tallest building in the world. At the top is a restaurant that inevitably revolves, though rather slowly; the prospect of a bungee jump from the outside viewing gallery is available to those with an even stronger yearning for action. The park itself, long since divested of its horticultural blooms, is a bland area of lawns and woody glades encircled by a miniature railway and enlivened by busts of international personalities whose political good deeds make them deserving of an appearance in the shadow of the tall UN buildings: a moustachioed Salvador Allende, the former president of Chile who killed himself during a military coup in his country in 1973, peers from a concrete plinth hidden by a glade of trees, while Simón Bolívar, who led South America's political struggle against Spanish rule in the early nineteenth century, stares blankly into the middle distance from another. Otherwise, the park is fringed by drab parking lots and tennis courts that stretch in one direction to the Alte Donau, and in the other to the Danube proper, or at least the busy highway that skirts its eastern shore. The constant grind of traffic absolves the park of any pretence at being a calm oasis in the hubbub of the city, but the odd UN worker can sometimes be glimpsed here at lunchtime, munching on sandwiches or prattling into a mobile phone.

## NAPOLEON ON THE DANUBE
Six miles downstream from the Donauturm the Danube flows past a district of dockyards and industrial facilities that spread out on both sides of the river. Two hundred years ago this area was a marshy wilderness well beyond the boundaries of the city; the place where the Donaukanal now merges with the twin channels of the river to form a single waterway was, then, an expanse of islands and lagoons. In1809 one of these lonely mid-river islands, named Lobau, became the scene of two major battles of the Napoleonic wars.

By the turn of the nineteenth century the Austrian Emperor Franz II, still nominally the Holy Roman Emperor, had emerged as a major adversary of Napoleon, who coveted Franz's land and imperial possessions. In

1805 Austria suffered two catastrophic defeats, firstly at Ulm, on the German Danube, and then at Austerlitz, in Moravia; the resulting peace treaty was signed at Pressburg, as the city of Bratislava was then known. Here, Franz was forced to make humiliating concessions to the victorious French, including relinquishing his title of Holy Roman Emperor, held by his family since the Middle Ages. Four years later, the French fighting machine was in trouble in Spain, and Austria seized the opportunity to seek revenge for the humiliation of Pressburg. But once again the Austrians marched into a defeat beside the Danube—this time, at Regensburg in Bavaria. After that drubbing they could do little to stop Napoleon taking Vienna, and the city capitulated on 10 May 1809.

Even so, Napoleon still had a large Austrian army, under the command of Franz's brother Karl, to contend with. On 20 May, ten days after the fall of the capital, Napoleon led some 40,000 French troops across the Danube, via Lobau Island, to engage Austrian troops on north bank close to the neighbouring riverside villages of Aspern and Esserling. The plan met with disaster for the French: the Austrians sent heavy barges downstream to disrupt the pontoons and inflicted heavy casualties. Six weeks later, in July, French forces regrouped, and once again crossed the river at Lobau, this time ramming palisades into the riverbed to block the flow of any heavy barges set loose by the Austrians. This second engagement, known as the Battle of Wagram, gave Napoleon one of his most famous victories, commemorated to this day in the name of one of the major boulevards leading towards the Arc de Triomphe in Paris. Following Wagram, Austria was once again forced to the negotiating table, and this time lost control of Galicia and Croatia to France. Napoleon, meanwhile, pulled his forces back from Vienna, once they had blown up the city's defences. Franz, however, was destined to have the last laugh: in 1814, following Napoleon's defeat at Leipzig and his exile to Elba, the emperor hosted a grand diplomatic shindig in the Hofburg known as the Congress of Vienna, which was to fix Europe's boundaries for much of the remainder of the nineteenth century.

## Chapter Five

# THROUGH THE BURGENLAND TO

# SLOVAKIA

### EAST FROM VIENNA: THE MARCHFELD

Once it has left behind the industrial sprawl that now blights the area around Lobau, the Danube flows into the Burgenland, Austria's easternmost province, and across a flat, fertile plain known as the Marchfeld. This is a quiet corner of Austria, a kind of no-man's-land between Vienna and the Slovak border. The Marchfeld derives its name from the River March (Morava to Czechs) that rises in the highlands of the Czech region of Moravia and flows into the Danube just west of Bratislava. The abundance of woodland, mainly birch, poplar and willow, has encouraged the Austrian government to create a national park in the Marchfeld, known as the Nationalpark Donau-Auen. The area's scenery can hardly compete with the national parks of Austria's Alpine regions, but the Marchfeld exudes a quiet tranquillity, particularly along the river itself, where luxuriant reed beds provide a habitat for beavers and nesting waterfowl. Unlike the reaches of the river that pass through Vienna, the Danube is allowed to flood here unimpeded, allowing wildlife to flourish in the wetlands that border its banks.

Away from the river bank nestle the hunting lodges that once belonged to rich Viennese, dating from the time when the Marchfeld was treated by city dwellers as little more than a fertile hunting ground. Now, with much of the woodland cleared, intensive arable farming has taken over as the mainstay of the economy. Soulless villages, linked to Vienna by the S-Bahn commuter railway, scatter the countryside, and wind turbines have sprouted amidst the fields, making good use of the strong but bitter gusts that can howl through these flatlands in winter. Vienna's international airport, Schwechat, also benefits from the level terrain, its runways beginning only a few hundred yards south of the Danube. On dull days the landscape of the Marchfeld can be dreary and uninspiring. But in the east of the plain the horizon is dominated by the low hills of Slovakia,

Devín Castle ruins

which provide a promise of more dramatic countryside to come.

The former Roman camp and settlement of Carnuntum provides the region's main historical focus. The remains scatter a three-mile stretch of the river's south bank, around the commuter town of Petronell and a neighbouring low-key spa town, Bad Deutsch Altenburg. In its heyday Carnuntum was one of the most important settlements along the entire length of the Roman *limes*. It was founded as a military camp for the fifteenth legion in 40 AD by Emperor Claudius, and just over sixty years later Emperor Trajan made it the military and civil capital of the province of Upper Pannonia. By then the camp and its associated town was home to a population of more than 50,000.

The soldiers posted here had the task of defending a frontier state of the empire in the era of its greatest spread. By the opening decades of the second century AD, Roman rule stretched from the Nile to the Rhine, and from Morocco to northern England. But along this reach of the Danube lawless, violent tribes from across the river gnawed away at the empire's defences as tenaciously as the beavers that now make their homes in the reed beds of the Marchfeld. A succession of emperors grappled with the threat from these tribes throughout the second century, most particularly Marcus Aurelius, who based himself in Carnuntum for three years' hard campaigning between 171 and 173 AD. His principal foes were the Marcomanni, a tribe that made its home in what is now Bohemia and Moravia and whose name translates as "men of the borderlands"; and the Quadi, who lived in the area slightly to the east, in what is now western Slovakia. In the end Marcus Aurelius made little headway in his efforts to subdue these tribes. His achievements never matched those of Trajan, who subdued the Dacian tribes north of the Danube in what is now Romania, and incorporated their territory into the empire.

But the achievements of Marcus Aurelius in another sphere were rather more enduring, for he was a philosopher as well as a politician and military commander. Between sorties across the Danube from Carnuntum he found the time to write part of his *Meditations* while staying in the camp. "We live for an instant," he wrote in his somewhat melancholic treaties, in which he denies the existence of an afterlife and welcomes death as providing an end to all desire. "Everything is by nature made to die," the philosopher-emperor went on. The *Meditations,* which Marcus Aurelius wrote as a personal reflection on life and death, were eventually published in Zurich in 1558, and were later championed by the philosopher John Stuart Mill, who likened them to the Sermon on the Mount. The Romans, however, preferred to remember Marcus Aurelius for his military exploits. They are recorded in graphic detail on the column of Marcus Aurelius, which stands to this day in the Piazza Colonna in Rome. The spiralling frieze on the column depicts an army crossing the Danube (probably at Carnuntum), and further along, a predictable melee of scourged barbarians, victorious Romans and horses, chariots and prisoners being led away in chains.

Carnuntum experienced its moment in the political spotlight twenty years after the departure of Marcus Aurelius. In 193 AD Septimus Severus, at that time the governor of Pannonia, was proclaimed the new emperor of Rome by the troops stationed in the camp, who were no doubt overjoyed to see a "local boy" elevated to the highest position in the empire. But in the following century the ebb and flow of history was to provide a downturn in Carnuntum's fortunes, when the town played a role in the divisions and in-fighting that accompanied the slow and tortuous unravelling of the empire. In 260 AD the troops here, shocked by the capture of Emperor Valerian by the Persians, proclaimed a senator named Regalianus as Valerian's successor. Coins bearing the head of Regalianus were minted at Carnuntum and have been unearthed by archaeologists investigating the site. But nowhere else were these coins produced: Regalianus seems to have been championed only in Carnuntum, and did not emerge as a serious rival to Valerian's son Gallienus. In fact, the schism seems to have been confined solely to this Danube encampment. After failing to seize the moment, Regalianus sank back into the obscurity from which he had emerged, and was killed some years later in a separate bout of imperial squabbling.

The following century, in the year 308, Diocletian chose Carnuntum as the place to host a conference that aimed to strengthen the empire in the era of the Tetrarchy when the sprawling Roman domain was split between four separate rulers. But by then the writing was already on the wall for the empire. Within a hundred years Carnuntum was finally abandoned to the tribes that Marcus Aurelius had campaigned so hard to subdue. As the barbarian hordes stormed across the river, the remaining Roman troops were moved upstream to Vindobona, and Carnuntum was allowed to sink slowly into the mud of the Danube floodplain.

Unlike other Roman camps along the *limes* such as Passau, Linz, Regensburg or Vienna, Carnuntum was not reborn as a Teutonic settlement in the Middle Ages. So when excavations began at Carnuntum in the nineteenth century, archaeologists were not faced with the prospect that much of what they were interested in was buried beneath modern buildings. Instead, it was centuries of mud, spilled by the Danube while it was in flood, which covered the old fortification walls, the bath houses, the amphitheatres and the shops and roads and houses. Indeed, the river, shifting and re-shifting its channel after each flood event, had swept much of the old settlement away. But a fair proportion of ruins remain, the bulk of them in Petronell, where the waist-high walls and chariot-wheel-scarred streets pop up between the commuter homes and the river bank, to be picked over by parties of schoolchildren, day trippers from Vienna and hardy archaeologists, who are convinced that the silt of the Danube has much still to yield. A drainage network has been found under the paved streets, and the old classical façade of the Temple of Diana has been reconstructed, partly with bricks fired in a modern kiln in temperatures of over one thousand degrees centigrade. Nearby are some public baths probably constructed (or at least significantly embellished) for Diocletian's grand political meeting in the fourth century.

Standing in the midst of deserted farmland a few hundred yards from the river is the Heidentor, a vast triumphal arch built by Emperor Con-

stantinus II (351-61) to commemorate his military achievements in Gaul. The structure is crumbling but the central arch, built of red brick, still remains, providing a grand gateway into nothing more than a ploughed field. Two huge lumps of masonry lie on the ground at the foot of the arch, abandoned where they fell. Patrick Leigh Fermor, visiting Carnuntum without the benefit of guidebooks, simply stumbled upon this remarkable feature, rising "alone, enormous and astonishing" from the flat countryside. Further away, two amphitheatres have been unearthed, one for the soldiers and one for the civilians in the adjacent town. Once the amphitheatres provided seating for thousands; now they are now little more than circles of freshly mown grass surrounded by rings of grey stones. The soldiers' amphitheatre has a tunnel that leads to the Danube, for quick and easy disposal of the dead.

Downstream from the second amphitheatre, in Bad Deutsch Altenburg, a museum built to resemble an ornate Roman villa lies a stone's throw from the river bank and is stuffed full of archaeological finds. The most striking exhibit is in the museum's foyer: a reconstructed Mithraic relief, depicting the Persian sun god Mithras slaying a cosmic bull, while a serpent and a dog drink from the bull's wounds and a scorpion pincers its testicles. The cult of Mithras was popular with soldiers, particularly those who guarded the borders of the empire, and reliefs of this kind can be found along key Roman frontiers such as the Danube and Hadrian's Wall. Little, however, is known about the cult, whose believers wallowed in ritual and superstition that encompassed the shifting constellations in the night sky and the passage between night and day. Newcomers into the cult were required to bathe in bull's blood in subterranean temples as part of their initiation ritual; and the relief in the museum at Bad Deutsch Altenburg probably comes from the dank walls of one such temple.

## Hainburg to Devín and Bratislava: Through the Former Iron Curtain

The easternmost town on the Austrian Danube is Hainburg, some thirty miles downstream from Vienna and a mere two miles beyond Bad Deutsch Altenburg. The town has had a long history of being in the thick of things, both militarily and politically. When it was attacked by Turkish forces heading upstream along the river in 1683 the inhabitants refused to surrender, and 8,000 of them were killed in retribution when the Turks finally broke through. Hainburg's medieval fortifications, including a sturdy thir-teenth-century gateway known as the Wienertor, are testament to its long role as a protective outpost of Austria. During the era of the Austro-Hun-garian Empire, with the Turkish threat receded, Hainburg fell into peace-able times again, only to have its frontline position resurrected after the Second World War when the "Iron Curtain" closed right beside it. Specifi-cally, the curtain came down along the Morava river, which flows into the Danube from the north immediately beyond Hainburg. The confluence is overlooked by the substantial ruins of Devín Castle perched on a rugged promontory. The castle is in Slovakia; the Morava marks the Slovak-Aus-trian border, and for four decades the small town of Devín, gathered like a skirt around the foot of the castle promontory, was the first glimpse behind the Iron Curtain for travellers heading downstream along the river.

The coining of the phrase "Iron Curtain" is most often credited to Winston Churchill, who used it in his famous speech delivered in Fulton, Missouri, in March 1946. But the phrase had been around for a number of decades by that time. In February 1945, just three months before the war ended, Goebbels commented in a speech that if Europe was occupied by Soviet Russia it would lead to mass slaughter being committed behind an "Iron Curtain" of Soviet rule. The socialist politician and writer Ethel Snowden also used the expression in her 1920 book *Through Bolshevik Russia*. Nevertheless it was Churchill who brought it into the popular lexicon, and it provided a neat summation of the division of Europe after the Second World War. "From Stettin, in the Baltic, to Trieste, in the Adri-atic, an Iron Curtain has descended across the continent," ran the text of his Fulton speech. "Behind that line all the capitals of the ancient states of central and eastern Europe—Warsaw, Berlin, Prague, Vienna, Budapest, Belgrade, Bucharest and Sofia—all these famous cities, and the popula-tions around them, lie in the Soviet sphere, and all are subject, in one form or another, not only to Soviet influence, but to a high and increasing measure of control." Churchill's words presaged the wrenching asunder of the continent's ancient *Mitteleuropa* heart.

It is interesting to see Vienna in Churchill's list of cities. In 1946, when he made the speech, it looked as if the venerable capital of the Aus-trian Empire would be dragged into the sphere of Soviet Europe. The country's first post-war government was sponsored by the Soviets, and the veteran social democratic premier Karl Renner was forced to give key ministerial posts to communists. For this reason the other three Allies refused to acknowledge the new government, fearing that Austria was slowly being sucked into the communist sphere of influence. When the war was over the country, like Germany, was carved up into four zones of occupation, with the Soviets claiming the eastern portion, through which most of the Austrian Danube flows. Vienna, also divided into four sectors, was marooned within the Soviet occupation zone, suffering exactly the same fate as Berlin. The Soviets began to asset-strip their occupation zone, sometimes moving entire factories back to Russia, but the opportunity to turn eastern Austria into another East Germany somehow slipped through their fingers after the failure of two attempted coups.

In May 1947 communist agitators helped to foment food riots throughout the country, and although rioters besieged the chancellery building in Vienna, they did not gain the support of the trade unions as the Soviets had hoped. The second coup attempt came in 1950 when US Marshall Plan aid money ran out and food prices rose sharply. Riots broke out in Vienna, but a general strike was called off after only one day, and once again the trade unions did not throw in their lot with the communists. By 1955, when Allied forces withdrew from Austria, the eastern sector had been bled dry by Moscow. Khrushchev had lost interest in creating a Soviet satellite state centred on Vienna and gave his support to the creation of a neutral, independent Austria. So although the Iron Curtain fell further east than was expected—Yugoslavia, of course, also proved a slippery Soviet catch—fall it did, and for forty years Europe was more divided politically, militarily and economically than it had ever been in its history.

The Danube played a tiny role in bridging that divide. During the Cold War it was a major artery for trade between western and eastern Europe. Soviet ships often ventured as far upstream as Regensburg, and ships from Austria and Germany regularly plied the waters of Romania and Bulgaria. But their cargoes were goods, not people or ideologies, and the European divide at Devín was as sharp as it was anywhere else along the entire length of the Iron Curtain. Crossing the border in 1985, on his trip along the Danube, Tristan Jones was surprised by the strong contrast he witnessed travelling from Hainburg to Devín, which was then in Czechoslovakia, one of the most repressive and hard-line communist states. The change "did not happen gradually," he wrote in *The Improbable Voyage*.

"It happened with a sudden change in the primal colours of the universe, like passing from sunshine into shade. It was something of the feeling I've had when I've walked into a butcher's freezer." To him, Devín looked "grey and dead and flat... The whole town seemed to have the look I have seen in the eyes of mugging victims in New York. It seemed to say 'Look what they've done to me.'"

It is all different now. Any traces of the border defences around Devín, the watchtowers and the fences and the searchlights, have been swallowed up by the thick forests that smother the countryside. The small town of Devín appears prosperous and bustling, and the castle, once marooned in a sensitive border zone, is nowadays a popular day-trip from the Slovak capital Bratislava, only fifteen minutes away by bus. The outcrop on which the castle sits bears witness to being settled 7,000 years ago. The Romans made it a key part of the *Limes Romanus*; it is rare to find Roman fortifications on the north side of the river, but clearly they could not resist making use of such a splendidly defendable outcrop of rock. The soldiers who manned the fortress were drawn from the Carnuntum garrison. When the Romans departed, the site fell under the control of the Great Moravian Empire, which ruled much of what is now the Czech Republic during the early Middle Ages. One frequent visitor during this time was a tenth-century prince, Vratislav, after whom Bratislava is named.

The current castle dates mostly from the thirteenth century, with additions made by later Hungarian overlords. It has been in ruins since its destruction by Napoleon in 1809. In the 1930s the government of Czechoslovakia bought the castle from the Hungarian family who owned it, and archaeologists have been picking away at it ever since, despite its sensitive position right on the border. One find includes a carbonized loaf of bread baked in the castle's bakery during the fifth century.

Although the castle is in ruins, those ruins are substantial, and among the most impressively situated on the Danube. The walls rise precipitously on the high slim rock that towers over the confluence, while a picturesque polygonal bastion known as the nun's tower perches on its own column of rock and provides the castle's most obvious photo opportunity. The hills to the north are dotted with villas and vineyards: the prosperous commuter hinterland of Bratislava. Slovakia is a mountainous country, and the hills here are the first peaks and ripples of the Carpathians, which sweep north in a giant arc, rising to the Alpine massif of the High Tatras in the north-east of the country (then the mountains swing south, and the Danube encounters the chain again, nearly 625 miles downstream from Devín, where the river wrenches itself through the high ground via a gorge known as the Iron Gates). To the south of Devín the land ripples away into steppe land.

The natural gateway that Devín guards, through which armies have poured and retreated, and along which borders have been drawn and defended, is known as the Porta Hungarica. The gateway is not only a political boundary, but a linguistic and cultural one too. Nowadays Devín and Bratislava are Slovak towns, but for centuries the region immediately downstream from the Porta Hungarica was a part of Hungary, and it is at the Porta Hungarica that the river changes its character completely. No longer is it a Teutonic river flowing across Germanic lands; from here to the Black Sea, the plains the Danube crosses and the hill ranges it cuts through are settled by quite different peoples, whose origins lie deep in eastern Europe and Asia: Hungarians, Romanians, Bulgars and Slavs.

*Part Three*

# INTO THE BALKANS
## BRATISLAVA TO BELGRADE

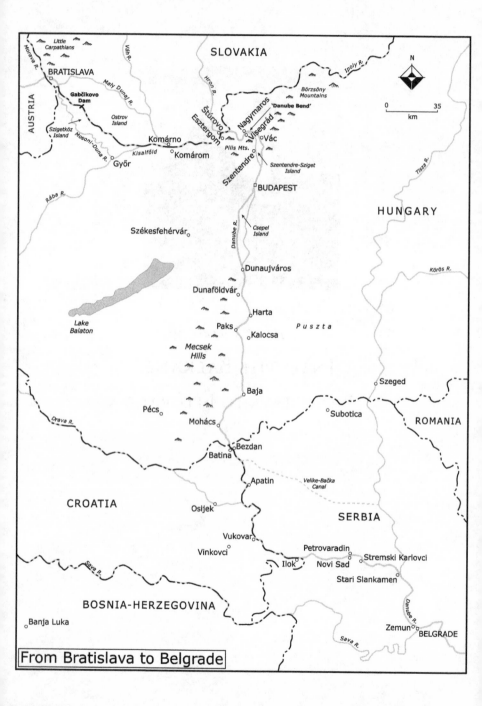

From Bratislava to Belgrade

## Chapter Six

# Bratislava and the Slovak-Hungarian Borderlands

### "East of Vienna, the Orient Begins"

Defining the landward boundary of any peninsula is always a troublesome affair, and the Balkans seem no different to any other peninsula in this regard. Where exactly can travellers on the Danube claim with certainty that they have reached the Balkans? On their trip by barge along the Danube in 1997 Bill and Laurel Cooper were firmly told that Austria was part of the peninsula. "Hier Sie lassen Europa," they were told by a customs official in Passau, who continued in English: "Here you are leaving Europe. Ho, Ho! Here at Passau the Balkans begin." But this does not seem very likely. The Balkans are defined by language and culture, not geography: the peninsula is Slav, Hungarian, Greek, Romanian, Albanian and Turkish, but not German. Austria's claim to be part of the region seems tenuous at best. But the country's capital has always been considered the last cultural stepping stone of Western Europe; the gateway to the Balkans. "Östlich von Wien, fängt der Orient an," wrote Metternich, the great nineteenth-century German statesman and diplomat: "East of Vienna, the Orient begins."

Anyone visiting Vienna who wants to gain a sense of that city's position on one of Europe's most conspicuous cultural fracture lines should go to Mexikoplatz, a windswept square overlooking the Danube just east of the Prater. In the distant days of the Cold War, traders from Russia and Georgia would set up stalls here selling jeans, watches, stereos and cheap clothing to Czech, Romanian and Hungarian visitors. The goods were shoddy and none could be returned if they were faulty, but the products sold in Mexikoplatz were far superior to anything that could be bought back in Budapest, Bucharest or Prague. Nowadays the Iron Curtain may have lifted but the traders of Mexikoplatz are still there, buying and selling in the shadow of the noisy flyovers that whisk traffic across the Reichsbrücke, one of the principal bridges over the Danube in the Austrian

capital. The Mexikoplatz market defines Vienna as a city that has historically looked in two different directions along the river: west, towards the
cultural heart of Europe, and east, to its impoverished hinterland. Of
course, the harshness of the boundary line has softened in recent years,
and in the future it might be rendered almost invisible. But in the past
the sense of Vienna being on the cultural frontline was unmistakable.

"You are on the edge of civilization now, in Vienna," Negley Farson
was told in 1925 while he sojourned for a few days in the city, before navigating his yawl east along the Danube towards Bratislava. There, as the
Donau became the Dunaj, Farson encountered a wholly different city. And
he was not the only traveller of that era to realize that a journey from
Vienna to Bratislava meant crossing a boundary that was much more than
just political or linguistic. "A different cast had streamed on stage and the
whole plot had changed," wrote Patrick Leigh Fermor after travelling the
short distance between the two cities. In Bratislava he saw dancing bears
in the streets, cohorts of beggars and chaotic tangles of children and
fortune tellers; in the air, he caught the vibrant tones of gypsy violins and
zithers; and in a cavernous Jewish coffee house the size of a railway station
he was aware for the first time of the strange guttural sounds of Yiddish,
and saw rabbis sporting long beards and covered in long black cloaks
hanging down to their heels. The sense of "otherness" in every square, in
every street, in every shop and bar and restaurant was palpable. This was
the Balkans: another Europe, wholly different to the one just upstream in
Vienna.

BRATISLAVA: "A DIFFERENT CAST HAD STREAMED ON STAGE"
Bratislava has been doused by the shifting cultural tides that have washed
over central Europe to an even greater degree than Vienna. This is most obviously apparent in the number of names by which the city has been
known. The Greeks knew the place simply as Istropolis: the City on the
Danube. To the Hungarians it was Pozsony; the first Slovaks called their
city Prešporok; and the Germans have always called the city Pressburg, all
of which are derived from the same Latin root, Posonium, which was the
name by which the Romans knew the city. The first Slavs, who arrived on
the scene in the very early Middle Ages, called their settlement Brezalaus-
purc. The city has only been known as Bratislava since the Treaty of
Trianon made it part of Czechoslovakia in 1920. The name is derived from

a Slav prince, Vratislav, who ruled the place over a thousand years before it was to finally bear his name. Indeed, the thousand-year gap between the era of Prince Vratislav and the signing of the Treaty of Trianon separates two distinct eras of Slav rule in Bratislava; the historical space between these two eras is filled by the Hungarians, masters of Bratislava from the ninth to the early twentieth century.

In 1920, at the end of the Hungarian period of rule, most of the inhabitants of Bratislava spoke German or Hungarian, and knew the city as Pressburg or Pozsony; Slovak was spoken by only one person in seven. Yet in the early decades of the twentieth century this trilingual nature gave the city its most distinctive character. In the 1920s Negley Farson wrote of the "three-name town, where all the signs in the streets, all the menus, are in three tongues... on one side [of a café] a painted bunch of grapes, with under it the names Vino-Wein-Bor; on the other side a painted glass of beer and Pivo-Bier-Sor." However, when Farson passed this way the city's days as a linguistic melting point were numbered. Bratislava was part of the newly created state of Czechoslovakia, and many Hungarians and Germans were preparing to move out. By the time of the Soviet liberation of Slovakia in 1944, the city was once again as Slav as it had been back in the days of Prince Vratislav.

Appropriately it was Vratislav who founded the most distinctive landmark in the city named after him: the castle that perches gloomily on a knuckle of rock above the north bank of the river. The castle in its present incarnation takes on a rather severe form, its high corner-towers making it resemble an upside-down table. But this is a result of the rebuilding work to which the structure has been subjected over the course of the twentieth century. The historical associations of the site more than compensate for the dourness of the castle's exterior, for the castle has witnessed the ebb and flow of well over two millennia of history from its rocky perch, during which time it has been occupied by the Romans, the Slavs, the Habsburgs, the Hungarians, the Slavs (again) and even the Soviets, who passed this way during the quashing of the 1968 reform movement in Czechoslovakia that came to be known as the "Prague Spring".

The prime defensive site on which Bratislava Castle now sits was first inhabited in the Stone Age. Later the Celts and the Romans constructed substantial forts to guard the settlement that grew up along the river bank in the shadow of the rocky promontory. With the collapse of the Roman

Empire the site was occupied by a number of migrating tribes, culminating in the Slavs, who trickled into this region from what is now western Russia during the sixth century. Vratislav, who was a prominent Slav prince, built a castle here to complement the one upstream at Devín sometime around the year 805. But Slavic control of the castle was only to last a few decades. Another tribe, the Hungarians, who were not Slav but instead traced their origins to central Asia, was in the ascendancy in central Europe. This fierce warrior people arrived on the shores of the middle Danube in the ninth century and were soon moving upstream, extending their territory by ruthless conquest; it was not long before they wrested control of Vratislav's castles at Devín and Bratislava from the Slavs. The Hungarians rebuilt the castle at Bratislava so solidly that it withstood fierce assaults by the Mongols, who made frequent raiding incursions along the Danube from what is now Romania during the early thirteenth century. Once the Mongols withdrew, riven by internal feuding and overstretched by the sheer size of their vast central Asian empire, the Hungarians were able to establish a wealthy and powerful state centred on Buda (now part of Budapest) in an era of comparative peace. During this time Bratislava sank into relative obscurity, overshadowed in Hungarian politics by Buda and other towns of the middle Danube.

When the Middle Ages were over, a new Asiatic foe emerged from the Balkans and encroached steadily up the Danube, just as the Mongols had once done: the Ottoman Turks. Recognizing that Vienna was in the firing line, the Habsburg ruler Ferdinand I decided that Hungary would make a good buffer zone. He proclaimed himself King of Hungary and flooded the country with Habsburg troops. But it was not enough. Turkish forces occupied Buda in 1541, and the Hungarian political establishment decided to move their capital upstream to Bratislava. Along with government ministers came the emblems of Hungarian statehood: the crown jewels, which were kept in Bratislava Castle between 1552 and 1784. During their stay in the castle the jewels were guarded by one hundred soldiers—fifty Austrian, and fifty Hungarian, an arrangement that was a sure sign that Hungary was by now fully a part of the Habsburg Empire. Even as the Turkish threat abated during the eighteenth century, the Habsburgs remained in Bratislava, and gradually converted the castle into a palatial residence. Maria Theresa, the builder of Vienna's Hofburg, presided over the most dazzling phase of rebuilding. As Queen of Hungary from 1740 she gave the castle its biggest makeover, and liked it so much that she spent as much time here as she did in Vienna.

In 1783 Buda was returned to its rightful role as capital of Hungary. Government functions moved back downstream from Bratislava to the restored capital, while the crown jewels were taken upstream and found a new home in the Hofburg. Bratislava declined in importance and by the turn of the nineteenth century the castle was home to nothing more glamorous than a seminary for Catholic priests. In 1802 the building was converted again, this time into a military barracks, and it was in this guise that it met its partial end in 1809, when it came under merciless cannon bombardment from Napoleon's troops. Two years later the wrecked castle burst into a fireball due to the carelessness of soldiers living the high life in what remained of Maria Theresa's rococo interiors. The fire was so bad that it spread down the hill to parts of the town; however, it was not so destructive as to render the castle uninhabitable. Throughout the rest of the nineteenth century the inhabitable parts of the building continued to be used as a barracks. In 1934 Bernard Newman, passing through Bratislava on his cycling trip down the Danube, thought the castle was a "mere shell— four outer walls and no roof or interior, more picturesque from a distance (particularly from the river) than in a close-up."

The state of Czechoslovakia was created in 1919, an ambiguous phoenix that rose from the ashes of the defeated Habsburg Empire as a result of the Treaty of St.Germain. By the terms of that treaty, Czech-speaking Bohemia and Moravia were bolted on to Slovak-speaking Slovakia to form a brand new and very elongated state stretching from lush pine forests bordering Bavaria in the west to the impoverished peasant communities of Ruthenia (now part of Ukraine) in the far east. The new state also included territory formerly part of Hungary, including Bratislava. The arrangements did not go down well in Slovakia. Many Slovaks feared their language and culture would be swamped by the Czechs, who formed the majority linguistic group, and the creation of the new state was marked by riots and demonstrations in Bratislava. The castle came under threat of demolition from the new regime in far-off Prague, but an alliance of Slovak historians and nationalists prevailed and the building became the subject of a preservation order.

Disaster befell Czechoslovakia in March 1938. Facing the threat of invasion and possible armed conflict, the Czechoslovak leadership capitulated to the Nazis, and Bohemia and Moravia became a protectorate of the Reich. Slovakia was not part of the new protectorate, but the Nazis sent a gunboat down the Danube from Vienna and had the vessel aim its guns at Slovak government offices. Cowed by the show of force, the Slovak leader Josef Tiso eventually proclaimed his state independent from Prague but politically allied to Berlin. For the duration of the war Slovakia remained a Nazi puppet state, unoccupied by German troops (until late 1944) but in thrall to the Nazis throughout the conflict.

When the war was over and Czechoslovakia was reborn as a Soviet satellite, the castle was opened to the public for the first time, and snail's pace restoration work began. The work was interrupted in August 1968 when the castle was once again commandeered as a barracks. This time the soldiers were from Warsaw Pact countries, part of the invasion force that the Soviets launched as a response to the reformist policies of the Czechoslovak president, Alexander Dubček. In all, 200,000 soldiers entered Czechoslovakia to bring the country back into line, in a brutal show of force that saw tanks rumbling up and down the streets of the country's main towns and cities; Soviet commanders dubbed the invasion "Operation Danube". Of course, the Soviet bullying tactics were successful. The programme of liberalization was ended, Dubček and other political reformists were imprisoned or sent to labour camps, and the quashing of the "Prague Spring" became the most notorious emblem of the Soviet stranglehold over Eastern Europe.

Although Dubček's liberalization programme was firmly terminated, the events of the summer of 1968 did at least alert the Czechoslovak political establishment to the desperate need for change in the country. This came the following year, when a Federation law dividing the country into two—the Czech Socialist Republic and the Slovak Socialist Republic— was signed in the historically resonant setting of Bratislava Castle. This was a separation, not a divorce; that was not to come until the "velvet revolution" of 1989 ended communist rule in Czechoslovakia. After that it was clear that the unhappy marriage was over, that separation was not enough, and that a "velvet divorce" was inevitable. The fully independent Republic of Slovakia celebrated its birth on 1 January 1993, and simultaneously Bratislava celebrated its role as Europe's newest capital city. Appropriately, dignitaries were called to the Knight's Hall of the castle to put their signatures to the country's new constitution. When they did so the project to reconstruct the castle that was begun in the 1950s was given a renewed impetus whose effects are still being felt. In 2008, as Slovakia prepared to adopt the euro as its national currency, the castle was shrouded in scaffolding as yet another rebuilding project was initiated. But this is only the latest phase in a continuous history of building and rebuilding that has reflected the changing fortunes of Bratislava since the days of the first Slavs.

Although the castle's spectacular setting above the Danube provides Bratislava with its most emblematic picture-postcard view, close-up the building is nothing to write home about. It is a mish-mash of styles, and really only the gardens, created by Maria Theresa and modelled on those in the Schönbrunn summer palace in Vienna, provide much in the way of interest. Inside, the whitewashed rooms have been given over to government offices and dreary historical displays. But Bablavého, the steep cobbled street that winds its way up to the castle from the foot of the hill on which it is built, is one of Bratislava's delights. The pastel-coloured cottages lining the street, spotless and gleaming in the sun, are home to a string of smart restaurants and buzzing antique shops; at the foot of the street is a tall, slim rococo building housing an engaging museum of clocks. The colourful façades of these graceful cottages mask an unsavoury past: once they were home to prostitutes who served the soldiers billeted in the castle. Walking up to the castle from the river in 1933, Patrick Leigh Fermor heard the "polyglot murmur of invitation" from women standing in the dingy doorways, and noted their peroxide hair and the "paint laid on their cheeks with a doll-makers boldness".

All of this took place in the shadow of the slim spire of St. Martin's Cathedral, the city's most prominent church, which is situated just across from the clock museum, and a couple of hundred yards from the river bank. This building is the most pertinent reminder of Bratislava's Hungarian heritage: between 1563 and 1830 nineteen kings and queens of Hungary were crowned in its airy but rather cumbersome interior. And, to go with a dreary interior, a grim fate has robbed the exterior of the church of any charm as well: the building is pummelled to its core by the pounding traffic on a four-lane motorway that skirts within a few yards of its front door. Perhaps the construction of this busy highway was intended by the Slovaks as a snub to the city's Hungarian past; or maybe it was just the city planning authorities reminding the Catholic Church who was boss back in communist days. To the north of the church an ancient section of city walls peeps out beside the screaming rows of traffic; but the walls seems just as forlorn in their setting as the cathedral.

The motorway that brushes St. Martin's Cathedral provides the approach to Bratislava's second architectural emblem, the Novy Most, or New Bridge, whose busy traffic lanes span the Danube immediately downstream of the castle. The most distinctive feature of the whitewashed cable bridge is its single pylon anchored off-centre, half-suspended over the southern bank and leaning back to take the straining weight of the gently arching roadways. The tilting pylon is crowned by a gleaming circular pod that resembles a flying saucer, and gives the bridge its popular name—the UFO bridge. When the bridge was built, in the dark communist days of 1972, it carried yet another name, the Bridge of the Slovak National Uprising, honouring the uprising of August 1944 led by Slovak partisans in the mountains, which paved the way for the liberation of the country by the Red Army. That the bridge was opened a few years after the creation of the Slovak Socialist Republic is no coincidence: as its original name suggests, it was intended as an ostentatious celebration of Slovak national

identity. Nearly forty years on the bridge remains a striking structure, a sleek and instantly recognizable city landmark, but as ugly and severe as the castle (whose ramparts provide the best views over it). At the southern end of the bridge, fast lifts whisk visitors up through the pylon struts to the UFO pod, where a glitzy restaurant and nightclub provide stunning views along the Danube far into Hungary and Austria.

The south bank of the Danube, facing the castle and the Old Town of Bratislava, features a less impressive legacy of Slovakia's communist era: phalanxes of grimly similar workers' apartment blocks that march in formation towards the distant horizon. This functional municipal housing, grey and savagely impersonal from afar, peeling and grimy up close, forms a prominent feature of every single Danube settlement from here to the Delta. It will take decades for cities such as Bratislava to rid themselves of the visual blight inflicted by socialist city planners for whom functionality and cheapness were everything, while anything that could be seen as a nod towards an aesthetically pleasing environment in which people could live was frowned upon as dangerously bourgeois. Although trees have been planted along the river bank, and some shiny new office towers have risen from the bleak jungle of faceless apartment blocks and blustery urban highways, Bratislava's southern suburb of Petržalka is every inch a reminder of those dreary days of communism.

Back then, Bratislava had something of a reputation for being a cold and unforgiving city, qualities that could be experienced to the full during the bitter winters as grey and endless as the Petržalka workers' blocks. Tristan Jones, heading downstream along the Danube in his boat *Outward Leg* in 1986, vividly caught the flavour of one of those bleak communist winters. He wrote that the view from the city's harbour was

> a gloomy vista of police barracks, cranes, silos, tall, grimy docks and jetties, a high wall with watchtowers surrounding all, and rows and rows of concrete workers' flats peeping over the grim walls like faceless prisoners peeping over a fence. Over all, from above, a thin, cold, sticky rain descended on and permeated everything… to me it looked one of the most dreary prospects I had seen since the Soviet port of Murmansk during World War Two. It had the same hopeless, suffering, miserable, *crying* air about it.

Jones' impressions of the city did not improve on leaving it: while he was navigating out of the port in a soupy mist, the Slovak harbour authorities caused him to collide with a huge industrial barge that they deliberately sent across his path—and then proceeded to arrest him for causing the accident.

How things change. When Jones came here, Czechoslovakia was one of the most doctrinaire communist states in Eastern Europe. By 2004, an independent Slovakia, divorced from its overbearing neighbour, was a member of Nato and the European Union and was busy hosting summits between George Bush and President Putin. The city has seventeen "twin" cities around the world, including three along the Danube—Vienna, Ulm and Ruse, the latter city over 800 miles downstream in Bulgaria. The grim workers' blocks remain on the south bank of the river, but the old centre of Bratislava, set back from the north bank by a few hundred yards, has been smartened up considerably, and now is as neat and as charming as anywhere in Germany or Austria. New office blocks are springing up all over the place and construction firms are being kept busy. The clubbing and restaurant scenes are lively and the tourists pour in. Many come on day trips from Vienna, while cheap beer and cheap airline fares also draw in dozens of noisy stag parties from Britain. The smart museums down by the waterfront—the Slovak National Gallery with its huge collection of gothic altarpieces, and the Slovak National Museum with its interactive displays that trace the history of the country from the Stone Age to the present—are unlikely to feature on stag weekenders' itineraries.

It is not only the stag weekenders who do not stay long. In truth, Bratislava exhausts its appeal faster than other European capitals, and there is much more to Slovakia than its often grey and chilly capital: Bratislava Castle, after all, is on a spur of the mountains known as the Little Carpathians, which arc north from here and eventually become the High Tatras, whose Alpine peaks occupy the true heart of Slovak national consciousness. Unlike Austria or Hungary, Slovakia is defined by its mountains, not its river—which only flows wholly within the country for a distance of some fifteen miles. As the tourists head away from Bratislava—north, into the mountains, or west, to Vienna—the river heads south-east, and even the slowest boats are passing lonely Hungarian farmsteads on the southern bank within an hour of leaving the Slovak capital.

## Beyond Bratislava: the Gabčikovo Dam

The Porta Hungarica, the narrow defile just west of Bratislava that ushers the river from German-speaking into Slovak-speaking lands, not only marks a linguistic and cultural boundary. It also announces a change in the character of the river itself. In Germany and Austria the river has largely confined itself to a single channel, prone to flooding certainly, but fixed firmly on its course once the floodwaters have drained away. But after Bratislava the Danube becomes a different river. Continuously clogging up its own course with silt from countless floods, it starts to branch and divide: channels diverge and forge their own path across the plains, sometimes to rejoin the main channel tens of miles downstream. On maps, cartographers no longer present the river as a single thin blue line, but as a myriad of channels threading themselves around shoals and islands: a broad blue stroke across the page that is perhaps the hydrological equivalent of middle-aged spread.

It is on the flat plains of the Kisalföld, east of Bratislava, that the river first gets to taste this new sensation of space, and to stretch itself out accordingly. Kisalföld in Hungarian means "Little Plain". But the Kisalföld is only little in comparison to the Great Plain of southern Hungary. In comparison with marshy plains further upstream, such as the Marchfeld in Austria or the Donauried in Bavaria, the Kisalföld is vast, and forms by far the widest area of plains the river has so far encountered. The flat expanse stretches across the whole of north-western Hungary and southern Slovakia, from the Bakony Hills bordering Lake Balaton to the foothills of the Tatras. This is a monotonous landscape of deadeningly flat horizons and vast skies, of productive farmland and dull, straggling villages. The waters of the Danube (known to Hungarians as the Duna) cross this area by means of three channels: the agitated and meandering Mosoni-Duna to the south, the calmer Malý Dunaj to the north, and the main channel with its shoals and islands situated between them. The Malý Dunaj is separated from its main parent channel by an island named Ostrov, some 55 miles long and nearly twenty miles wide in places; the southern channel in turn creates another island, a smaller expanse known as Szigetköz, famed for its wetlands and abundant birdlife.

As its two errant children disappear over the horizon, the main channel of the Danube has a chance to relax and become sluggish, its waters continually diverging and converging to weave a tortuously difficult course for boats to navigate. Tristan Jones discovered this the hard way as he steered *Outward Leg* along this reach of the river in 1986. "At some places the channel was marked, at others it was a matter of by-guess-and-by-God," he wrote. "At one or two stretches we managed to sight a descending tug convoy before it disappeared into the mist or rain ahead of us and these gave us some clues as to where the safe passages lay." And Jones also noticed how empty the place seemed: the result of generations of impoverished peasants fleeing the grinding poverty of the Kisalföld for better lives elsewhere. "On the Hungarian side there was only one building the whole way from Hrušov to Komárno," he wrote. "That was a river control post. The lone Hungarian at its window waved to us as we passed. Otherwise Hungary seemed to us, from the deck of *Outward Leg*, to be one vast, flat, empty plain of wavering grass. There were no people, no animals, nothing but a few stumpy trees here and there."

Negley Farson, travelling the same route some sixty years previously, also noted the apparent emptiness of the place. "For forty miles we did not see a house, but a close inspection of the thick beech forest on the banks showed soldiers every now and then peering at us from the bushes." Farson seemed to have more time for the scenery here than Jones, though. "Travellers have described this part of the Danube as being uninteresting and monotonous," he wrote.

> And I suppose travellers, satiated with pine-forests and mountains—which seem to be the only scenery in Europe that is ever visited—would feel a little depressed by this stretch of deep beech forest criss-crossed with waterways. But from close at hand, on the *Flame*, we could see… black cormorants fishing, and the motionless herons in the green bayous beyond.

He goes on to mourn the fact that he had no canoe to explore the numerous secret channels that wandered around the deserted islands and marshy shoals.

The main channel of the Danube forms the frontier between Slovakia and Hungary as it flows across the Kisalföld. (That was why Farson saw so many soldiers peering at him from bushes.) In doing so the river also draws a cultural and linguistic boundary between the Slavs and the Hungarians. But this frontier is a recent one. Back in the tenth century, when the Hungarians were engaged in a relentless period of expansion, the river formed no barrier to their territorial ambitions. For centuries the whole of the Kisalföld, and the high mountains beyond it, formed part of the Kingdom of Hungary. The Danube did nothing more than mark a convenient border between neighbouring Hungarian provinces. But disaster came when Hungary was dragged into the First World War through its allegiance to the central powers. On its defeat the country was forced to acquiesce to the Treaty of Trianon, which awarded two-thirds of Hungarian territory to newly created countries that were intended to be "successor states" to the old Habsburg Empire. The biggest loss to Hungary was Transylvania, which was incorporated into Romania; Yugoslavia was awarded the corridor of land that had given Hungary access to the sea; and the Kisalföld and the Tatras, along with Bratislava, went to Czechoslovakia. The border between that country and Hungary was drawn along a ninety-mile reach of the Danube, stretching from Bratislava in the west to Esztergom in the east, where the river makes a dramatic turn and plunges south into Hungary proper. Many Hungarian speakers left Slovakia after the creation of this new frontier, heading across the river to establish new lives in burgeoning Hungarian cities. But plenty stayed. To this day around one in ten inhabitants of Slovakia still speak Hungarian as their first language, and many towns and villages on the Slovak side of the Danube remain majority-speaking Hungarian.

Modern Hungary, meanwhile, is a rump of its old self, landlocked and bereft of its former cities such as Bratislava. But the territory of the country today roughly equates with that settled by the first Hungarian tribes in the ninth century, shortly after they arrived here from the shimmering steppe lands east of the Caspian Sea, and began to farm the flat plains bordering the middle course of the great river.

After the Second World War relations between Hungary and Czechoslovakia were often strained. Hungary agitated over the rights of Hungarian speakers living north of the Danube, while in the 1970s the two countries developed a very different style of governance: Czechoslovakia's oppressively hard-line stance contrasted with the "goulash communism" of Hungary, where the government tolerated limited freedom of speech and allowed private firms to flourish within its command economy.

However, in 1977 the governments of the two countries managed to overcome their differences and give the go-ahead for one of the most controversial river control schemes ever constructed on the Danube. The Budapest Treaty of that year initiated the construction of a huge dam at Gabčikovo, thirty miles downstream from Bratislava in the heart of the Kisalföld, along with a secondary dam at Nagymaros, over sixty miles further on, below the Hungarian city of Esztergom. The dams would alleviate the flooding that plagued the area, and improve navigation in anticipation of the opening of the Rhine-Main-Danube canal. Most important of all, though, the dams would generate huge amounts of electricity. It was anticipated that the plant at Gabčikovo would have eight turbines providing a total of 720mw of electricity. The second dam at Nagymaros would be smaller and would be principally charged with stabilizing the water levels in the reach of the river between the two dams, though it too would have turbines built into it. The dams were to be built using Austrian technology and money; in return, some of the electricity would be fed into the Austrian national power grid.

This arrangement incensed many in Hungary: was not Austria simply reviving the old colonial relationship between the two states, which had seen Hungary so exploited during the days of the Habsburg Empire? A mischievous whispering campaign began: it was said by those who opposed Austrian involvement in the dam that the old Austro-Hungarian emblem *K und K*, standing for *Kaiserlich und Königlich* (Imperial and Royal), now stood for Kreisky and Kádár, referring to the leaders of the two countries who worked closely together on infrastructure projects such as the Gabčikovo dam, and ensured that relations between their two states were as cordial as the Cold War could allow them to be. But hard as the Hungarian leader Janos Kádár might have tried, the relationship was always destined to be rather one-sided: Austrians were able to travel easily into Hungary, and used the country as a place for cheap holidays on Lake Balaton, cheap food shopping and cheap dental treatment. No wonder that the plans for the dam caused many Hungarians to wonder whether much had really changed since Habsburg days.

For a time it looked as if the ambitious scheme on the Danube would go ahead. But then goulash communism got in the way. In 1984 a protest group against the dam was formed in Hungary, known as the Danube Circle (Duna Kör). The country's comparatively liberal stance on free speech meant that the group could orchestrate a reasonably coordinated campaign (unlike the protest movement against the dam in Czechoslovakia, which was organized by the human rights group Charter 77 and was much more low key). Environmentalists protested against the dam on several fronts: valuable wetlands and historical sites would be drowned, and Budapest's water supply could be poisoned. Charter 77 drew attention to the damage that would be inflicted on large areas of Slovak forest and farmland, scheduled to disappear under the waters of an enormous lake. Austrian environmental groups also became involved in the protest, hoping to drown the proposal in the way they had a previous dam at Hainburg, just west of the Slovak-Austrian border. But even liberal Hungary would only tolerate so much in the way of protest. Concerns from environmentalists were ignored and building began, albeit rather slowly.

In the end it was a change in political fortune that sealed the dam's fate. In 1989 the new democratically elected government of Hungary decided to yield to the environmentalists, and announced the abandonment of the project. The government of Czechoslovakia, however, decided to press ahead with it, although without the water control dam at Nagymaros the structure at Gabčikovo ended up much smaller than originally envisaged. With the birth of Slovakia in 1993, the government in Bratislava took a keener interest in the dam than their old masters in Prague had done. They brought the matter of Hungary's abandonment of the project in front of the International Court of Justice in The Hague. After four years of deliberations the court judged in 1997 that both parties had reneged on their original agreement. But the judgment was not backed up with any force and to this day the matter remains unresolved: the Slovak government has made its position clear—that the Hungarians should construct their dam at Nagymaros—but the Hungarians have intimated that this is a project that is now dead in the water. Meanwhile the dam at Gabčikovo is up and running, producing just over one-tenth of Slovakia's electricity needs. The wide lake associated with the dam, stretching as far back as the suburbs of Bratislava, and the twenty-mile-long, arrow-straight conduit that channels the water to the turbines, have alleviated the problems of navigating this reach of the river previously encountered by Tristan Jones and others.

## Komárom/Komárno: Fortress City on the Danube

Some 25 miles beyond Gabčikovo the Danube flows through a grimy port town known as Komárom in Hungarian, and Komárno in Slovak. It is the

only settlement of any size fronting the river between Bratislava and Esztergom, still about thirty miles distant. The town spreads itself on both sides of the river and, until 1920, formed a single municipality; the northern part of the town, on the Slovak side, is still home to a high number of Hungarian-speaking residents. A bile-green girder bridge, 1,640 feet in length, spans the river, linking Komárom with Komárno. The Slovak bank of the Danube is crammed with rusting cranes and deep concrete docks, while the Hungarian side is a humdrum sprawl of railway yards, grey apartment blocks and dreary shopping complexes. Neither part of the town is inspiring; these are the peeling provincial backwaters of Eastern Europe, deprived of the makeovers that have so transformed central Bratislava or Budapest, and touched by no aspect of capitalism more engaging than a Tesco supermarket.

Komárom's selling point as far as visitors are concerned is a fortress whose origins date back to the time of the Mongol invasions in the Middle Ages. Much later on, in 1848, the fortress was the scene of an important victory for revolutionary Hungarian forces fighting the Habsburgs in pursuit of independence. Although the revolution failed, and Hungary was to remain part of the Habsburg Empire until the First World War, the forces defending Komárom against the besieging Habsburgs never capitulated; defeat elsewhere in Hungary brought an end to the independence movement, and the heroism and fighting spirit of the defenders of Komárom have ensured a place for the fortress in Hungarian legend.

Writers of a romantic turn of mind dubbed the place the "Gibraltar of the Danube", and Komárom earned itself a motto—*Nec Arte, Nec Marte*, ("Neither by force nor by tricks"). A pity, then, that what there is to see in Komárom now is a rather dour fort named Monostor, constructed between 1850 and 1870 by the Habsburgs to stop any river-borne invasion force heading for Vienna. Built from harsh grey stone, the fort is crudely functional and not at all romantic or inspiring. But it is impressive enough, particularly as it is only one part of the defences built by the Habsburgs. Two more forts were built across the river in Komárno, and they form a whole with a separate series of bastions and interconnecting walls that encircle Komárom. The whole complex formed the largest army base in Hungary and included a highly sophisticated system of trenches and gun emplacements as well as over two miles of underground tunnels. But all the construction work was in vain, for the fortress never saw action in its rebuilt state and has acted, variously, as an army training centre, a prison, a refugee camp and, during the Cold War, as one of the biggest Soviet arms dumps in the whole of Eastern Europe. The place has been tidied up since the Soviets took all their weaponry away, and highlights at Monostor now include an outdoor concert venue housed in one of the larger bastions and a museum in the old barracks bakery. But much of the fort consists of windswept parade grounds and peeling barrack blocks; only the river, pounding away a few steps beyond the perimeter wall, softens the scene.

Komárom once acted as the customs post where ships heading along the river checked into or out of Hungary. That role is now largely gone: no border controls remain between Hungary and Slovakia, and the old passport huts on the bridge across the river have been abandoned for some years. But in the past the business of registering vessels with each customs station along the Danube was a tiresome but necessary one. When he passed this way in 1985 Tristan Jones was able to note the contrasts between Czechoslovakia and Hungary as he hung around in the customs house at Komárom. "Very high on one wall was a large picture of Lenin," he recalled. But whereas in Bratislava the probing eyes of the communist state seemed to miss nothing, here in Hungary things were different." According to Jones, Lenin "was leering through the picture windows across the river towards Czechoslovakia, and seemed to be ignoring Hungary altogether. His steady, slit-eyed gaze shot straight over the heads of everyone in the room." Jones was an acutely perceptive observer; by that time, the mid-1980s, Hungary had fully established itself as the most liberal of all the Soviet bloc regimes.

Only a couple of years after Jones registered Lenin's curiously benign gaze in the Komárom customs house, Budapest was awarded the dubious privilege of playing host to the first McDonald's in Eastern Europe (opened on a street a stone's throw from the Danube), and two years after that, in May 1989, the Hungarian government cast one of the opening salvos in the demise of East European communism when it threw open the country's border with Austria. Thousands of East Germans poured into West Germany via Czechoslovakia and Hungary, and no government seemed able or willing to stop them. Six days after the opening of the border, popular opinion forced János Kádár from office; he had been installed in power by the Soviets after the 1956 uprising but, with some irony, later became the architect of Hungary's liberal version of communism. A month after Kádár's departure, on 16 June, Imre Nagy, the reformist Hungarian premier whose liberal stance had inspired the uprising, and who had been executed on Kádár's orders in 1958, was reburied with full state honours.

With the Iron Curtain now lifted and Hungary setting the pace for reform, East European communism began to unravel at an astonishing pace: Poland already had a non-communist prime minister in the form of Tadeusz Mazowiecki; in October the Hungarians went one step further and announced free multi-party elections; the next month the Berlin Wall came down and the hard-line regimes in Prague, Warsaw and East Berlin finally acknowledged that the game was up. But although central Europe launched itself peacefully into a bold new era, it was not the same further downstream along the Danube, where the demise of communism was to bring bloodshed and violence to Yugoslavia and Romania.

## Chapter Seven

# Through the Hungarian Uplands

### Esztergom: "a celestial city in a painting"

A low fold of distant hills can be seen from the girder bridge at Komárom; they form the westernmost limb of an arc of uplands that curve through north-eastern Hungary. These uplands are split into a number of different ranges. At the point where the Danube cuts a swath through the high ground, it is the Pilis hills that rise from the southern bank of the river, while the Börzsöny Hills rise from the north. Neither range is particularly high; but although the summits barely touch 2,600 feet, the scenery is more dramatic than the numbers on the contour lines suggest. Up in the hills, forests of beach and oak, foraged by red deer and wild boar, occupy the craggy limestone slopes. But the most dramatic scenery is claimed by the river itself as it cuts through the massif by means of a winding gorge known as the Danube Bend. Standing at the gateway to the gorge, at the

place where the river moves off the plains and the hills begin to close in, is the city of Esztergom, its magnificent domed basilica an appropriate beacon that heralds the true start of the Danube's Hungarian journey.

Esztergom is the place where Hungary was born. Stephen, the first King of Hungary and now the country's patron saint, was crowned here by an emissary of the pope on Christmas Day in the year 1000. Stephen holds an exalted position in Hungarian history. It was he who welded the various Magyar fiefdoms into a unified state, and it was he who began the conversion of the Magyars to Christianity. (His religious zeal had cruel overtones: when it seemed as if his throne would pass to a pagan, Stephen made sure it did not by blinding the man and pouring molten lead into his ears.) Stephen's coronation regalia, on show today in the houses of parliament in Budapest, represent the most potent talisman of the Hungarian state, and his mummified hand, kept in the capital's main basilica, is its most revered holy relic. Previous to Stephen's momentous coronation at Esztergom the site had been settled by the Celts, and then by the Romans, whose garrison was known as Strigonium; Emperor Marcus Aurelius spent time here in the second century and wrote some of his *Meditations* in Salva Mansio, the town that grew up next to the Roman camp.

Six centuries after the departure of the Romans, the site caught the attention of the earliest Hungarians. Stephen's father, Prince Géza, established his court here, and so naturally chose the cathedral he had founded on the hill overlooking the Danube as the place where his son should receive papal blessing as the first King of Hungary. For over 200 years following Stephen's coronation Esztergom was invested with twin roles, as both the capital of Hungary and its principal religious centre. Change came in the thirteenth century, when Mongol encroachments forced the removal of the royal court downstream along the river to Buda (now part of Budapest). The clergy stayed put, but even they could not survive the Turkish onslaught three centuries later, when Esztergom became an Ottoman stronghold subject to constant attacks by Christian armies. In the 1820s, with the Turkish occupation a distant memory, the city regained its position as the Primal See of Hungary, and the current basilica began to rise on the same high rock that had once supported the original cathedral of St. Stephen. Nowadays Esztergom, with its cluster of monasteries, libraries, palaces and theological colleges, is to Hungary what Kraków is to Poland, Reims is to France or Toledo is to Spain.

The town's focus is on its enormous domed basilica. It is one of the most dramatic structures anywhere along the entire length of the Danube. As usual, Patrick Leigh Fermor captures the scene with a verbal flourish. "A cliff loomed over the long sweep of the river," he wrote, "and on this ledge was perched a white fane that resembled St Peter's in Rome. A light circle of pillars lifted a gleaming dome into the sky. It was dramatic, mysterious, as improbable as a mirage… [for over a thousand years] history has been accumulating here and entwining itself with myth."Negley Farson, approaching by boat rather than on foot, saw the towering dome for the first time at sunset, "like some strange mirage… iridescent, and unreal against the bronze Hungarian mountains". The basilica's massive dome, which can be seen from miles around, hovered "above water and timber and fen as though upheld, like a celestial city in a painting, by a flurry of untiring wings". Claudio Magris was less impressed. "The vast neo-classical cathedral which looms above the Danube has all the cold, dead monumentality of a cenotaph," he writes in *Danube*. "It beams forth a glacial temporal power, or insolence."

Although impressive, the basilica is a curious structure. Its exterior is rather harsh, with severe straight lines of monumental grey stone, and the dome is far too big for the rectangular box on which it sits. Inside, it is the scale of the building rather than its beauty that is most striking. The monumental height and breadth, the massive columns and the high windows all serve to awe worshippers into a humble reverence. Decoration is for the most part rather plain, although a flourish is provided by the altarpiece, painted by a Venetian, Michelangelo Grigorletti, whose inspiration was a painting by Titian, *The Assumption*, which hangs in the Friari church back in his home town. But the altarpiece can not offset the heaviness of the rest of the building, with its profusion of dour red marble and dark mosaics. Downstairs, the crypt is on a similarly massive scale, the thick walls and unadorned columns all adding to an even gloomier ambience than in the church itself.

Amid a myriad of tombs of dead prelates in the crypt, one stands out, that of a cardinal named József Mindszenty. He dared to speak out against the communist takeover of Hungary and in 1948 he was tortured and then sentenced to life imprisonment. He was freed during the 1956 uprising and then spent fifteen years in refuge in the American Embassy in Budapest, before the Hungarian government finally agreed that he could live out his final years in Austria. Mindszenty died there in 1975, and was reburied in Esztergom amid huge celebrations in 1991, a hero of free Hungary finally laid to rest in the nation's spiritual birthplace. Nearly twenty years later his tomb still attracts pilgrims by the busload. The Hungarian tricolour, with its red white and green stripes, the bunches of flowers, photographs and candles that all hang around the tomb provide the only semblance of light and warmth and colour within the stone-cold darkness of the crypt.

As for the rest of Esztergom, pastel nineteenth-century buildings mingle with churches, gardens, museums, palaces and cobbled streets to create one of the most beguiling small towns in Hungary. Spires and domes punctuate the skyline. A grassy embankment lines the river and small boats bob around in a side channel of the Danube known as the Kis-Duna. In fact, the only sour note in Esztergom is provided by the view across the river to the Slovak town of Štúrovo. Here tall industrial chimneys, pencil-thin in the distance, overlook phalanxes of peeling communist-era housing blocks in a town whose colours seem to have been bleached out by decades of economic stagnation and neglect. The place can not have looked so bedraggled in the 1930s when Patrick Leigh Fermor chose to end his book *A Time of Gifts* standing on the bridge linking the two settlements, the sounds of the bells of Esztergom ringing in his ears. But shortly after he passed through, the bridge was destroyed in the Second World War, and it was not until 2002 that it was rebuilt, much in the style of the one upstream at Komárom. Nowadays cars stream continuously across the cantilever structure. But the bridge seems to have done nothing for Štúrovo, which languishes under a thin white pollution haze in a remote backwater of Slovakia while Esztergom buzzes with prosperity. In that town's streets and squares and supermarkets, Hungary's post-communist economic success chimes louder even than the bells in the basilica.

## THE DANUBE BEND

For a few miles beyond Esztergom the north bank of the river continues to be Slovak territory. But the basilica at Esztergom seems to act as a beacon to the river, reminding it that it has a Hungarian destiny to fulfill. As the Ipoly river joins the Danube from the north, the land on both sides becomes Hungarian territory. And soon after passing the first Hungarian settlement on the north bank, a melancholic-sounding village named Szob, the river embarks on the extraordinary looping manoeuvre that forms the Danube Bend.

For many the scenery here is the very best the Danube can offer on the entire length of its journey. With its steep wooded valley and pretty red-roofed villages, the area is similar to the Austrian Wachau. But the valley here is deeper than in the Wachau, the river wider and the surrounding countryside more ruggedly beautiful. Beyond the river the forested hills rise steeply and then begin to fold and curl like waves on the open sea. Each ridge of the Pilis or the Börzsöny seems higher than the last, giving a depth and drama to the countryside that the Wachau lacks. Only the gorge of the Iron Gates, 375 miles downstream from here, gives the Danube Bend a run for its money in terms of scenery; and somehow, because of the graceful curve of the river that gives the landscape such a deep perspective, and because of the rippling hills and the thickness of the forests smothering them, the Danube Bend emerges the winner.

Writers have long extolled the grandeur of this scenery. Bernard Newman, for example, was lucky enough to witness a magnificent sunset here as he cycled through the gorge in the 1930s. "Anything more beautiful I have yet to see," he wrote in *The Blue Danube*. "Mountains silhouetted beyond; the water gleaming with a thousand reflected shades; wild, deserted nature trumpeting displeasure at our invasion through the shrill throats of waterfowl: a scene for poets and painters." But the scenic beauty of the Danube Bend means that the place is no secret: barely thirty miles from Budapest, the area is swamped in summer by day trippers and ramblers, who arrive by the boat, bus and car-load and head into the hills along the walking trails that start at every railway station and bus stop and landing stage. The village at the heart of the Danube Bend is Visegrád, whose guesthouses and holiday cottages and restaurants groan under the weight of visitors in summer. It is also in Visegrád that the main historic sights of the Danube Bend are to be found: the remains of the once-magnificent Visegrád Palace, down beside the river, and above it the older and more impregnable citadel.

The name Visegrád derives from the Slav word for "high castle", and indeed the Slavs were the first to build a fortress on the citadel site, taking advantage of the commanding view along the river valley. Later on, King Stephen adopted the thick forests of the Pilis range as his hunting ground, and converted the citadel into a grandiose hunting lodge. In the thirteenth century, with the threat of Mongol and Turkish incursions growing, the pendulum swung back, and the citadel once again adopted a defensive role. Throughout the centuries that followed, the triangular fortress was variously adopted as a royal refuge, a repository for the Hungarian crown jewels and a monastery, before the Turks finally captured the place. They left it in ruins, and the citadel would gradually have crumbled to dust had not a local priest alerted the Hungarian government to the historic building's state of decay. Restoration and in some cases wholesale rebuilding work on the citadel started in 1870 and continues to this day.

Now, after years of rebuilding, the line of defensive walls that tumble down the hillside from the citadel to the Danube waterfront look formidable enough to repel the most determined army. The walls finish at a sturdy water bastion right beside the river. Above the bastion is the octagonal bulk of Solomon's Tower, which guards the approaches to Visegrád along the Danube valley, and recalls King Solomon's imprisonment here by his cousin Ladislas early in the twelfth century. Like the water bastion, the redoubtable tower has been the subject of some fairly crude restoration work. In the citadel itself, many of the walls have been reconstructed from the foundation of the originals, and the resulting structure is a mish-mash of terraces and medieval fantasy architecture. Courtyards give access to rooms full of waxworks wearing medieval garb. Visitors dutifully drift through these and then head on into the dubious exhibition halls crammed with medieval torture instruments. But if the interior of the citadel is a fake reconstruction, none of this diminishes the quality of the views from the outdoor terrace, which stretch along the curving river and over the roll and swell of the hills: there is perhaps no more spectacular vista along the entire length of the Danube.

The Palace of Visegrád, which occupies a ledge of land below the citadel right beside the river, started life as a defensive castle constructed in response to the Mongol incursions of the thirteenth century. But as the Mongol threat diminished, this lower fortress was transformed into a glorious and luxurious royal palace. Work on this remarkable change of fortune was begun in 1316 by the Hungarian monarch of the day, Charles of Anjou, who decided to make Visegrád his main royal residence, the home of a medieval court that would be the envy of Europe. Each successive monarch who followed Louis felt the need to outdo his predecessor in endowing the palace with yet more layers of luxury and opulence.

The panoply of fountains, gardens and palatial rooms grew ever more ostentatious as the Middle Ages gave way to the Renaissance.

By the era of King Matthias in the fifteenth century, the royal court had moved downstream to Buda, and Visegrád was relegated to the status of country residence. But it was a glorious one, according to contemporary accounts. In 1488 János Thuróczy, a Hungarian aristocrat and the author of a book entitled *Chronicle of the Hungarians*, described the "upper walls stretching to the clouds floating in the sky, and the lower bastions reaching down as far as the river." A few decades later, Miklós Oláh, Archbishop of Esztergom and a prolific writer, remarked that "this royal palace has so many luxurious quarters that it undoubtedly surpasses buildings in other kingdoms."

Yet at the time these words were written, Visegrád's fortunes were about to change once more. In 1543 the palace was abandoned in the face of the gradual Turkish onslaught along the Danube, and after the Turks were gone, the buildings were never reoccupied. Over the following centuries locals plundered the crumbling palace for building stone, while landslides careering down the near-vertical slope above the building caused it to sink gradually into the mud. The magnificent gardens were reclaimed by the forest while weeds choked the flagstoned floors and opulent fountains. In 1702 the parts of the palace that remained were blown up on the orders of the Habsburg Emperor Leopold I, who was concerned that the walls and bastions might be used by rebel forces fighting for a Hungary independent of the Habsburgs.

Once Leopold's gunpowder had done its work no trace of the palace remained. In fact, its very existence began to assume a somewhat mythical air: many archaeologists came to Visegrád and searched for evidence of the building, but none found any. Then, in the early 1930s, one archaeologist got lucky. János Schulek, who had been hunting for the ruins for some time without success, made his startling discovery in the wine cellar of one of the houses in the village of Visegrád. He had been looking for some wine for a New Year's party; he noticed that the walls of the wine cellar were formed from ancient building stones, and guessed at once that they were the foundations of the lost palace. Schulek and his team began excavating the site soon after, and gradually the fabled Palace of King Matthias began to emerge from its muddy tomb.

The historic palace on show today is a mixture of bold reconstruction

and careful excavation. Some of the walls of the tiered structure, which creeps up the steep hillside on a number of different levels, are barely waist-high. But rising amid the crumbling walls is a wonderful Renaissance courtyard, a cool, whitewashed two-storey space surrounded by arched *loggias* that has been reconstructed more or less from scratch and would not look out of place in Rome or Florence. The central feature of the courtyard is a replica of a fountain that used to spout wine instead of water. Close by is another replica, that of the lion fountain, a red marble basin resting on sleeping lions that was once the showpiece of the formal gardens of the palace, and which gushed water channelled down from the citadel via an elaborate network of gutters. Both fountains postdate the most famous event staged here, a great medieval gathering known as the Visegrád Congress, which took place in 1335. The focus of the congress was supposed to be the discussion of new trade routes across Europe affecting the territory of the Kings of Bohemia, Poland and Hungary. But the three kings dragged retinues numbering hundreds to Visegrád, and the congress turned into a two-month, drink-sodden orgy of feasting, jousting and debating.

Over six centuries later, in 1991, the castle played host to another political conference, which had a remarkably similar guest list—namely, the leaders of Czechoslovakia, Poland and Hungary, who met here to thrash out a joint campaign for their countries to join the European Union. The group was christened the Visegrád Triangle, a neat designation that had to be abandoned when Czechoslovakia split in two in 1993. The four countries of the re-named Visegrád Group (or V4) eventually joined the European Union in 2004. But the group did not wind itself up once its original aims had been met: today the V4 continues to promote the integration of former communist bloc countries into the European economic and political spheres, and also manages a fund (based in Bratislava) awarding grants, scholarships and artistic bursaries to institutions in Slovakia, the Czech Republic, Poland and Hungary.

Across the river from Visegrád, and linked to it by a car ferry, is the village of Nagymaros, once famous as an artists' colony, but now destined to be known as the site of the abandoned dam that would have formed the downstream section of the great Gabčikovo-Nagymaros barrage project. The barrage, had it been completed, would have ruined the great gorge of the Danube Bend, and even in an era dominated by the search for alternatives to fossil fuels there are few who would lament the consignment of this project to history. The half-completed dam constructed here was blown up in 1994 and a resurrection of this project seems highly unlikely. The straggling village of Nagymaros itself sits on the outside of a great curve of the river, the last in the tortuous series of dog-legs that form the Danube Bend. After this final right-angle kink the river finally makes up its mind which direction it should go, and turns south, the direction it will maintain with steadfast determination until the Croatian city of Vukovar, some 220 miles downstream.

VÁC

As the river flows past Nagymaros it divides into two channels that enclose a long, curving, wooded island known as Szentendre Sziget. Barges have to follow the more easterly channel, while pleasure craft are relegated to the narrower, shallower western channel. By the time the main channel flows past Vác, six miles beyond Nagymaros, it has left the hills behind it, and is heading southwards, making straight for Budapest.

Vác is another former Roman garrison town, but unusually it is situated on the river's left rather than right bank, which would have meant that barbarian attackers did not need to cross the river to engage the Roman legionaries in combat. The Romans, for their part, would have had to fight with their backs against the watery barrier that elsewhere gave their garrisons protection. No trace of the Roman settlement remains, and there is no trace from the Turkish occupation either, when Vác was endowed with no fewer than seven mosques and a public hamam. Like the Roman remains, these have long since been reclaimed by the muddy floodplain of the Danube.

Instead, Vác is known for its wonderful main square, a tapering, spacious, irregular space lined with handsome pastel buildings from the baroque and rococo eras and fringed, in summer, with outdoor cafés that spill picturesquely onto the cobblestone of the plaza. Fountains and greenery abound, cooling the square on hot days in summer when Vác hums with tourists who make the short trip here by boat or train from the stifling capital. In the centre of the square are knee-high remnants of buildings that stood here in the twelfth century, when the Bishops of Vác were engaged in a fierce rivalry with those of Esztergom, and busied themselves founding churches and ecclesiastical colleges. A few steps down from the square is the river, wide and luxuriant and verdantly fringed with trees. A car ferry, little more than a floating platform onto which a dozen or so cars can squeeze, chugs to and fro from here to the forested shores of Szentendre Sziget.

A short distance upstream from the ferry terminal, along a shady stretch of embankment perfectly suited to the Hungarian equivalent of the Italian *passegiata* (summer evening stroll), the scene abruptly changes. A prison occupies the river bank, its high wall separated from the water by only a thin sliver of greenery. Vác is by far the most notorious prison in Hungary, for it is here that the dictator governments of the country incarcerated their political prisoners. During the brutal regime of Admiral Horthy, the pro-Nazi ruler of Hungary during the Second World War, those imprisoned here included the future media tycoon Robert Maxwell, then using his original name of Ludvik Hoch. After the war the prison's cells played host to hundreds more dissenters, this time opponents of the communist regime. In 1956, during the Hungarian uprising, prisoners were able to see and hear evidence of the revolution from their cells—flags waving, protest songs being sung—and staged a mass break-out which, like the revolution itself, was brutally crushed.

One of the prisoners at this time was a Hungarian-born Englishwoman and communist sympathizer named Edith Bone, who was serving a sentence for spying. She had travelled to Hungary in 1949 to work as a translator and to research articles for the *Daily Worker* newspaper. As she tried to fly out of the country she was arrested by the police and was subjected to a farcical trial, during which the nature of her supposed offence was never made clear to her. She served her sentences in gruesome prisons in Budapest and Vác. "I was in what was known as the special section [in Vác]," she wrote in *Seven Years Solitary*, her 1957 book about her experiences. "It was completely separated from the rest of the prison... even the exercise yard was sealed off from the rest of the prison by a completely blank wall as high as the prison building itself." Bone, in her sixties, suffered dreadfully in the bitter winters and was finally released and deported during a general amnesty of prisoners that followed the uprising.

Today, the building still functions as a prison and bristles with security cameras and barbed wire. The political prisoners have long since been released, of course, but the prison provides a potent reminder of the dictatorships that governed Hungary for more than fifty years. The building itself was originally an elite boarding school, founded by the Empress of Austria, Maria Theresa; a rather plain triumphal arch, built in neoclassical style and dating from the time of her visit to Vác in 1784, sits rather incongruously next to the prison, on the landward side. Later on the school was converted into a barracks, and it was only in the nineteenth century that it began to earn notoriety as a place of internment.

## SZENTENDRE

When the Turks withdrew their forces from Hungary during the late seventeenth century, the opportunity arose for substantial resettlement of the fertile plains surrounding the Danube. However, it was not Hungarians who repopulated the area, but Germans. In particular, impoverished Swabian peasants floated here from the upper reaches of the Danube in the flat-bottomed boats known as Ulm boxes. As Swabians settled along the Danube Bend (and in many other towns and cities in Hungary away from the Danube), a separate wave of migrants moved into this same part of

Hungary, from the south. Like the Swabians, the Serbs came by boat. Unlike the Swabians, they were forced into flight along the Danube by the Turks. It was the capture of Belgrade by Ottoman forces in 1690 that precipitated this new migration. Some 30,000 Serb and Bosnian refugees, led by their patriarch, Arsenije Čarnojević, fled the fighting and the ensuing occupation, and around 6,000 ended up in Szentendre (Sentandreja in Serbian), less than twelve miles upstream from Budapest. (The town already had a substantial Serb community at the time: waves of refugees had been absorbed from the Middle Ages onwards, the first in 1389 when the Serbs were defeated by the Turks at the Battle of Kosovo.) More waves of migrants followed, and during the eighteenth century

Szentendre became the seat of the exiled Serbian Orthodox Church, and the community here prospered as traders and vintners. Soon a community of merchants from Albania, Bosnia, Armenia, Dalmatia and Greece joined them, all refugees from the Balkan and Turkish conflicts. This multicultural community was granted protection by Emperor Leopold I and later this was confirmed in the form of a permanent contract by Empress Maria Theresa. Yet as the ensuing decades and centuries passed, a combination of flooding, intolerant Habsburg opinion and the vine-blight phylloxera meant that many began to trickle home. By 1890 only a quarter of the inhabitants were Serb, and now only around ten Serbian families remain.

The era of the Serbian settlement left a decisive mark on this riverside town, in the form of Orthodox churches and a rich collection of townhouses built by the merchants. Streets curve and twist up the hillside to the most dominant building in the town, the russet and cream Belgrade Cathedral, built in the eighteenth century and surmounted by an onion dome and spire. Prominent Serbs are buried in the surrounding graveyard. But the Serbian heritage is not the most immediately obvious feature of Szentendre: dominating the town's personality today is the preponderance of artists' workshops and galleries, all of which date back to the first decades of twentieth century when the town gained a new lease of life, and a new existence, as an artists' colony.

Today the town is still home to 200 working artists, and over a dozen galleries and museums celebrate the work of Hungary's principal sculptors and painters, many of whom lived and worked in Szentendre. Now the tiny lanes, the galleries, the churches, the cobbled squares and the fine setting beside the Danube provide an irresistible magnet for tourists; the place is busy all year, and is positively overflowing with visitors in the summer, when a festival of theatre, music and dance, and a one-day festival of Serbian culture, draw yet more crowds, making Szentendre one of the top tourist draws in Hungary. They flock here from Budapest by boat, and also on the capital's clanking suburban rail network, of which Szentendre is the final outpost.

Close to the landing stages where the boats deliver visitors is a tiny square whose fourth side opens on to the river and whose tiny iron cross commemorates one of the most important figures of Serbian culture associated with Szentendre. King Lázár was beheaded by the Turks after the Battle of Kosovo in revenge for the death of their sultan, Murad. The reliquary containing the king's body was brought to Szentendre by survivors of that battle and buried in a wooden church that stood beside the river here. In 1774, with the Turkish threat abated, his body was moved back to Serbia and an iron cross erected where the church had been. But the inconspicuous cross is ignored by most visitors now, as they swarm along the cobbled lanes that wind up from the river to the town's wonderful main square, known as Fő tér, a triangular open space lined with pastel houses, street cafés and clopping horses pulling carriages full of tourists. Glimpses of the Danube, only a hundred yards away, can be caught from the lanes leading away the square, whose centrepiece is an enormous and effusively decorated plague column. It was placed there by the guild of merchants after Szentendre managed to escape one of the lethal epidemics that raged around the Danube basin during the eighteenth century. The merchants who erected the column were a powerful and ostentatious group; above one former merchant's house just off the square is a rune-like symbol carved into the stonework of an elegant portal, depicting the Orthodox Patriarchal Cross superimposed with designs representing an anchor and the number four. The symbol was the signature of the guild: the anchor represented trade along the Danube, and the figure four the percentage profit which members of the guild thought was due to them when they traded in the bounteous goods the river brought them.

Two remarkable buildings lie between Fő tér and the river, one a reminder of the town's Serbian Orthodox heritage, the other an emblem of the artistic community that has flourished here for nearly a century. The tiny Blagovestenška Church, with its single nave and its extraordinary iconostasis, is a surprise in Catholic Hungary, and is one of seven Orthodox churches in Szentendre. The iconostasis, which separates the altar from the worshippers in Orthodox churches, takes the form of a richly coloured screen that stretches from floor to ceiling; dark greens, sumptuous reds and fine gold leaf form a background to icons depicting major Christian figures. The church dates from the 1750s and replaced an earlier wooden structure built by the waves of migrants who came here in 1690. On the outside wall of the church, faded Greek lettering on a tombstone marks the burial place of a Greek merchant who made his home in Szentendre.

Across the narrow lane from the church is one of the most popular galleries in the town, dedicated to the sculptor Margit Kovács, a highly-regarded cultural figure in twentieth-century Hungary. Her sculptural figures express an extraordinary gamut of emotions—hard work, grief, joy, concentration, laughter—all suggested through a few deft strokes of the sculptor's knife through clay. But suffering is Kovács' principal theme. Claudio Magris wrote that the suffering experienced by her figures seems both "dumb and inexplicable... but in that silence there is an unshakeable dignity even more mysterious than sorrow, the enigma of existence and even of happiness in spite of tragedy." The scenes and figures on display in the gallery are often fashioned with an engaging rustic simplicity, awash with flowers that form the background to the themes that inspired Kovács: religion, love, motherhood and legend.

# *Chapter Eight*

# BUDAPEST AND THE HEART OF HUNGARY

### THE "PEARL OF THE DANUBE"

Budapest is the loveliest and most elegant city on the Danube. Vienna turns its back on the river; Belgrade and Bratislava are gruff, rather charmless cities; Passau and Regensburg are pretty but lack any sense of expansive grandeur; but Budapest, with its magnificent riverside cluster of palatial buildings and fine churches, takes the Danube to its heart. The river strings itself through the city like a thread through a bead; the city, in turn, gravitates towards the waterside. The Danube is present at every turn, dominating the city's triumphant and tragic history, providing the grandest views, forming its iconic heart. Many say the river is seen to best effect when illuminated by the brilliant starbursts of fireworks that explode above the water on 20 August, Hungary's national day; but it can look equally lovely on a bright afternoon in February, when the bridges and

embankments are draped in a white mist that softens the harsh winter light on the pale buildings.

It is true that other beautiful cities have a river flowing through their hearts, defining them; but Paris or London are flat, and the Thames or the Seine are only ever seen close to. Budapest, with its precipitous hill flanking one side of the river, giving extensive views up and down the ribbon of water, allows for a complete appreciation of just how much the river seems to be cradled by its city. It is as if the Danube is flowing, steady and implacable, through a cupped hand. In fact the river's dominance of Budapest is so complete that the most magnificent way to enter the city is by boat, as the writer and traveller Bernard Newman discovered in 1935. "The whole of the city was brilliantly lit; on either bank the national buildings were picked out in floodlight," he wrote in *The Blue Danube* after arriving in the city along the water, at night. "The general effect, with graceful suspension bridges illuminated by tiny lights, daintily reflected in the river... reminded me inevitably of a fairy city. He who enters Budapest by night and by river will never, never forget it."

Not only is Budapest the Danube's most engagingly beautiful city: it is also its most eclectic. The warrens of medieval lanes on the Castle Hill are a world away from the wide Parisian boulevards on the opposite side of the river. Working-class districts wrapped around the city's port seem to be part of a wholly different city to the wealthy villas on the Buda Hills, whose picture windows offer their well-heeled residents a tantalizing glimpse of the river through stands of trees. This eclecticism stems in part from the fact that the two halves of the city—Buda in the west, and Pest in the east—developed separately, and were not officially united until the late nineteenth century, shortly after they were linked by a bridge for the first time. Buda is the older: the Celts, the Romans, and then the Magyar tribes were each drawn in turn to the steep hills on the river's west bank on which, over 2,000 years, a succession of castles, forts and palaces have been constructed. Pest, meanwhile, developed from a medieval town of artisans and merchants into the commercial heart of the second city of the greatest empire ever established in central Europe. Nowadays Buda basks in its history, while Pest—noisy, brash and modern—is where modern Budapest happens: the shops and nightclubs, banks and businesses, the great museums and the government buildings, all of which define a city that for two decades has been emerging from a troubled recent history of dictatorship and war.

## ROMAN AND MEDIEVAL BUDAPEST

Two hills dominate the west bank of the Danube as it flows through Budapest. To the south is Gellért-hegy, a precipitous lump of limestone whose sides rise vertically from the river bank; to the north is the more expansive Várhegy, on whose summit plateau sits Buda Castle. Aeons ago both hills formed the bed of the ancient sea that covered what is now the great Danube plain. Then, just over 200 million years ago, this part of the seabed was wrenched into the knuckle-like formations of today by tectonic forces deep within the earth. When humans began organizing themselves into defensive groups the hills provided just the right sites to build forts.

Stone Age and Celtic settlers on the hills were followed by the Romans, who defended the *Limes Romanus* from this high ground. The Hilton Hotel, whose copper-glass frontage is a distinctive feature of the Várhegy, proudly displays a stone from Roman times in its lobby that once marked the edge of the empire. But the Romans chose to site their principal encampments on the flat ground beside the river rather than on the hills above it. During the first centuries AD, for example, Colonia Septima Aquincum, their riverside garrison town north of the Várhegy, grew into one of the largest Roman encampments along the entire length of the Danube. As usual, the bulk of the camp was on the west bank, since the enemy hordes occupied the east. Evidence of the settlement now lies scattered through the workaday Budapest suburb of Aquincum, situated some twenty minutes north of the Várhegy on the city's HEV suburban train network. Two grassed-over amphitheatres languish here, marooned among villas and woodland; further inland, hidden by grey high-rise estates, is a villa with a third-century mosaic depicting Hercules about to vomit at a wine festival.

Throughout the modern district of Aquincum lonely columns rise up in the midst of suburban shopping precincts, while the paltry remains of bath houses cluster beneath flyovers. The ruins of the civilian town of Aquincum, once the capital of the Roman province of Pannonia Inferior, lie next to a busy road some 800 yards west of the Danube: a spread of waist-high lines of stone that were once the foundation walls of law courts, marketplaces, baths and sanctuaries where Epona and Fortuna Augusta were worshipped. The rest of the town still lies beneath the mud of the Danube floodplain. Every so often the construction of yet another glitzy shopping mall in this part of Budapest yields more booty for museums. But, partly because of its location in the busy suburbs, Aquincum seems rather forgotten now; not many tourists make it out here.

The ruins of a satellite fort, Contra Aquincum, established by the Romans on the opposite bank of the Danube, seem even more ignored: the site consists of a few stone walls in a sunken park on a square, Marcius 15 tér, less than 150 feet from the Danube riverfront in central Pest. But in the end, all this stonework may not even be the Romans' most enduring legacy in Budapest, for they unwittingly also gave the city its name. When they abandoned Aquincum and Contra Aquincum, the last Romans left behind a number of lime kilns, which the Slavs, several hundred years later, were able to use for themselves. It was the Slav word for kiln, *Pec*, later transmuted into Pest, which gave the east bank of the city its name.

Shifting groups of Germanic and Slav tribes settled on the plains of the middle Danube after the Roman era. No one tribe became dominant until the first Magyar tribes arrived on the scene in 896: the clan of one Magyar chieftain, Árpád, settled on Csepel Island just south of Gellért Hill, while his brother Buda brought his tribe to the other side of the river and gave the settlement on the west bank its name. Over time these two brothers, the founders of Hungary and of its capital, have assumed a mythical status in Hungarian history, not least because legend tells that they were sired by a giant eagle that had raped their grandmother. In the nineteenth century this mythical eagle (Turul in Hungarian) was championed as a symbol of Hungarian national identity during the struggle for independence against the Austrians. Today a giant statue of a fierce Turul glares across the river from the heights of the Várhegy, a sword clasped in its talons. Unfortunately, the iconic bird has been commandeered by Hungary's skinheads as their emblem, somewhat comprising the mythical resonance of this great winged beast.

Árpád's great-grandson Prince Géza invited the first Catholic missionaries to Hungary, and Géza's son King Stephen, crowned at Esztergom in the year 1000, became the country's first Christian monarch. But the Hungarian peasantry did not take kindly to Christian preaching. In 1046 one of the first missionaries, a Venetian prelate named Ghirardus (Gellért in Hungarian), was tied to a barrel studded with nails by vengeful heathens and pushed over the more southerly of the two hills in Buda to a watery death in the river. The hill, Gellért-hegy, is named after Gellért and there is a restrained statue of the martyred bishop half way up the slope, nestling among beech trees and a trickling waterfall. Gellért's statue depicts him thrusting a crucifix towards the heavens and gazing across the river towards the Belváros parish church on the Pest shoreline, where the saint was buried. Although this church is reckoned to be the oldest in Pest, very little remains of the original structure, and the current building on this site, situated right on the river bank adjacent to the paltry ruins of Contra Aquincum, is rather plain and dates from the eighteenth century. The precise burial place of Gellért within the church is unknown but some of his relics were returned to Venice and interred in a number of churches there.

Over time more missionaries followed in Gellért's footsteps and were rather more successful at spreading the Christian word. By the thirteenth century the new Hungarian state was thoroughly Christianized; but then an era of comparative peace and prosperity was shattered by the Mongol incursions. Sweeping across the Danube plains from the east, the Asiatic warriors sacked Pest in 1241, forcing King Béla IV to fortify the Várhegy, or Castle Hill, on the Buda bank. Although nothing remains of Béla's fortress, the antler-like spread of gently curving streets that form the Var, or Castle District, date from the time of his fortification of the flat summit of the hill. Béla also founded a church on the Várhegy, officially dedicated to the Virgin Mary but popularly known for the past five centuries as the Matthias Church (Mátyás templom) after the great fifteenth-century Hungarian king, Matthias Corvinus. (Although the Matthias Church is today a dominant feature of the Várhegy skyline, and looks resplendent when viewed across the Danube from Pest, only a tiny part of the present building dates from the time of Béla.)

With the Mongol threat persisting, Béla decided that more was needed to see them off than stone fortifications. He made a vow that if the next Mongol advance was successfully repelled, he would express his gratitude to God by placing his young daughter Margaret in a convent. The Mongols were indeed beaten back, and Béla's nine-year-old daughter Margaret duly found herself installed in a Dominican convent on an island in the Danube whose southern tip is just visible from the Várhegy.

When the saintly Margaret grew up she earned a reputation for curing lepers and never washing above her ankles. Her former convent was destroyed in the seventeenth century by the Turks, and is now visible as a jumble of low walls set in a glade of trees in the northern part of the island named after her: Margitsziget. Margaret's supposed resting place is under a simple granite plinth replete with flowers, exposed to the elements in one of the monastery's roofless former rooms; she had to wait seven hundred years, until 1943, for her canonization. Her island has fared rather better than the monastery: splitting the Danube into two channels for more than two miles, but never more than 1,000 feet wide, Margaret Island serves as a vehicle-free city park, with an outdoor theatre, thermal baths that cater for the needs of rich Europeans, tennis courts, jogging tracks, picnic lawns and splashing fountains hidden among quiet reaches of woodland.

As the Middle Ages gave way to the Renaissance era, and the Hungarian capital was moved from the ancient royal stronghold of Székesfehévar near Lake Balaton to Buda, an enemy even more determined than the Mongols began to set its sights on Hungary. The Turks had begun to extend their empire north along the Danube during the early fifteenth century. In 1456 their ambitions were temporarily thwarted by an army led by an ambitious Transylvanian warlord named János Hunyadi, whose defeat of the Turks outside Belgrade led to his being celebrated as a Hungarian nationalist leader and a saviour of Christendom. Hunyadi's son, Matthias Corvinus, basking in his father's glory, ascended the throne of Hungary after a coup orchestrated by his uncle, and he rebuilt the old medieval palace on the Várhegy as a glorious Renaissance showpiece, replete with fountains that reputedly flowed with wine. The reputation of the court's opulence that grew up around this remarkable monarch spread throughout Europe, and artists and scholars flocked to the great palace at Buda from all over the continent. But the Turkish threat, temporarily arrested by Matthias' father, did not go away. In 1526 the Ottomans finally defeated a Hungarian army under King Louis II near the Danube town of Mohács, 125 miles downstream from Budapest, and in 1541 they took control of Budapest. It was one of the most decisive moments in Hungarian history: the Turks were to remain in control of the country for the next century and a half.

## THE TURKS IN BUDAPEST

The Turkish conquest of Budapest marked the apogee of the Ottoman Empire. The empire of Suleiman the Magnificent (1520-66) now stretched from the lush plains of Hungary to the deserts surrounding Baghdad and the Persian Gulf. Ottoman rule in Hungary has been portrayed, perhaps rather unfairly, as a time of utter devastation. It is true that a great deal of destruction was wrought. The former Hungarian capital, Székesfehévar, was levelled to the ground, as was the glorious wine-flowing royal palace of Matthias Corvinus on the Várhegy. Elsewhere in the Hungarian capital, the island where saintly Margaret once converted lepers became a harem for the Turkish pasha, while Margaret's former convent was abandoned and a medieval church in the northern part of the island was razed. (The ruins of the latter were excavated in the 1920s and the church was rebuilt almost from scratch; an ancient fifteenth-century bell, found tangled up in the roots of a walnut tree uprooted in a storm, was re-hung in the tower, and the church now occupies a quiet part of Margitsziget, a stone's throw away from the waterside.)

Even so, the Turks were tolerant of religious pluralism. Communities of Sephardic Jews and Armenian Christians flourished on the Várhegy, living in houses lining the medieval streets laid out during the reign of Béla III. And some churches were converted rather than destroyed. The capital's two great churches, the Matthias Church on the Várhegy and the Belváros parish church beside the river in Pest, both served as mosques. A preserved *mihrab*, or prayer niche, can still be seen in the wall beside the altar of the latter church, taking the form of an arched recess inscribed with Arabic text from the Koran. This is just one example of the cultural and architectural legacy that Turkish rule stamped onto the city.

Sometimes the legacy is just in the detail: turbaned heads carved in the stonework above the portals of doorways in the Várhegy, or a collection of small plinths dug into the ground behind a riverside museum in Buda that on closer inspection are revealed to be Turkish gravestones. To the north of the Várhegy, however, is a more substantial monument: on a quiet hillside overlooking the river is the tomb of Gül Baba, a Sufi dervish who participated in the capture of Buda and who died during the thanksgiving service afterwards. This small octagonal shrine, with splashing marble fountains and adorned with arabesque tiles and beautiful calligraphic script, is the world's most northerly place of Islamic pilgrimage. Restored with funds from the Turkish government, it is also one of the most surprising sights in the whole of Budapest. But few tourists go there. They are much more interested in the other legacy of Turkish rule in Budapest that has become one of the city's most enduringly iconic features: the preponderance of bath houses.

Bath houses can be found all over Budapest. But the greatest concentration is on Margitsziget and along the Danube waterfront in Buda. From the Danubius Grand Hotel on the northern tip of Margitsziget to the famous Gellért Baths at the foot of Gellért Hill, Budapest's tourists and residents spend hours lounging in the swimming pools, saunas, steam baths and massage rooms that constitute a typical bath house. A succession of Roman-style dips in warm, hot and then near-scalding water, followed by a cold plunge before you start it all again, is the usual way of passing an afternoon in one of these establishments. Medical facilities and specialist staff offer specialist programme for those with muscle or back problems, including the application of mudpacks or underwater massage; some of the baths also serve as gay pick-up joints.

The Turks were not, in fact, the first to exploit the mineral springs that bubble beside the Danube here. The Romans knew all about their curative properties in Aquincum (whose name translates as "Five Waters"). But the Turks, who as Muslims were required to bathe five times daily in preparation for prayer, developed the ritual of the bath into a virtual art form, and the tradition has remained in Budapest ever since. Two of Buda's riverside baths, the Rac Baths and the Rudas Baths, still retain their octagonal stone bathing pools and other features from Turkish times. Here, bathers wallow away for hours in sixteenth-century tiled pools as steam billows around them and shafts of light pour in from star-shaped apertures in the domed ceiling.

In 1683 a pan-European army put an end to Turkish expansionism by subjecting Ottoman forces to a crushing defeat outside Vienna. Turkish expulsion from Hungary came three years later when a Christian force under the nominal command of Pope Innocent XI besieged the Várhegy for six weeks and eventually captured the hill after eleven unsuccessful onslaughts. According to legend, a statue of the Virgin Mary that had been bricked up in the Matthias Church suddenly appeared to Turkish worshippers as the Christian forces massed at the bottom of the hill. The collapse of the wall and the spectacle of the Virgin watching over the besieged Turks foretold the imminence of the Christian victory.

## HABSBURG BUDAPEST: EXPANSION AND REVOLUTION

At the head of Pope Innocent's victorious army was a dashing young commander named Eugene of Savoy, a Habsburg prince who became a hero of Christian Europe (and who later in his career commanded Austrian forces at the Battle of Blenheim). After his victory in Budapest, Eugene chased the Ottoman forces down the Danube, defeating them again at Zenta in 1697 and finally recapturing Belgrade in 1718. Along the way he forced the Turks to accede to the Peace of Karlowitz, signed in 1699, which transferred Ottoman possessions in Europe to the Habsburgs. As such, control over Hungarian affairs was passed from one imperial power to another.

Resentment at the continued denial of independence was to prove a prime mobilizing force in Hungary during nearly two and half centuries of rule from Vienna. The resentment and simmering nationalism first boiled over into an independence war in the early eighteenth century, which saw the destruction of Visegrád Castle by Habsburg forces. Then a full-scale revolution was attempted in 1848, taking its cue from the revolutionary fervour that galvanized Europe that year. Those events saw a Hungarian count, Louis Batthyány, take over as nationalist prime minister. But Batthyány's rule lasted only a matter of weeks before he was publicly executed by the Habsburgs in a square in Pest in front of baying crowds. Despite many concessions granted after the attempted coup, such as the end of serfdom for the Hungarian peasantry, the Habsburg order was quickly and in some instances brutally restored.

Buda and Pest continued to develop separate identities during the Habsburg era. Pest, bursting at the seams, began to expand beyond its crumbling medieval walls. These had been laid out in the form of a backwards letter C, with the Danube closing off the defences in the open part. Now the walls were replaced by a broad avenue, the Kiskörút, echoing Vienna's Ringstrasse, and the city spilled out beyond the new avenues on all sides. The Belváros, fronting the river, hummed with trade and commerce. Buda, on the other hand, kept its head in the clouds. Empress Maria Theresa, palace builder and Danube straightener, realized that Budapest could showcase Austrian lavishness just as well as Bratislava and

Vienna. She levelled the old Renaissance palace of Matthias Corvinus, which the Turks had left largely in ruins, and ordered another palace to rise in its place on Buda Hill, sporting over 200 rooms, an enormous dome and a brazenly magnificent façade to remind upstart traders across the river in Pest who was in charge. But Maria Theresa never lived in the new building. Instead, the absurdly grandiose palace became the home of the Habsburg viceroy, and its crypt, lurking within the foundations of previous forts and palaces on the Várhegy, became the burial place of various prominent Habsburgs. Meanwhile, Maria Theresa's other achievement in Budapest was to put a stop to the witchcraft that was apparently rampant on Gellért Hill and was sullying the old stamping ground of Hungary's first Christian missionary.

By the middle of the nineteenth century it was clearly high time that Buda and Pest should be linked by a permanent bridge. Until then, floating pontoons had been slung across the river to allow passage between the two settlements. The instigator of a permanent crossing was an anglophile and innovator named Count István Széchenyi, who founded the Hungarian Academy of Sciences and, among his many achievements in the field of engineering, brought steam engines to Hungary. He was also the

author of a tract entitled *Hitel* ("Credit") that blamed the country's woes on a still-active feudal system—radical opinions for a member of the aristocracy to put forward.

In the 1840s Széchenyi commissioned the British engineer William Tierney Clark to design the first bridge linking Pest and Buda. Clark had come to Széchenyi's attention by designing two bridges over the Thames in England: London's Hammersmith Bridge in 1827, and a bridge at Marlow, between London and Reading, nine years later. Hammersmith Bridge was rebuilt in the 1880s but the bridge at Marlow survives, taking the form of an elegant suspension bridge whose single-lane roadway is slung between two sturdy arched stone towers. It was, and is, a marvel both of engineering prowess and aesthetic sensibility.

The bridge that Clark designed to link Buda and Pest was a wider and longer version of the earlier commission at Marlow. Known as the Chain Bridge, it was completed in 1849, with the work overseen by another British engineer, Adam Clark (no relation). Adam Clark also built the tunnel under the Várhegy that gives access to the bridge (a local joke tells that the tunnel was built to store the bridge in when it rained).

In 1848, as the bridge was nearing completion, anti-Habsburg forces attempted to destroy the structure during the independence struggle; but Adam Clark personally thwarted the dynamiters by flooding the bridge's chain lockers with water, drowning any possibility of an explosion. Not surprisingly he was proclaimed something of a national hero. (Clark later married a Hungarian woman and lived in Budapest for the remainder of his life.) His contribution to the riverscape of Budapest is acknowledged in the name of the square sandwiched between the bridge and the tunnel mouth: Clark Adam tér. The name of the square serves as a reminder not only of his work but also of the curious convention of reversing forename and surname that is uniquely Hungarian.

The Pest end of the bridge opens onto traffic-clogged Roosevelt tér, whose fourth side is open to the river. (The decision to name the square after the American president was made in 1947; the name stuck throughout the communist era, an unusual instance of Cold War civility.) The square is lined with buildings that reflect the confidence and grandeur of late Habsburg Budapest. On the east side of the square, facing the bridge, is an Art Nouveau building commissioned by a British insurance company in 1904 and rather grandly named Gresham Palace, after the financier Sir

Thomas Gresham. His portrait can be seen on the façade of the building; inside, the glass-roof arcade and stained glass windows typify the Art Nouveau style that became hugely popular throughout Europe during the turn of the century. The building currently serves as a luxury hotel. Another side of the square is occupied by a stately nineteenth-century pile that is home to the Hungarian Academy of Sciences, an institution which came into being after Széchenyi pledged a year's income from his extensive estates towards its endowment.

Roosevelt tér today serves as a busy traffic interchange, buzzing with cars and trams and pedestrians, but in the nineteenth century it was free of clutter and in 1867 was the scene of an unusual ceremony. In that year Franz Josef, Habsburg emperor and King of Hungary, commanded that soil from every corner of Hungary should be piled into a mound in the centre of the square. When the pile was complete he solemnly waved the ceremonial sword of King Stephen over it, declaring to the gathered dignitaries that as monarch he would defend his kingdom from all its enemies.

The 1867 ceremony in Roosevelt tér was prompted by that year's momentous division of the Habsburg Empire into two unequal parts. Absolute power was to remain with the emperor in Vienna, but Hungary, in the terms of the famous "compromise" negotiated by the nationalist politician Ferenc Deák, was to attain a significant degree of autonomy. Few were enamoured with the arrangement. In his book *The Man without Qualities* Robert Musil observed that the two parts of the new Austro-Hungarian Empire "matched each other like a red-white-and-green jacket and black-and-yellow trousers. The jacket was an article in its own right; but the trousers were the remains of a no longer existent black-and-yellow suit, the jacket of which had been unpicked in the year 1867." But the arrangement did unleash a new wave of Hungarian self-confidence. Soon after Hungarians gained the autonomy they craved, the citadel on the summit of Gellért Hill, an ugly concrete bunker built by the Austrians to subdue the capital following the failed coup of 1848, was stormed by a mob of angry citizens anxious to show that Habsburg power no longer held sway in Hungary. (In the event, Habsburg troops were to remain stationed in the citadel until 1899.) More positively, Hungary's new political status led to the official unification of Buda and Pest in 1873, creating the city of Budapest, and shortly thereafter the most prominent architectural dividend of the dual monarchy started to rise up on the Pest bank of the river.

With its riverside location and its neo-gothic forest of pinnacles and flying buttresses, Budapest's parliament building bears an inescapable resemblance to the Palace of Westminster in London. Only the fantasy-castle turrets and the enormous dome set it aside from its cousin beside the Thames. Patrick Leigh Fermor was certainly a fan of the building. In his book *Between the Woods and the Water*, the sequel to *A Time of Gifts*, he described it as a "frantic and marvellous pile" crowned by "an egg shaped dome that might more predictably have dominated the roofs of a Renaissance town in Tuscany, except that the dome itself was topped by a sharp and bristling gothic spire. Architectural dash could scarcely go further." The Hungarian poet and novelist Gyula Illyés, who died in 1983, was less keen: "no more than a Turkish bath crossed with a Gothic chapel" was his dismissive verdict.

Whatever the architectural merits of the building, it is impressive, and its grandeur and distinctive style makes it one of the most iconic buildings along the entire length of the Danube. The frontage, built of cream-coloured stone with russet for the domes and roofs, stretches over 800 feet along the embankment; the cupola on the dome soars to a height of 96 metres (315 feet), an allusion to the conquest of the Danube Basin by Magyar tribes in the year 896. However, the parliament that has convened here for over a hundred years has had something of a chequered history. It was nothing more than a rubber-stamp body during the fascist and communist eras, although it began to come into its own as communism started to unravel in the late 1980s. Nowadays, of course, it has a huge significance as the embodiment of Hungary's new and confident democracy.

Since 2000 the building has also served as the repository for the Hungarian crown jewels, on show to tour groups and guarded by soldiers with sabres permanently drawn. St. Stephen's crown, the centrepiece of the regalia, has led an extraordinarily peripatetic life since being placed on the head of King Stephen at Esztergom in the year 1000 and being put on show in the parliament building exactly a thousand years later. At various times it was buried for safekeeping in Transylvania, kept under guard in Bratislava, Visegrád and Vienna, taken to Germany by Hungarian fascists, stored in Fort Knox after it came into American hands as war booty, and then displayed in the Hungarian National Museum in Budapest after the Americans kindly returned it in 1978. According to tradition, the bent cross on top of the crown is a result of it being hidden away for a period inside a baby's cradle.

In the latter part of the nineteenth century, the creation of the dual monarchy, and the official unification of the two parts of the capital, also gave an impetus to various rebuilding projects in the city, many of which involved the river. The Matthias Church on the Várhegy, left in ruins after the Turkish occupation, was rebuilt in neo-gothic style by the architect Frigyes Schulek. With its slender spire bristling with pinnacles, and its gaudy, multi-coloured tiled roof, the church hovers high over the Danube waterfront. The interior of the rebuilt church is a rich confection of striking designs: painted leaves climb up columns on curling branches, geometric motifs adorn the walls, the arrangement of floor tiles creates yellow, red and green interlocking petals, while frescoes cover the ceilings.

Another part of the redevelopment of the Várhegy was the construction in 1870 of a funicular, the Budavári Sikló, up the steep side of the hill facing the river. The lower station is adjacent to the mouth of Adam Clark's tunnel, while the upper station brings passengers out onto the heart of the

Várhegy, right next to the brooding Turul eagle that symbolizes the clans of Árpád and Buda. At the time of the funicular's construction there was only one other like it in the world. Its instigator was Ödön Széchenyi, son of István, and clearly a chip off the same block. At first the passenger cars were dragged up the slope by a steam engine; nowadays it is an electric winch that hauls brightly painted wooden cabins laden with sightseers up to the Vár.

The final addition to the Várhegy skyline from Habsburg days is a whimsical one. Along the edge of the plateau, whitewashed turrets linked by ramparts are strung out like beads in a necklace above the sheer drop that overlooks the Danube embankment. The structure is known as the Fishermen's Bastion, recalling the days when Danube fishermen were responsible for defending the city's fortifications. The turrets (there are seven of them, representing the seven Magyar tribes) resemble inverted ice-cream cones, while the crenulated walls come straight out of an illustration from a book of fairy tales. Whimsical though it is, the views from the bastion are breathtaking: the ribbon of the Danube stretches north into the hills that form the Danube Bend and south into the hazy flatness of the Great Plain, while Pest stretches out on the east side of the river. King Stephen prances away on a magnificent horse just close by, his statue at the centre of the Vár's most attractive plaza. The assortment of views, buskers, statuary, street artists and restaurants ensures that this is the heart of tourist Budapest.

## BUDAPEST SINCE 1918: DECADENCE, TRAGEDY, DICTATORSHIP AND DEMOCRACY

During the 1920s Budapest made a reputation for itself as one of the most stylish and sophisticated cities in Europe. Negley Farson, who visited in 1926 as he navigated his yawl down the Danube, caught the mood of this vibrant era perfectly. In *Sailing across Europe* he described a city that was "infinitely more beautiful than Vienna, refreshingly cleaner, and gives one a feeling of security, contentment and well-being almost unknown in the Austrian capital… Budapest seems the most adorable, bewitching city in Europe. It is all that Vienna might have been—but isn't." No building in Budapest is more symbolic of this decadent era than the Gellért Hotel and the adjacent baths, opened in 1918 and sandwiched between the foot of Gellért Hill and the Danube. The hotel is a grandiose Art Nouveau pile whose façade opens onto the river. Behind it, the focal point of the bath complex is a Roman-style columned bath house where debutantes once danced the evenings away on a glass floor laid over the pool. Now the place is something of an overpriced tourist haunt; there is even an outdoor pool with a wave machine behind the bath house. But the Gellért has undeniable style: a forest of columns support the high, curving roof of the bathing house's cavernous hallway; an ocean of stained glass throws soft pools of light onto the cream and russet-brown tiles; and bathers can have their massage oils scented with a choice of lavender, camomile, camphor or eucalyptus. The hotel also played a role in Budapest's dark post-imperial history: this was where, in November 1919, Admiral Miklós Horthy, leader of the fascist Arrow Cross party and future ally of the Nazis, established his command during the early weeks of his rule as the premier of an independent Hungarian Republic. His premiership was to set the seal on Hungary's dark twentieth-century fate.

During the opening phase of the Second World War Horthy's Hungary proved itself a worthy ally of the Nazis, but by 1944 Horthy's loyalty to Berlin was wavering. Hitler, losing patience with the regime, encouraged more radical elements within the Arrow Cross movement to stage a coup. By October of that year Horthy was out of office, the Germans were in control of Budapest and the Soviet Red Army had launched an invasion of Hungary from the east. Five months of violence and savage mayhem were then inflicted on the capital. The main victims were Budapest's Jewish population, who until this time had been spared the fate of Jews elsewhere in Europe. Outside a gaudy-roofed church on Szilágyi Deszö tér, on the Buda river bank, hundreds of Jews were murdered by the Nyilas, fascist gangs allied to the Arrow Cross regime. Victims were tied together in threes and forced to stand at the edge of the Danube embankment. One of the victims was then killed with a single bullet, whereupon all three plunged into the river and drowned. What made these murders particularly poignant was the fact that many Hungarian Jews had lived securely in Budapest in the early part of the war under Swiss, Swedish or Vatican protection; but with the Nazis in full command of the city protection by neutral powers counted for nothing.

One key figure to emerge from the tragic months of late 1944 and early 1945 was Raoul Wallenberg, a Swedish national who helped Jews by giving them Swedish papers and hiding them in safe houses. His efforts staved off at least some of the murders and deportations. After the Soviet invasion Wallenberg was arrested as a spy by the Russians and incarcerated in a Siberian gulag. A memorial to him sits on a plinth in a public park overlooking the Danube in the north of Pest, facing Margitsziget. The memorial was commissioned in the 1950s but it was hidden away for decades during the communist era and only placed on public view for the first time in 1999.

Soviet forces began to close in on Budapest in January 1945. Some of the fiercest fighting was across the Danube itself, with tank and mortar shells hurled from one side of the river to the other. The Germans blew up all the bridges, including the Chain Bridge, in the hope of halting the advance of the Red Army. Pest's Belgrád rakpart, which before the war had been the city's most attractive and stylish embankment, was completely destroyed. The palace of Maria Theresa on the Várhegy, along with most of the other buildings in the Vár, was also reduced to rubble as the Germans dug themselves in for a last-ditch defence. Capitulation finally came in February, when the Germans lost control of their last redoubt, the old Habsburg citadel on Gellért Hill. As the Russians took control of the capital the fascist era in Hungary came to an end and the communist era began.

Both the fascist and communist eras in Hungary are oddly commemorated in one of the most unusual riverside monuments in Budapest. At the summit of Gellért Hill, high above the statue of Bishop Gellért, a monument from the Horthy era was refashioned shortly after the war to celebrate the victory of the Red Army. Originally, the monument was commissioned by Horthy to commemorate his son who had been killed in an air crash. When she first looked over the Danube from atop a high plinth the long-skirted woman who takes centre stage in the monument held an aircraft propeller in her outstretched hands. After the war, the propeller was replaced by a palm frond, while a phalanx of Red Army soldiers appeared around the base of the monument, in celebration of the Soviet victory. The soldiers have now gone, although they can be seen in a park on the outskirts of Budapest where all statuary and memorials from the communist era have been moved and are on display. But the woman with her palm frond remains, a bombastic reminder of the two rival dictatorships that Hungary endured during the twentieth century.

The years after the war were marked by a painstaking reconstruction of the monuments destroyed in the fighting. The Chain Bridge was rebuilt to its original design and traffic was rumbling across it again by 1949, its centenary year. The same happy fate befell most of the other bridges, the exception being the Erzsébet Bridge, which crosses the Danube from the Belváros parish church to the Gellért Hotel. The original, constructed at the turn of the twentieth century, was for many years the largest arched bridge in the world; the rebuilt structure dating from the early 1960s is completely different: a wide, sleek suspension bridge whose towers and cables gleam a brilliant white in the sunshine.

Further north, the damage inflicted on the Várhegy during the war was so great that only one in four houses on the hill remained habitable in 1945. But decades of restoration work have turned the Vár into an outdoor museum of Renaissance and baroque architecture. Handsome, pastel houses line the cobbled streets laid out by Béla IV. Cloistered courtyards and quiet squares mingle amid the patrician houses. Surprisingly perhaps, there are corner shops, and even schools; the Vár still has a resident population, and when the tourists are gone, people walk their dogs and children play in the shadows of centuries of history.

The royal palace of Maria Theresa was rebuilt too, and still glows with the opulence of the Habsburg era. Its vast wings and palatial façade dominate the view of Buda from the Pest bank of the Danube. The palace now houses the Hungarian National Gallery, a treasure trove of art from all over Hungary, including some stunning gothic altarpieces, and examples of Hungarian impressionism and twentieth-century abstract art. A bronze equestrian statue of a prancing Prince Eugene stands outside the entrance to the gallery, looking out over the river. Other wings of the palace house the Budapest History Museum and the National Library, whose founder was the father of Count István Széchenyi.

Elsewhere on the hill, the "Castle Caves", a network of tunnels and passages dissolved in the limestone by hot spring water, and then later widened and extended for a whole range of uses, are a popular attraction. During the Second World War, members of the Jewish community sought refuge here, and the tunnels were later used as air-raid shelters during the fight for the city. Now they form a contrived labyrinth, the dank walls and dingy rooms enlivened by copies of the Lascaux cave paintings and a "house of horrors" collection of masked figures.

The postwar restorers also set to work on the damaged streets and buildings on the river bank. After decades of work, a succession of elegant squares linked by rows of tall nineteenth-century apartment blocks once again established the unique character of riverside Budapest. One square in the Watertown district, between the Várhegy and the river bank, commemorates a leading figure in the 1848 revolution—and has played its own part in more recent displays of disaffection, too. Like most squares along the Danube, Bem tér opens out onto the river and is expansive enough to incorporate a small pocket of greenery in its centre. It is named after the Polish general József Bem, who supported the nationalist cause in the 1848 revolution. The plinth of his statue is inscribed with words by the poet and revolutionary Sándor Petöfi, who served as Bem's adjutant, and it was around this statue that crowds gathered during the uprising in 1956, ready to march on the parliament building and holding aloft Hungarian flags whose central hammer and sickle icon had been removed. In the 1980s the square was again the focus for demonstrations, this time against the Nagymaros Dam.

Despite the handsome appearance of squares such as Bem tér, other riverside areas have not fared so well. In particular, Budapest lacks a stylish riverside thoroughfare for strolling or eating. Unfortunately, the Belgrád rakpart, the elegant embankment that was bombed to pieces in the war, was redeveloped as a frontage for two giant luxury hotels, the Marriott and the Intercontinental. The chain of bland outdoor cafés and car rental offices outside the hotels today provide no hint of the era when Budapest's wealthiest citizens would parade up and down on fine summer evenings.

The Danube, and the buildings along it, is Budapest's showpiece. Not even the broad, straight avenues laid out in Pest during the nineteenth century, modelled on Haussmann's avenues in Paris, can compete with it. Beyond the shopping streets of Pest and the tourist haunts of the Várhegy, the riverside residential suburbs of Budapest stretch to the north and south along the ribbon of water. The suburbs are surprisingly varied and even during communist times distinct working-class and middle-class areas were apparent.

South of Gellért Hill the Danube splits into two channels that flow around Csepel Island, home to Budapest's sprawling and grimy river port, marooned amidst a sea of tenement blocks. During the early twentieth century the island gained the nickname "Red Csepel" because of the left-leaning attitude of the dockworkers here. North of the Várhegy is a very different residential district known as Rózsadomb. In communist times this was where the party functionaries lived, in hillside villas whose picture windows allowed for a spectacular view of the Danube. Some of the villas were rumoured to have tunnels and secret exits to allow party leaders to escape in the event of a civil disturbance.

Now the district is the most fashionable in Budapest and is home to film directors and entrepreneurs. Narrow lanes wind between high-walled villas where access from the street is often through the top floor, while the rest of the house lies in the floors below, propped up against the hillside. These disparate parts of the city—Rózsadomb with its hillside villas, Csepel with its grey rows of workers' housing, the Belváros with its dour nineteenth-century apartment blocks—are linked by an extensive network of rumbling trams, smoky buses and a glacially efficient metro whose construction was funded by the Soviets in the 1960s. The second metro line, connecting Déli station in Buda with Keleti station in Pest, passes through the only tunnel to have been built under the Danube anywhere along its length.

The demise of communism has brought even more change in Budapest. The rebuilders have their work cut out once again but this time they are repairing decades of neglect under communism rather than damage from a war. Shiny new office blocks now line the streets of central Pest while gleaming shopping malls have sprouted in the suburbs. The city centre boasts night clubs, international banks, swish hotels, smart restaurants and fashion boutiques. Budapest is busy cultivating for itself a reputation for hedonism and style, as it did in the 1920s. But the glitzy, new Budapest is to be found away from the banks of the Danube, in central Pest or on the landward side of the Várhegy. The riverfront itself, a museum piece that is the product of 2,000 years of history, remains largely unchanging as the city around it reinvents itself as one of the booming centres of a reborn *Mitteleuropa*.

## Along the Edge of the Great Hungarian Plain: Budapest to Mohács

The *Puszta*—the Great Plain of south-eastern Hungary—opens out as the river flows south from Budapest and leaves the urban sprawl of the capital behind it. The plain is a region of vast skies and distant pancake-flat horizons, baking hot in summer and often bitingly cold in winter. Once again, the river divides and splits into multiple threading channels as it spreads itself over the plain, crisscrossing a landscape of reedy ponds and spongy marshland that is a haven for waterfowl. Not surprisingly, travelling along this lonely reach of the river has caused many writers to spin evocative descriptions of the remarkable landscape through which it flows. Don Maxwell, who recorded his 1905 journey by boat along the Danube in his book *A Cruise across Europe,* dubbed this reach of the river "a land of a thousand islands" where "great forests of uncut willow, fantastic in sunlight and ghostly in shade, clothe the islands and the shore." Maxwell found navigation difficult: there were "such multitudinous channels that it was impossible to tell whether the boat was in the river itself or in one of the thousand backwaters," he went on, before describing a period when he became helplessly lost and spent days drifting across what appeared to be flooded farmland. Henry Rowland, an American adventurer and writer who navigated his motorboat *Beaver* along the river at around the same time, described "the wonderful beauty of mornings on the Danube" as he crossed the vast plain. "The dawn comes with a crimson glow above a thick blanket of baffling mist," he wrote in *Across Europe in a Motorboat.* "Birds cry from all about: the liquid whistle of curlews, and the clear, keen, notes of snipe and plover... Suddenly a vista appears, and a glimpse of the river, a dazzling mirror leading through a vague, misty effulgence straight to the sun, a Jacob's ladder without the steps."

Negley Farson, following the same route across Europe as Maxwell and Rowland some two decades later, wrote of the "long, lonely stretches of this river, untouched, unspoilt... today we came down through a wilderness of willows where the Danube wandered between low, sandy islands, where it broadened, and seemed to halt in half-mile-wide, satin-green pools, like a lake." Farson longed to explore the myriad of creeks and side channels by canoe: he could hear the "rhythmic thud of the paddles like distant drums in the night" as parties of German canoeists paddled past. "No wonder this enchanted river makes Huck Finns of otherwise industrious Germans," he continued. "It was created for sport and adventure. A man could paddle his canoe, fish, shoot and explore these wandering estuaries—and never get through in a lifetime."

The plain is not a static landscape. In the Middle Ages its ecology was an expanse of forest and fenland, most of which has now vanished. The two great rivers that cross the plain, the Danube in the west, and the Tisza in the east, regularly inundated the area in those days, sometimes cutting off entire towns for months at a stretch. But when the Turks invaded Hungary, they were wary of the trees, fearing that stands of forest could shelter the rebel Hungarian groups fighting a partisan war against their occupation. So the trees were cut down, leaving behind a wasteland that people called the Puszta—the Hungarian term for "abandoned"—once the Turks were gone. (Officially, the region is known as the *Alföld*—the "Great Plain"—to distinguish it from the "Little Plain" of north-western Hungary.)

Then, in the nineteenth century, flood control on both rivers allowed wide expanses of dry grassland to flourish, and people began to repopulate the area. Soon, huge estates, the preserve of the aristocracy, were supporting cows and sheep on the lush pastureland; farmers took to horses to herd the animals, further enhancing the reputation of Hungarians for horsemanship. With the advent of communism after the war, these farms were collectivized, and peasants, deprived of their livelihood, were moved into the new apartment buildings that sprouted on the edge of the old market towns of the Puszta.

Settlers have traditionally shied away from living alongside the branching channels of the Danube, or on the marshy islands between them. But along the western edge of the main river channel the flatness of the plain is broken, sometimes abruptly, by folds of low, sandy hills that reach their highest point in a picturesque range known as the Mecsek, a favourite haunt of weekend hikers from Budapest who resent the overcrowding in the Danube Bend. These hills provide a vantage point along the watery ribbon of the river and over the plain to the east, and they also allow for settlement above the level of floodwaters. As a result, a string of towns can be found along the west bank of the river as it flows through this Hungarian heartland, while the east bank fringes nothing more than stands of ash and willow that give way to the lonely expanses of the plain.

None of these towns on the hilly west bank is particularly remarkable. The first is Dunaújváros, located some forty miles downstream from Budapest. Just north of the town an arm of the Danube known as the Ráckevi Duna rejoins the main channel to close off Csepel Island, which stretches all the way from here to the foot of Gellért Hill in the capital, making it one of the longest and widest islands along the entire length of the river. Dunaújváros translates as "Danube New Town" and the settlement was constructed more or less from scratch in the 1950s around a new riverside steelworks. The town was intended to be the lynchpin of Hungary's postwar drive to industrialize. Originally it was named Sztálinváros, as it was founded at a time when Stalin's economic policies were enthusiastically embraced by the country's postwar communist rulers. The steelworks remains to this day, belching a cloud of grey smog into the otherwise clear skies of the Hungarian plain. To the north of the works, row upon row of sludge-coloured apartment blocks spread out over a high ledge above the river. Originally built to house the influx of new workers attracted here from the countryside, the blocks line windswept, near-identical streets laid out in a ruthless grid pattern. At the end of one street a group of standing figures sculpted from dark iron overlooks the Danube from a high cliff: the figures, men and women holding agricultural and industrial tools, have a strange primitiveness about them, with outsized breasts and buttocks creating startling body profiles. Dating from communist times, they represent the workers and farmers who forged the postwar socialist state and form part of a weird outdoor gallery of sculptures fashioned from iron from the foundry. Far below the group of figures, the Danube flows past a scruffy freight terminal, while the plain, unbroken, stretches away into nothingness beyond the far bank.

The chimneys of the Dunaujváros steelworks can be seen from Dunaföldvár, eleven miles downstream. After Belgrade fell to the Turks, Hungarian forces retreated here and constructed a fort to protect the Danube, the vital route to the capital. All that remains of the fort are some foundation walls and a squat lookout tower, now a museum, with a commanding view of the river from its top gallery. A green box girder bridge crosses the river below the tower, and behind it the peaceful town settles around a pretty central square lined with mustard-yellow buildings from Habsburg times.

Next along is Harta, a small town on the opposite bank a little way downstream. It was settled by Germans in the eighteenth century, who replaced the Turkish communities that moved south after the Ottomans were forced out of Hungary. Paks, back on the west bank, is famous for two things, both dependent on the river—its elderly nuclear power station, built to a Soviet design, whose pressurized water reactors provide some forty per cent of Hungary's electricity; and, more palatably, a tradition of fish soup. Ten miles further on, the river used to flow past the town of Kalocsa—but over time the Danube has shifted its course on the muddy plain, like a lazy snake, and now the town, which lies in the heart of paprika growing country and boasts the world's only paprika museum, sits on nothing more than a muddy creek. Guidebooks highlight its tradition of folk art and its baroque cathedral.

Pressing on south, Baja too is a little inland; the town's expansive cobbled square with its pastel-and-grey civic buildings opens out onto a quiet side channel known as the Sugovica Danube, while the main channel of the river flows past humdrum residential districts on the out-skirts of the town. Here a sturdy bridge carries both a road and a railway line over the river, while grain silos rise above an untidy cluster of loading quays and timber yards. But Baja is a river town in the best sense of the word: its culinary speciality is a soup known as *halászlé*, a mix of carp, catfish, pike-perch and paprika, and in July there is even a fish soup fes-tival, when cauldrons bubble away on the town's main square. Another festival here celebrates St. John Nepomouk, the patron saint of fisher-men, whose effigy is carried along the river by a procession of small boats on his feast day.

Baja is the home town of the poet Karl Beck, who first coined the phrase "the Blue Danube"—and it boasts a unique place in history, too, for it was in this quiet and unassuming town that Habsburg rule in Europe reached a decisive conclusion. Karl I of Austria (who was also Karl IV of Hungary), the last Habsburg ruler of Austria-Hungary, who had abdicated the imperial throne in 1918, came here three years later to join up with a small force committed to restoring Habsburg rule. But after a skirmish Karl was evacuated from Baja by a British gunboat and, following a journey by river and sea, he finally ended up in exile on Madeira along with his wife, Empress Zita.

The last town on the Hungarian Danube is synonymous with defeat. Mohács was where a highly organized Ottoman army defeated a rather less disciplined force of Hungarian troops in 1526, heralding the eventual Turkish occupation of Budapest. The Hungarian king at the time, Louis II, was an ineffectual ruler who could not raise an army from the ranks of his bickering nobles; so the army that he eventually marched south from Budapest under his command consisted in the main of German merce-naries. Most of them were to perish in the battle, and Louis himself was

killed when his horse fell and crushed him in a stream. It is said that the monarch knew he was doomed: before leaving home he left careful instructions for the care of his beloved hunting hounds.

The battlefield itself is a fair distance to the west of the Danube, and little can be seen in the sleepy town of Mohács relating to the event beyond a domed and rather graceless commemorative church. Yet Mohács is a river town, like Baja, and the highlight of its calendar is the waterborne Busójárás Carnival, which celebrates the beginning of spring: masked figures bearing fiery torches set sail on the Danube on bobbing wooden boats to chase away winter—and no doubt to see off the Turks as well.

## Chapter Nine

# THROUGH THE FORMER YUGOSLAVIA

### EUROPE'S MOST RECENT WAR ZONE

Like Czechoslovakia, Yugoslavia was an unwieldy federation that emerged from the ashes of the Austro-Hungarian Empire. Serbia, formerly a powerful and independent kingdom, was always destined to be dominant within the new federal state, while the former Habsburg territories of Bosnia, Croatia and Slovenia, along with Montenegro and Macedonia, were never going to be anything more than its political underlings. On its foundation in 1918, the new nation was christened the Kingdom of Serbs, Croats and Slovenes. Belgrade, an ancient city situated on the confluence of the Sava and Danube rivers, and formerly the capital of Serbia, became the federal capital, and a Serb monarch was made the first head of state. In 1929 the country was renamed Yugoslavia—the "Land of the South Slavs". But the political arrangement was to remain an unhappy one.

On the outbreak of the Second World War, Yugoslavia was initially persuaded to form an alliance with the Axis powers. But popular anti-Nazi

protests in Belgrade, and a political coup, led Hitler to believe that support from his Balkan ally was wavering, and he ordered German forces to invade Yugoslavia in the spring of 1941. A bloody conflict between Nazi occupation forces and partisans under the communist agitator Josip Broz Tito raged until the Red Army liberated Yugoslavia from Nazi rule in 1944.

When the war was over it looked as if the country would join its eastern neighbours as a Soviet satellite state, but Tito manoeuvred himself into the presidency and began to adopt a very different form of communism to the one propagated by Stalin. Yugoslavia was expelled from Cominform, the Soviet-controlled collective of East European states, and for a while it looked as if Soviet forces might invade the country to unseat Tito and put one of Stalin's supporters in power. But Tito held firm, and was to rule Yugoslavia until his death in 1980.

After Tito's death the presidency of Yugoslavia rotated between the leaders of the constituent republics. This awkward arrangement began to unravel as communism was swept aside across Europe. First Slovenia, and then Croatia, took advantage of the new political climate and began to agitate for independence from the federation, and it looked as if other states would soon follow. As the old federation came apart at the seams the Communist Party chairman in Serbia, Slobodan Milošević, took it upon himself to campaign for the rights of the Serb minorities in the breakaway republics, and in the summer of 1991 the Serb-dominated Yugoslav Peoples' Army moved into Croatia to protect the interests of Serbs living there. Skirmishes between Serb forces and Croatian police soon erupted into full-scale war, and a number of Serb-dominated Croatian cities, particularly Vukovar on the Danube, were subjected to a ferocious Serb bombardment.

The fighting continued until 1995, and when it was finally over, the conflict in Croatia had claimed the lives of at least 10,000 people, and had created hundreds of thousands of refugees. In the late 1990s the arena of conflict in the Balkans shifted again, this time to Kosovo, when Milošević's efforts to protect Serb minorities there resulted in yet more bloodshed. Meanwhile, Yugoslavia died a slow and painful death: in 2003 Serbia and Montenegro—the only two republics that remained in the federation—finally dropped the name, and three years later split to form independent states.

Although Bosnia, Kosovo and the coastline of Croatia lie far from the Danube, some of the early battles of the Yugoslav war were fought along the banks of the river in the northern part of the former federation. Even after Serbian troops had left Croatia and retreated back across the Danube, the region remained dangerous and unstable for years. On their journey along the Danube in the mid-1990s, Bill and Laurel Cooper faced innumerable difficulties along this stretch of the river. Serbia was under UN sanctions at the time and any boat passing through Serbian territory was seen as a potential vehicle for smugglers. The Coopers describe how the entire contents of their boat had to be logged by an international team of customs officials at Mohács and the manifest sealed in an envelope, ready to be presented and checked by another customs team when they left Yugoslav territory. Once over the Hungarian border the Coopers faced an ever-present threat from Serbian pirates who, at gunpoint, would demand diesel from passing boats.

Travelling the river was particularly precarious because for eighty miles the waterway divides two of the former warring republics: Croatia on the west bank, and Serbia on the east. Yet now, a decade and a half after the end of the conflict, these two states, once engaged in fierce and bitter conflict, are now fully-fledged independent democracies, and the countryside through which the Danube passes is once again peaceful. It is also, however, rather dull. The Croatian bank of the river is marked by folds of sandy hills supporting vineyards and straggling, one-street villages. The landscape here is as distant from the travel brochure image of Croatia as it can be imagined: the azure blue Adriatic with its sun-drenched resorts is a world away from this forgotten region of bleak agricultural plains and scruffy villages. On the opposite bank, the self-governing Serb province of Vojvodina mostly comprises the same drearily flat scenery as the Hungarian plain. Few settlements are attracted to either bank of the river along this reach. But many of those that are—particularly Vukovar, on the Croatian shore—still reveal the scars of the vicious conflict that raged here in the early 1990s.

## Mohács to Vukovar

The Hungarian border lies some six miles beyond Mohács; here, the Hungarian *Dunaj* becomes the Serbian-Croatian *Dunav*. A short distance downstream from the border are the first riverside villages of Croatia and

Serbia: Batina and Bezdan respectively. An end-of-the-line patina of neglect hangs over them: life in Serbia and Croatia is clearly going on in places other than these quiet border settlements. A smart new road bridge, rising and falling in a sleek, single arc, and unusually painted red, links the two banks of the river but the access roads to the new bridge bypass the villages, compounding the sense of despondency.

Things were very different in the past when Bezdan was the focus of a network of natural and artificial waterways that spread across northern Serbia. The Velike-Bačka Canal built in the nineteenth century to link the Danube and its tributary the Tisza, joins the river here, and a second canal runs south across the plains of Vojvodina to rejoin the Danube further downstream at Novi Sad, providing a short cut for river traffic; but neither canal is used much these days.

On the Croatian bank, on a sandy hill above Batina, is another reminder of a more remarkable past: an imposing monument from communist times comprising a statue of a woman poised dramatically atop a concrete spike. The woman's skirts appear to billow in the breeze as she holds aloft a five-pointed star and gazes east over the river. The memorial commemorates the fact that it was here, in November 1944, that the Red Army crossed the Danube as it swept across Yugoslavia. The Soviet soldiers met fierce resistance from the German forces embedded along the river's wooded banks. Nowadays the monument is remarkable for its views up and down the curving river, and over the awesome flatness of the plains that stretch away into Vojvodina.

Heading downstream from Bezdan, the next Serbian settlement the river flows past is Apatin, which like many towns on this reach of the Danube was settled by Germans in the eighteenth century. The settlers came here at the behest of Maria Theresa and her son, Emperor Joseph II. Many came from Swabia, in south-western Germany, and floated here in the makeshift rafts known as Ulm boxes. The migrations caused a mingling of German cultural traditions with those of central Europe and provide an endless source of fascination for Claudio Magris in his book *Danube*. "The river... draws German culture towards the east," he wrote, "mingling it with other cultures in hybrid metamorphoses in which it finds its fulfilment and its fall... those Donauschwaben, Swabians of the Danube, were to make a basic and important contribution, now erased, to the culture and life of the Danube basin."

One writer who witnessed this cultural metamorphosis at first hand was Lovett Fielding Edwards, who came to Apatin in the 1930s and was surprised to find that "in the streets one hears mostly the curious sing-song Schwab German. The faces of the people, too, are kindly and German." Edwards, who published an account of his journey upstream and downstream from the Yugoslav capital in a book entitled *Danube Stream*, had cadged a ride here on an industrial barge that he boarded in Belgrade. He was not impressed with Apatin: the mosquitoes "hung in grey transparent shimmering clouds over the still reaches of the river," he complained. The buzzing swarms caused the whole town to shut its doors and go to bed early on summer evenings. Nowadays Apatin lies in the centre of a watery wilderness that spreads over both side of the river: the Kopački Rit Nature Park, on the Croatian shore, is teeming with birdlife that includes cormorants, grey herons, stalks, and, in the autumn, flapping flocks of ducks and geese. Signs in multiple languages warn visitors not to stray off paths in the reserve as many areas are yet to be cleared of mines.

A little further downstream the Drava joins the Danube from the west. The Drava is one of the Danube's principal tributaries, and the merging of the two streams slows both rivers, and creates the swampy backwaters of Kopački Rit that occupy the narrow "V" of the confluence. The Drava rises near Klagenfurt, on the eastern fringes of the Austrian Alps, and just before emptying into the Danube flows through Osijek, which has been a busy river port from Roman times until the present day.

In 1991 Osijek, and the towns of Vinkovci and Vukovar to the south, found themselves in the frontline of the first Yugoslav war. This region of Croatia had a substantial Serb minority that sought protection from Serb-dominated Yugoslav forces as Croatia jostled for independence. All three cities bear scars from these days but the port town of Vukovar, the largest settlement on the Croatian Danube, suffered the most. Like Apatin, it was once a German town, associated with an aristocratic family, the Counts of Eltz, whose palace sits close to the river. As Yugoslavia began to break up, Vukovar was nothing more than a reasonably prosperous industrial town beside the Danube. But just over a third of its population was Serb. In April 1991 the town became a battleground as Croat extremists launched rockets into Serb-held areas, and Serbian snipers responded by shooting at Croat police. By September the Yugoslav army had encircled the town while Croat forces hunkered down in the centre. The resulting siege dragged on for eight weeks until, on 18 November, Yugoslav forces finally broke through and took control of the town. By then around 2,000 Croatian soldiers and civilians had died defending Vukovar, and the town was virtually destroyed.

Bill and Laurel Cooper witnessed the resulting devastation from their barge a few years later:

> On the outskirts [of the town] is a burnt-out factory with shellholes in its walls, then a gutted apartment building seven stories high... On the commercial quays the cranes stand, twisted, hurt like wounded herons. Further on an elegant waterside promenade is littered with debris, its lamp standards bent or broken...Vukovar is a devastated town, not a building left intact; if the walls are standing the windows are blackened by fire, the roof has collapsed, and the splintered rafters poke the sky like spillikins thrown by an angry child.

At the time the Coopers passed through Vukovar it was in the hands of UN peacekeeping forces; the town was returned to Croatian control in January 1998.

More than ten years later the river front still carries the scars of the siege: a brick tower, half-collapsed, sits beside the water, surrounded by

buildings that are little more than charred shells. An old water tower is pockmarked with bullet holes. A new shopping complex and a plush riverside hotel have risen from the ashes of the town centre but the overwhelming impression of wholesale destruction will take decades to erase. Whole streets are still lined with buildings that are little more than rubble, while bullet scars can be seen peppering the sides of apartment blocks. On a breakwater beside the entrance to the town's harbour is a stout cross fashioned from gleaming white limestone commemorating all those who died in the conflict known to Croatians as the "Homeland War". The memorial is hard by the waterfront so it can be clearly seen from the Serbian bank. But, perhaps surprisingly, a hundred yards upstream from the cross is a customs station and the slipway for a car ferry, for the Danube is championed nowadays as a river of peace and unity after so many years of war and division. Even so, despite the efforts of the local authorities—founding a new university, and trying to get some tourism off the ground—Vukovar remains a shadow of its former self: the town is two-thirds the size it once was, and contact between the Serb and Croat communities that remain is minimal.

## INTO SERBIA: VUKOVAR TO BELGRADE

The last town on the Croatian Danube is Ilok, a former Roman settlement crowned by a castle that is now a Franciscan monastery, although the town only features in the guidebooks as a road crossing into Serbia. Once past Ilok, and for just over 125 miles, the Danube flows wholly within Serbia.

The origins of this troubled nation date back to the very early Middle Ages, when Slavic tribes trickled into this region from north-eastern Europe. By the thirteenth century a fully-fledged Serbian kingdom occupied the south bank of the Danube as it flowed through this part of the Balkans. Territorial extremities of the kingdom extended and shrank over time. For many centuries the Serbian reach of the Danube separated the Hungarian Empire to the north and the Byzantine and Ottoman empires to the south. The river here still acts as border to this day—separating Serbia proper from its northern, self-governing province of Vojvodina. The capital of Vojvodina, Novi Sad, is the second city of Serbia, and sits on the Danube some fifty miles upstream from Belgrade.

Novi Sad is a grim commercial city, where a few elegant nineteenth-century buildings make a concerted effort to remain distinctive amid an ocean of soulless apartment blocks and riverside industry. The tourist board seems keen to advise visitors that Novi Sad is the home town of the tennis player Monica Seleš, and also of Albert Einstein's wife, Mileva. Einstein himself, who was born in Ulm, some 800 miles upstream, lived in Novi Sad for a few years in the early twentieth century. But the tourist board faces an uphill task attracting visitors. The town is a hard place to like, and Lovett Fielding Edwards was quite dismissive of the place when he passed by in the 1930s: "In spite of its long and inspiring history, Novi Sad has little to show for it," he said. "It was not particularly depressing: merely boring." Edwards failed to recognize that Novi Sad had by then become the cultural centre of Serbia—but then, there is little evidence of this in the city's appearance.

The centre of Novi Sad is several hundred yards or more from the river's west bank; the suburb on the east bank, Petrovaradin, is dominated by a walled citadel of the same name that, like so many forts along the Danube, watches sternly over the river from a high plateau. The first fortress known to have been built here was named Peterwardein, the watchtower of Peter, after Peter the Hermit who in 1096 chose this place to marshal the rag-tag army that was to form the disastrous first crusade. Six centuries later, Eugene of Savoy, the Habsburg commander who chased the Turks out of Budapest and down the Danube after relieving Budapest, asked the great French military architect Sébastien Vauban to rebuild the fortress after it came into Hungarian hands—and later on Empress Maria Theresa also gave the place a substantial makeover. Her main architectural contribution was the construction of a vast network of passageways and dungeons under the castle, built over a period of eighty years by prisoners, thousands of whom died in the process. Now they are used as a tourist attraction and as a location for shooting horror films.

For a time, when Vienna was threatened by Napoleon, the fortress was also used to hide the Austrian crown jewels, and as an unusual tax-raising ploy: anyone living in the city who could see the fort's enormous clock tower from their home was forced to pay a special "clock tower" tax. During the later nineteenth century the fort was the headquarters of the *Grenzer*, soldier-settlers who were given the job of guarding Habsburg lands from Turkish incursions, and who paid no taxes in return for their readiness to take up arms. But by the turn of the century the place was used simply as a barracks and a prison: one inmate here, in the late 1920s,

was the young Tito, imprisoned after the banning of the nascent Yugoslav Communist Party.

Today the fortress consists of mustard-yellow Habsburg buildings nestling behind Vauban's massive walls. A museum and a hotel occupy the buildings, but the fortress is much better known for the EXIT pop music festival, staged for the first time in the year 2000 by two students eager to create a focus for opposition to the Milošević regime (the previous year all three bridges across the Danube in Novi Sad had been destroyed in a Nato bombing raid). Since then the festival has gone from strength to strength attracting tens of thousands of festival goers, who sleep the day away in huge tented cities across the river, and at night head across the rebuilt bridges towards the performance stages.

Between Novi Sad and Belgrade the Danube flows past the small baroque town of Stremski Karlovci (Karlowitz in German), where in 1699 Austria, Poland, Venice and Turkey put their names to a treaty that passed many of the former Turkish possessions in the Balkans to Habsburg control. The Treaty of Karlowitz effectively placed the entire reach of the Danube from Passau to Belgrade in Habsburg hands. Nearly twenty miles further downstream is Stari Slankamen, where Turkish control of Serbia met its decisive end, in a battle fought in 1691 that saw Ottoman forces chased down a hill and into the Danube. A few miles further on, amid bleak and marshy countryside, the Tisza (Tisa in Serbian), the Danube's longest tributary, joins the river, after a journey that brings it from the Carpathians in Ukraine, through the wine-making region of Tokaj in Hungary and across the eastern part of the Hungarian plain. Zemun, one of the outermost of Belgrade's sprawling suburbs, lies 25 miles further on from the confluence.

## BELGRADE: "ONE OF THE UGLIEST CITIES IMAGINABLE"

At Belgrade the last of the Danube's Alpine tributaries joins the river. The Sava rises in the beautiful Julian Alps of north-western Slovenia, and flows through Zagreb and the plains of Eastern Slavonia before merging with the Danube below Belgrade's historic fortress, the Kalemegdan. The city that stretches around the confluence is not a pretty one, an impression common to most travellers who have passed this way during the twentieth century. "One of the ugliest cities imaginable... It is absolutely devoid of charm!" Negley Farson remarked. "Here is a capital with no aristocracy, built by peasants, for peasants, and ruled by peasants. It suits them... [The city has] an enchanting situation, if they had made the right use of it." Nothing much seems to have changed in the ensuing decades: one contemporary guide book to Serbia suggests that visitors spend most of their time in the country's capital underground, sampling the legendary and thriving club scene. Above ground, Belgrade seems bleached of colour, a smudge of grey and brown where occasional hints of Turkish and Habsburg days merely serve as a reminder of how unappealing the modern city is.

Perversely, the reason why Belgrade looks so modern is because it is so ancient. Since 300 BC more than a hundred battles have been fought over the rock on which the Kalemegdan fortress is built, and Belgrade's position in the path of armies passing from Europe to the Balkans and vice versa has resulted in the city being destroyed and rebuilt some forty times. Lovett Fielding Edwards' visit in the 1930s coincided with one of these rebuilding phases: "[Belgrade is] in the midst of change, rapid and violent," he reported. "Every year familiar landmarks disappear and new ones grow up with bewildering rapidity... There are whole new quarters with the paint scarce dry, and new ones are springing up like an American 'boom' town."

There was then still a substantial Muslim community: the "trim red fez [was] an exotic note" in this rapidly changing city, Fielding Edwards noted. These Muslims were probably Turks who had remained in Belgrade even after the official withdrawal of Ottoman forces from the city in 1867. At that time the Turks had been in control of Belgrade, on and off, since 1521: in 1683 the sultan had waited here while the grand vizier marched his army upstream along the Danube on the final doomed onslaught on Vienna. But the Turks were not the only power who coveted Belgrade.

For the past millennium and more control of the city has yo-yoed between various Balkan powers with bewildering rapidity: it was Byzantine in the seventh century, then Slav, Byzantine again from 1018, Serb from 1403, and then Hungarian from 1456 until the Turkish era. As Ottoman control began to weaken, Belgrade was Habsburg from 1688, Turkish two years later, Habsburg again from 1717, then Turkish, Habsburg and Turkish again until the decisive date of 1867 was reached. Each time the Turks took control, mosques and bath houses sprung up around the city, and each time the Habsburgs wrested control from them, the mosques and bath houses went and churches and palaces appeared in their place. As if all of that was not enough, Belgrade has been subject to two phases of aerial bombardment in the twentieth century, by the Nazis in 1941 and by Nato forces in 1999, the latter forming part of the international effort to force Serbia to end the war in Kosovo.

Of the two rivers that pass through Belgrade, the city seems to pay more attention to the Sava: that river is fronted by a trendy contemporary art museum and numerous riverside restaurants, whereas the Danube waterfront is largely closed off behind a complex of dockyards and harbours. The clearest view of the Danube comes from the summit of the Kalemegdan fortress, where Belgrade's history begins. The fortress takes its name from two Turkish words: *Kale* meaning "field", and *megdan* meaning "battle", a neat indication of Belgrade's war-torn past; Turks also knew the place as *fécir-bajr*, the "hill for meditating". Centuries before the Turks came here, this was the site of the Roman settlement of Singidunum; Trajan based one of the Danube fleets at the foot of the fortress, and there was a bridge across the river to a second garrison encamped at Zemun. Seven centuries later the first Slav settlers named the place "White Town", or "Beograd", after the white limestone walls of the fort.

The current appearance of the fort dates from the eighteenth century, when the Austrians gained control of the place, and sturdy ramparts, with expansive views over the river, now enclose a peaceful city park, where

shady paths run between stands of birch and chestnut trees. In summer, peanut vendors, restaurants, and impromptu music groups add life to the place; in winter, however, the fort seems as stern and bleak as the city beyond its landward gates.

From the great walls of the Kalemegdan two towers can be seen: one is the squat and sturdy Nebojša tower, constructed by the Turks in 1460 on the flat land between the fortress hill and the river, to protect the approaches to the fortress; the other is several miles away, on the opposite bank of the Danube, on a hill above the river overlooking the prosperous waterside settlement of Zemun. This second tower can only be seen from the Kalemegdan in clear weather. It is a slender red-brick structure, bristling with a faintly ridiculous forest of turrets and pinnacles, but neglected and graffiti-covered. The tower was built by the Hungarians in 1896 to mark the one thousandth anniversary of the foundation of the Hungarian state. Although constructed as a showpiece, Hungarian troops used this so-called "Millennium Tower" to spy on the military goings-on across the water in Serbia.

The tower's existence is an indication that Austro-Hungary was at loggerheads with Serbia from the day of that kingdom's foundation in 1882. At the time of the tower's construction the carnage of the Somme and Verdun was still two decades into the future, but even in the late nineteenth century the seeds of conflict between Serbia and the Habsburg Empire were already sown. Boiling point was reached in June 1914, when Archduke Franz Ferdinand of Austria was assassinated by a Bosnian Serb in Sarajevo, igniting a war that was to result in fifteen million deaths and untold misery across Europe and beyond.

*Part Four*

# GORGE, PLAIN AND DELTA

## FROM BELGRADE TO THE BLACK SEA

# From Belgrade to the Black Sea

UKRAINE

Debrecen

CHISINAU

MOLDOVA

HUNGARY

Cluj

Szeged

ROMANIA

Siret R.

Prut R.

Brațul Chilia

Vilkovo

Timisoara

Tamis R.

Giurgiulesti

Galați

Ismail

Brațul Sulina

Sulina

Novi Sad

Noviodunum (Roman Camp)

Brăila

Tulcea

Halmyris (Roman Camp)

BELGRADE

Pančevo

Moldova Veche

Iron Gates gorge

Orșova

Iron Gates Barrage

Brațul Sfântu Gheorghe

Sava R.

Smederevo

Veliko Gradiste

Golubac

Lepinski Vir

Dobreta-Turnu Severin

Harsova

BUCHAREST

Cernavodă

Constanta

Kladovo

Rasova

Danube Canal

Donji Milanovac

Vidin

Danube R.

Silistra

Morava R.

Kozloduj

Girgiu

Ruse

Artchar

Lom

Nikopol

Novae

Svishtov

Varna

Danube Plain

SERBIA

Black Sea

KOSOVO

SOFIA

BULGARIA

ALBANIA

SKOPJE

Plovdiv

MACEDONIA

TURKEY

Istanbul

N

GREECE

0    70
km

Thessaloniki

# Chapter Ten

# EASTERN SERBIA AND THE GORGES

LEAVING BELGRADE: THE GREAT FORTRESS AT SMEDEREVO
Downstream from Belgrade the Danube, swelled by the waters of the Sava
and the Tisza, widens further and flows languidly between muddy, wooded
banks. Now the river is broad enough to dwarf the barges and at times it
can appear as wide and as still as a lake. The countryside through which it
flows remains flat and intensively farmed. But these plains are the last the
Danube will pass through for a while, as over the flat horizon lie the
Carpathians, and it is through these high mountains that the river cuts
one of its most dramatic gorges.

But all that must wait: before the mountains close in, the Danube
passes through an industrial region whose smoke-belching factories have
rendered this one of the most polluted reaches along the river's entire
length. The town of Pančevo, ten miles downstream from Belgrade at the
confluence of the River Tamiš with the Danube, is one of the worst of-
fenders. For decades its petrochemical plant has been pouring waste sludge
into the Tamiš and belching noxious fumes into the sky, making local
people ill and inflicting ecological catastrophe on the rivers and farmland.
In April 1999 a Nato bombing raid on the plant, part of the West's military response to Serbian aggression in Kosovo, led to the release of mercury,
ammonia and acids that caused yet more damage, from which the region
has yet to recover.

Things brighten up a little at Smederevo, twelve miles downstream
from Pančevo—but only a little. Here, the all too familiar ranks of drab
apartment buildings wrap themselves around a surprise, for in the centre
of Smederevo, right beside the water, is a colossal medieval fortress, one of
the largest along the length of the River Danube. Its construction dates
from 1427 when Smederevo was made the capital of Serbia, following the
fall of Belgrade to the Hungarians. A formidable redoubt was needed to
protect the town against two threatening powers—the Hungarians to the
north and the Turks to the south. The instigator of the fortress was a notorious Serb despot named Djuradj Branković, who forced the peasants

building it to supply their own eggs to put in the mortar mix, and ensured that any worker who died during the construction was bricked up inside it. The fortress was completed at break-neck speed, and in 1435 Branković chose it as the venue for the signing of a peace treaty with the Venetians. He must have enjoyed showing off his new palace, with its colossal walls, double ramparts punctuated by sturdy lookout towers, and its bastions alongside the river where ships could load and unload. Branković had amassed a vast fortune through gold and silver mines in Serbia, and he used the profits to fund this grandiose scheme. But fortune did not smile kindly on him in later life: he died in his fortress in 1456, by which time he was a prisoner of the Hungarians, who despite the formidable defences had managed to take control of the place.

Three years later the fortress fell to the Turks, who maintained a garrison here for the next three and a half centuries. They left in 1805, when the fortress was returned to Serbian control, and was allowed to fall into ruin. The Second World War ravaged what remained of it: a large part of the structure was destroyed when a cache of arms being stored here by the Germans was blown up, killing hundreds of people in the process, and three years later it was bombed during an Allied raid on what was then Nazi-occupied Yugoslavia. But not even these events could put an end to the great fortress.

Now its remains are surrounded by an ocean of railway sidings and dockyards, with the town, river and industry pressing in from all three directions. Many of the towers are somewhat the worse for wear; some even lean precariously over the remains of the moat, teetering in a state of near-collapse. The ancient walls retain their colossal dimensions, however, and even amidst a landscape of cranes and railway yards they are overwhelming; a stroll around the perimeter covers a distance of a mile. One of the towers still bears an inscription that refers to the completion of the fort in 1430—although the date as written in the stonework is 6938, the number of years reckoned by the Orthodox Church to have elapsed between the creation of the world and the completion of the fort.

The walls enclose a sizeable triangle of parkland, dotted with hot-dog stalls and a few lines of rubble that an information board helpfully points out is all that remains of a Turkish bath house. In summer funfairs are set up here, and couples canoodle among the crumbling stonework. But the best view of the fortress is from the river, where the water laps away at the

foot of the ramparts: approaching Smederevo on his yawl, Negley Farson initially mistook the fortress for a collection of grain towers, until up close he realized that he was looking at "the most astounding array of battlements conceivable... a veritable whale of a fort" that has lain beached on the flat shores of the Danube for nearly six centuries.

## The Iron Gates and Kazan Gorges
Just over thirty miles downstream from Smederevo a tributary named the Nera joins the Danube from the north. The Nera marks the border between Serbia and Romania; the border continues along the Danube after the confluence, and for the next 430 miles the river once again marks an international frontier, first between Romania and Serbia, and then between Romania and Bulgaria. In the days of the Cold War, the stretch of the river marking the border between Romania and Yugoslavia effectively formed the Iron Curtain. Then, every inch of the river was fringed by minefields, policed by patrol boats and observed from lookout towers. Tristan Jones noted the defences as he navigated *Outward Leg* along these waters in 1985.

"Between the Romanian towns and the river there was a long barbed-wire fence about ten feet high," he wrote. "At regular intervals along the fence there was a military watch tower; and atop the watchtowers, inside the little shelters with their roofs shining green, was a solider with a gun… it was like cruising on the coast of some nightmarish penal colony." But this frontier paranoia seems to be something of a tradition that pre-dates the Cold War. In *Danube Stream*, published in 1940, Lovett Fielding Edwards wrote: "The Romanians have the reputation of shooting first and then inquiring afterwards when they see anything unusual on the river."

Six miles downstream from the Danube's confluence with the Nera, the small Serbian village of Veliko Gradiste, at the mouth of the gold-bearing River Pek, serves as the customs station for boats entering and leaving Romania. The Romans maintained a fort near this second confluence, known as Punicum, and written records suggest that Emperor Trajan built a bridge across the Danube here, although no archaeological evidence remains. Even if any evidence did survive, it would have been submerged by the waters of the Danube by now, for Veliko Gradiste marks the furthest upstream extent of the lake created behind the Iron Gates hydro-electric barrage, an enormous dam built jointly by the governments of Yugoslavia and Romania in the 1960s.

The lake behind the dam is over sixty miles long and its creation has altered forever one of the most beautiful—and dangerous—reaches of the entire river. The danger came from the whirlpools and torrents in the two gorges that the river cut as it forced its way through this arm of the Carpathians: the Kazan Gorge first, and then the Iron Gates (the gorges are known as the Djerdap in Serbian and the Portile de Fier in Romanian). Now both are partly submerged beneath the waters, and villages, archaeological treasures, islands and a whole way of life have all been drowned. The destruction has resulted in the barrage's notoriety as by far the most controversial control scheme on the entire length of the Danube. But the scenery upstream of the dam remains undeniably wonderful, and, between Veliko Gradiste and the barrage, the lake formed by the swollen river occupies a deep, sheer-sided valley as grand and as overwhelming as a Norwegian fjord.

Hair-raising accounts of passage by boat through the gorges, prior to the construction of the dam, are legion. Most boat captains engaged pilots to guide them through the succession of whirlpools and eddies, but even the pilots could be challenged by the turbulent, frothing waters. Negley Farson described the channel through the gorges as "a frantic pent-up flood of rock-rippled waters… [that race] in a white sea through the black teeth of the dreaded Iron Gates" and wrote of the "sensation of taking a craft of this size through a whirlpool. It is like a succession of mechanical disasters— as if something has gone wrong with the ship. She strains, the steering gear doesn't answer, and the engine goes crazy." Mariners faced the twin perils of fast rapids and sharp teeth-like rocks lying just beneath the surface, ready to puncture boats as they plunged and rolled in the vicious swell. As Farson approached the most formidable section of the rapids, all he saw was "a long line of rocks tearing into a splashing torrent of water… *Flame* fought away from the down-rushing suck of the rapids, won the curved end of the stone-walled channel cut through the gates—and we shot down a swirling cascade."

In *Between the Woods and the Water* Patrick Leigh Fermor describes a similarly fraught passage by boat through the upper gorge, the Kazan, whose name means "cauldron" because the frothing, churning water appears always to be on the boil. "The slimy bed hardens to a narrow trough crossed by sunk bars of quartz and granite and schist, and between them deep chasms sink… The river welled angrily through the narrows, and the pilot stylishly outmanoeuvred them with swift twirls of the wheel." Then, in the most fearsome part of the narrows, he experienced a "sudden flurry around our vessel… the upheavals in the stream-bed stirred up fierce and complex currents. For hundreds of years rocks like dragons' teeth had made the passage mortally dangerous, only to be navigated when the water was high."

The American traveller Henry Rowland also enjoyed writing about a death-defying trip through the gorges, even if the experience itself, on his boat *Beaver*, was somewhat fraught. "The *Beaver* is caught in the suck," he writes breathlessly.

It rushes forward with giddying speed, her high, sea-going bows plunge into the stationary waves, a back swash from the rocky rampart spins her head, the pilot catches her with the wheel, back comes the eddy from the other bank… the towering, rocky walls, with their deep gloomy caverns, rise straight from the stream, cut off the vivid daylight, and fill the place with the subdued tints of twilight. Then suddenly a broad vista opens ahead, and we shoot out into another sheltered lake of wild and romantic beauty.

Bernard Newman, who cycled down the Danube in the 1930s, could not resist a boat ride through the gorges—but soon regretted his decision. He paid a Turkish boatman to take him out onto the water and they soon "found themselves in the swirl of the current." His skipper was alarmingly out of his depth: "'Allah!' he cried. 'Another two minutes and we shall be in the gates. Help me pull!'" But it was no use: they had to shoot the rapids. "At that moment I felt that disaster was inevitable," Newman recounts in *The Blue Danube*.

> I had already taken off my shoes and was prepared to swim for my life. Time after time the rough sides of our crazy boat scraped the jagged rocks. Time after time it seemed that the moment had come. I have never travelled in a boat in such crazy fashion... I could see people on the banks watching us. I wondered how far down the river my body would be carried... I have never fancied a watery grave.

But remarkably, Newman, his pilot and their boat survived the experience. Newman finishes his description of his unintended rollercoaster through the gorges with the rueful comment, "If anyone wants a real thrill let them go to the Iron Gates."

Yet other travellers seem unperturbed by the whole experience. Donald Maxwell, sailing his boat *Walrus* through the gorges in 1905, wrote in his book *A Cruise Across Europe* that the rapids of the Kazan were "easy... it's not so bad as it looks. Those rapids are nothing to a sea-built boat." Later, he looked "innocently the other way" while passing Orşova where people hailed him from the bank in a desperate effort to persuade him to take on a pilot. In the Iron Gates gorge "there was not sufficient disturbance to interrupt the progress of tea... the mate, who was at the helm, steered with his feet and continued eating as if nothing had happened... without knowing it, and during the uninterrupted progress of afternoon tea, [we] had braved the terrors of the Iron Gates."

From the Middle Ages until the eighteenth century the historical masters of the two great gorges were the Turks. By nature Turks were reluctant river boatmen, and preferred to move their goods and soldiers by land rather than river; so they did nothing to ease the risks faced by ships on this reach of the Danube. It was not until the late nineteenth century, when the northern bank of the Danube here formed part of the Kingdom of Hungary, that serious attempts were made at easing the problems. In the 1880s the vicious but invisible underwater rocks along a two-mile stretch of the Kazan Gorge were dynamited to create a safe passageway for boats that became known as the Stenka Channel. The following decade an artificial channel of similar length, the Sip Canal, was blasted out of the rock adjacent to the foaming river in the lower part of the Iron Gates gorge. At first ships were dragged along this canal by a tugboat named *Vaskapu* guided by a chain sunk into the water. Later, a railway line was built next to the canal and barges were attached to snorting steam locomotives. "It must be the most repetitive and shortest railway journeys in the world," John Marriner wrote after seeing his boat, *September Tide*, hauled along the Sip Canal this way in 1965. But together these waterways had drawn the most troublesome teeth from the jaws of the two gorges.

With passage by boat so dangerous there was an obvious need for a roadway to be constructed along the gorges. The Romans built the first of these roads. Running along the southern bank, it connected Belgrade with the various forts along the Bulgarian stretch of the Danube. Construction of the Romans' extraordinary route was initiated by Emperor Tiberius, continued by Vespasian and Domitian, and eventually completed by Emperor Trajan in around 105 AD. Along some parts of its length the road was hewn out from the solid rock of the cliff face. In others it consisted of a wooden causeway built on beams jammed into drilled-out holes in the rock. This arrangement would have caused the builders considerable difficulty, and would have involved boats fighting to remain stationary in the fierce current while the beams were manhandled into position. To complicate matters further the wooden sections of the road then had to be roofed over to prevent soldiers being attacked from above.

All trace of this road has now disappeared beneath the new lake, but Patrick Leigh Fermor recorded seeing the scant remains of it in 1933. He described the ancient road as "an intermittent causeway hewn just wide enough for two to march abreast along the perpendicular face of the right bank. Sometimes its course was traceable only by slots in the rock where beams had once supported a continuous wooden platform above the river." John Marriner, travelling along this reach of the river as the dam was being built, also saw the holes in the cliff and realized he was "looking at some of these things for the last time. Sometimes the holes would cease and would be replaced with an actual bit of road itself, cut out of the rock face."

The fact that the Roman road was built from wood for much of its length meant that it quickly disappeared after the Romans had gone. Indeed, the builders of the second road alongside the river, this time on its north bank, would have been scarcely aware of it. This road was built in the nineteenth century on the instigation of Count István Széchenyi, the Hungarian innovator, who also commissioned the building of the Chain Bridge in Budapest some 450 miles back upstream. Leigh Fermor thought that this second road was one of the most impressive sights along the entire length of the river. "It had been prised and hacked out of the perpendicular flank of the mountains, built up sometimes over the flood on tall supporting walls and sometimes lifted on arches," he wrote in *Between the Woods and the Water*. "Sometimes it plunged under caves scooped through towering headlands." Travelling along the road, precariously suspended between the plunging river and the mountain crests, must have been an extraordinary experience. "Shadowy mountains soared out of the glimmering water below, leaving only a narrowing band of starlight overhead, as though the two cliffs might join."

We will have to rely on Leigh Fermor's description of Széchenyi's remarkable road: like Trajan's it has long been submerged beneath the rising waters that rose behind the great barrage at Gura Văii, at the lower end of the Iron Gates gorge. The dam was conceived by the governments of Romania and Yugoslavia in 1956 and opened fifteen years later. It is the largest dam in Europe (outside the former USSR) and produces over ten billion kilowatts of electricity per year, divided between Romania and Serbia. The dimensions of the structure are breathtaking: it is 230 feet high and nearly 4,300 feet long. The barrage complex incorporates cavernous locks for ships, and a roadway runs along the crest, providing an international crossing point between Serbia and Romania.

The construction of the dam brought an end to navigational difficulties along the gorges, and reduced the time taken for barges to pass along this reach of the river from four days to fifteen hours. But there were huge drawbacks. More than 20,000 people on both sides of the river had to be resettled, and whole towns, such as Orşova in Romania and Donjii Milanovac in the former Yugoslavia, had to be rebuilt from scratch at a higher level. A new road and railway line had to be constructed to replace those that were flooded, and a number of archaeological remains from Mesolithic and Roman times were lost forever. Patrick Leigh Fermor lamented the creation of the lake in *Between the Woods and the Water*, a book that was written after the construction of the dam but which recounted a journey taken decades beforehand.

> [The dam] has turned a hundred and thirty miles of the Danube into a vast pond which has swollen and blurred the course of the river beyond recognition. It has abolished canyons, turned beetling crags into mild hills… others have done as much, or worse; but surely nowhere has the destruction of historic association and natural beauty and wildlife been so great… myths, lost voices, history and hearsay have all been put to rout, leaving nothing but this valley of the shadow.

But for once Leigh Fermor might be overstating his case. The scenery is still breathtaking, and a trip by boat along the finger lake that winds between high and occasionally sheer-sided mountains is something to savour. Tristan Jones considered it "some of the finest river scenery I have seen anywhere in the world. It can only be described in superlatives. It was often overwhelming. Nature showed us what pygmies we really are."

## BENEATH THE WATERS: THE SUBMERGED VILLAGES AND ISLANDS OF THE FLOODED GORGES

Before the flooding of the gorges, the villages along the banks of this reach of the Danube were isolated communities whose livelihood depended on sturgeon caught from the river, and the consequent export of caviar. In 1926 Negley Farson spent time with some of the fishermen of this region, "ragged-looking men", according to him, who baited their fishing lines with "white grubs they had been kedging out of the mud—horrible-looking things like small dragons." Farson considered the sterlet (young sturgeon) caught by the men to be an ugly-looking fish with "a head as hard as steel, a line of those star-shaped, hard scales on his back, another line down his sides, and two little lines on both sides of his tummy… and skin raspy as a shark, and a sharks' mouth underneath." When the men took Farson back to their fishing village, he was struck by how destitute it seemed. He thought the village dwellings were little more than "straggling huts, like native huts" gathered around "a few paths of dust [that] wandered through the village." A customs official serving in the village, "who evidently detested his billet", simply told Farson, "this place is awful."

John Marriner also noted the poverty of the riverside villages in 1965. By that time the dam was under construction and the people living by the banks of the Danube knew that their settlements were doomed. The Serb village of Donji Milanovac was at that time famous for its caviar production, but when the dam was ready there would be no more sturgeon as the creatures could no longer swim upstream from the Black Sea. "When the dam was built and the lake was born, so would Donji Milanovac die," Marriner wrote. "No wonder the mourners went about the streets. Why repair your house, why paint the church, why stock up the shops and why mend the roads, when soon all this would lie full fathom five?"

At least two islands were submerged beneath the great lake created by the dam. At the very northern end of the lake is, or rather was, an isolated mid-channel rock known as Babakai. The island's sunken position is marked by Golubac Castle, a redoubtable medieval fortress perching on the Serbian bank of the river, above the level of the inundation. Negley Farson recalled seeing the formidable islet of Babakai "standing up in the Danube like a spear" below the castle as he approached the gorges.

A famous story is attached to the island—and also accounts for its name. Once, it is said, there was a Turkish governor of this region, an Aga who had seven wives, of whom the beautiful Zuleika was his favourite. While her husband was away on a military campaign Zuleika eloped with a Hungarian count, and went with him to live in his court. On his return her husband, angry and heartbroken, became determined to reclaim Zuleika for himself. He sent a janissary to the court of the Hungarian. The janissary disguised himself as a peasant and gained an audience with the count by pretending to present him with a complaint about bands of Turks ruining Christian land. Then with a flash of a scimitar the janissary killed the count and seized Zuleika. But on her return to him, the Aga was horrified to discover that Zulekia had converted to Christianity. He begged her to reconvert to Islam but the woman refused. So the Aga tied her to the isolated mid-channel rock in the Danube and told her she would not be freed until she had repented of her sins.

But now the Aga was in for a shock: it was not the Hungarian count the janissary had killed, it was his aide-de-camp, and once the count heard of Zuleika's plight he commandeered a barge and rescued her. On seeing the island deserted, the Aga assumed that Zuleika had broken free of her bonds and had died in the river. But soon afterwards he was in for his second surprise. Within a week, the Christian and Turkish armies met on the field of battle, and the Aga, mortally wounded, was brought to the Hungarian's camp to have the truth revealed to him. The Hungarian count told the dying Turk that Zuleika was once more with him, and further-more, had no intention of renouncing her new faith. It is, of course, im-possible to verify this story, and besides, the island of Babakai is submerged now, and has taken its secrets with it, but for many years after the creation of the lake, the tops of the trees on the island would appear above the water surface when the river level was low, providing a haunting reminder of this lost island and of the fabulous tale attached to it.

The island of Ada Kaleh is very different. Now located beneath the southern extremity of the lake, just four miles upstream from the barrage, Ada Kaleh was blessed with a unique history and culture that made its loss beneath the waters the single most devastating consequence of the dam's construction. In Turkish its name means "Fortress Island", a reference to the island's origins as a military base established by fifteenth-century Ottoman commanders who had their sights set on conquering the Balkans. Four hundred years later, as the Turks withdrew from the Balkans, the descendants of soldiers who had fought with the armies of Sultan Murad I or Sultan Bayazid I simply never left the place. In 1878, when the fate of the former Turkish possessions in Europe was decided at the Con-gress of Berlin, Ada Kaleh was somehow overlooked. The island and its Turkish-speaking community remained under the loose protection of both Turkey and Austria-Hungary until the Treaty of Trianon in 1920, when it was officially made part of Romania.

Throughout this period the various political masters of the island in Budapest, Bucharest and Istanbul paid it scant attention. In fact, the island's community thrived here until the 1960s, when the inhabitants were forcibly resettled as the waters began to rise around them. Many is-landers were given new homes in the city of Constanţa on the Romanian Black Sea coast. The change must have been unbearable, and not surpris-ingly, many decided to leave Romania altogether, and seek new homes in Turkey. Also rescued from the encroaching flood was the principal building on the island, the stone fortress built by the Habsburg commander Eugene of Savoy; it was dismantled and reconstructed on the island of Ostrov Şimian, just downstream from the dam. (This island is now a military base, and the fortress cannot be visited, although it is clearly visible from the river bank.) All the other buildings on Ada Kaleh were simply abandoned to their watery grave.

Fortunately, many writers visited Ada Kaleh before the waters finally rose to cover it, and their description of life there provides a vivid memorial to the community that is no more. Foremost among them is Patrick Leigh Fermor, who was beguiled by the unique linguistic and cultural heritage of the island. One of the first things he saw when stepping off the boat in 1934 was men sitting at a coffee shop in the main village, wearing "bulky scarlet sashes a foot wide gathered in the many pleats of their black and dark blue baggy trousers... [and] faded plum-coloured fezzes with ragged turbans loosely knotted about them." But, on closer scrutiny, centuries of island living had clearly taken their toll on the community. According to Leigh Fermor, the "four or five hundred islanders belonged to a few families which had intermarried for centuries, and one or two had the vague and absent look, the wandering glance and the erratic levity that sometimes come with ancient and inbred stock... an atmosphere of pre-

Ada-Kaleh.

historic survival hung in the air as though the island were the refuge of an otherwise extinct species long ago swept away."

Cut off from the outside world by water, and surrounded by a sea of Romanian, Hungarian, German and Bulgarian speakers, the islanders spoke a language that had "drifted far from the metropolitan vernacular of Constantinople or remained immovably lodged in its ancient mould, like a long-marooned English community still talking the language of Chaucer." Their language was written using Arabic script, instead of the new Latin alphabet that Kemal Ataturk had made compulsory in Turkey. Strangely, however, Leigh Fermor does not indicate that the island was attracting a fair number of tourists. Bernard Newman visited the island around the same time and in *The Blue Danube* he describes the souvenirs on sale in the bazaar. In particular, he was delighted to find that Turkish Delight was on sale for only seven pence a pound.

In his 1938 book *Romanian Journey*, Sacheverell Sitwell remarked that the island's inhabitants made "their living as human curiosities, by supplying Turkish coffee to the tourists. Their indolence is to be envied in a totalitarian world." Lovett Fielding Edwards recalled in his book *Danube Stream* that Ada Kaleh was "the greatest tourist attraction on the Danube, a tiny Garden of Eden... Ada Kaleh lives on the tourist as much as Biarritz or Brighton, but it does so in an easy and dignified manner." Like Leigh Fermor, Lovett Edwards was charmed by the place. "We sat and drank Turkish coffee and ate sherbet ices in a vine-covered café," he recalled. "It was good Turkish coffee, made as only Moslems seem to be able to make it, Heaven knows why!"

John Marriner must have been one of the last westerners to visit the island, in 1965. He found the place "far more beautiful than any of us had expected" and goes on to give an extraordinary account of being invited to a circumcision party in the village. Two boys, aged around seven and twelve, were the centre of attention at this busy jamboree, which is still a rite of passage that most young boys in modern-day Turkey must undergo. "The elder boy was wearing some sort of very tarted up fez, covered with embroidery," Marriner recollects. "Neither looked at all concerned, though the gang of admiring children that followed them everywhere was no doubt quite aware of the solemn events in prospect... the 'surgeon' was in real life the village postman." The ceremony took place in a "small room in the best-preserved house in the village... Most of it, like a whore's in

Bayswater, was taken up by a gigantic bed, decorated in the same sort of taste that a professional lady might also show. A four poster, it was a mass of pink ribbons, too many cushions and thrilling eiderdowns." Marriner and the crew of his ship did not stay for the surgical part of the ceremony. But when they were invited back into the room after it was all over, he saw that

> on the great bed, his knees up and half covered in a sheet, sat the older boy. He looked exactly the same as he had always done since I had seen him… Still the serious elderly expression, still the non-committal gaze. I bowed and shook hands and he inclined his head from the bed. On his brow, like a martyr's crown, was a brilliantly embroidered fez. He had become a man.

### Above the Waters: from Veliko Gradiste to the Iron Gates Barrage

The distance between Veliko Gradiste, the small Serbian customs town at the northern end of the new lake, and the Iron Gates barrage, is just under seventy miles. Steep mountains rise abruptly from the shoreline of the finger-like lake all the way along its length. Modern roads, built to replace those submerged beneath the water, run along both banks, often zigzagging their way up and down the contours as they cross the tributary valleys that feed the river. The towns alongside the lake are mundane affairs, built since the 1970s to replace those drowned at lower levels. But the scenery is an unending succession of spectacular and dramatic views, whether seen from the lakeside roads or, even better, from the water itself.

Seven miles downstream from Veliko Gradiste is the Romanian port town of Moldova Veche. In former times this was where ships heading downstream through the gorges were required to take a pilot on board. The Turks created a fortified settlement here, but nothing of it remains. The main feature of the town is the grimy port facility, developed to transship the molybdenum and copper once mined nearby. The miners lived in the familiar grey municipal housing blocks while the Old Town was mostly inhabited by Serbs. With the mines now worked out, however, a rather neglected air hangs over the town, and it is as grim and as unappealing as any other industrial town on the Danube, despite its setting amid fine scenery.

Beyond Moldova Veche the formidable but ruined hulk of Golubac Castle looms on the Serbian bank. (Beneath the water here is the submerged island of Babakai.) Golubac, perched on a steep rocky bluff like the castles of the Austrian Wachau, and set in a rugged landscape, was even higher above the water level before the dam was built, and occupies the site of a Roman fort named Columbarium. The name of the castle is a reference to its lofty location: in Serbo-Croat the word *golub* means "dove" and the castle is also known as the "dovecote". The castle seen today was built in the late Middle Ages by the Hungarians and consists of nine defensive towers linked by a string of formidable walls. It was captured by the Turks as they advanced through the Balkans in the fourteenth century, and abandoned as they engaged in a temporary retreat two and a half centuries later, after which time it fell into ruin. But this ruinous state is part of the castle's appeal: crumbling walls and sheer drops abound and make it easier to believe in the legends attached to the place.

One legend tells that St. George slew the dragon here but forgot to throw the carcass into the river. This oversight accounts for the plague of giant mosquitoes that infect the area: over the centuries the creatures have grown fat by feeding on the rotting carcass. Lovett Fielding Edwards believed that these airborne creatures were capable of "laying waste the countryside. They move in huge swarms and their attack means death and destruction to cattle, horses and lesser beasts. They have even been known to attack human beings and sting them to death."

Immediately south of Golubac, the river flows through a deep chasm, only 500 feet wide, fringed by near-vertical slopes that soar 2,000 feet towards the sky. It is a silent, eerie place, alive with bird calls echoing from cliff to cliff. Before the construction of the dam this was a very dangerous section of rapids but today ships glide easily along this reach, floating on the still waters and dwarfed by the rocky chamber that threatens to entomb them.

The river widens out as it reaches the Kazan Gorge. An extraordinary sculpture of the bearded head of the Dacian chieftain Decebalus, forty metres high and the tallest rock sculpture in Europe, overlooks the water here from the Romanian bank; it is the product of ten years' work by twelve sculptors and was completed in 2004. Decebalus was the nemesis of the Romans in this part of the world, and he glares across the water at a Roman cliff carving on the Serbian bank: this takes the form of a me-

morial tablet sitting just above the waterline and framed by stone columns. The words *Tabula Traiana* are carved at the top of the memorial in block capitals. This is Trajan's Tablet, erected to commemorate the construction of Trajan's extraordinary road along the gorges. That road is submerged now, and the tablet would have been drowned along with it had it not been hewn from the rock by archaeologists and re-installed in its current position above the water line. In its original position the tablet had been used as a fireplace and cooker by wandering fishermen, so archaeologists took the opportunity to clean it up while it was repositioned.

The tablet is best seen from a boat; in fact, tourist launches from the Serbian village of Donji Milanovac and the Romanian town of Orşova, both on the lake shore, bring trippers out here on a daily basis in summer specifically for that purpose. In translation, the Latin inscription on the rock reads, "The Emperor Caesar, son of the divine Nerva Trajan Augustus Germanicus, High Priest and for the Fourth Time Tribune, Father of the Country and for the fourth time consul, overcame the hazards of the mountain and the river and opened this road." The tablet is the single most valuable Roman monument along the flooded area of the gorges. Although many other Roman remains were found at various sites along the river, including a Mithraic relief, all of them have long since sunk below the waves.

Also beneath the water is much of the valuable Mesolithic-era archaeological site at Lepenski Vir, on the Serbian shore near Donji Milanovac. This site was only discovered in the 1960s, during construction work on the dam, and consists of the remains of dwellings of an ancient culture that lived along the Danube around 5000 BC. Horseshoe-shaped settlements faced the river, perched on a narrow ledge of rock between the cliffs and the water, and the inhabitants, whose culture bridged the gap between hunter-gatherer societies and settled farming communities, lived largely on fish caught from the river. The dead at Lepenski Vir were buried in a rudimentary cemetery beside the settlement, although village elders appear to have been interred within the dwellings in fireplaces. The discovery of fish and deer bones in large numbers suggest that Lepenski Vir served as a site of religious sacrifice, though nothing is certain. Before the site was lost to the rising waters, part of it was moved to higher ground, while the most valuable finds, including extraordinary gargoyle-like sculptures of human heads with bulging eyes, fish-like lips and half-open mouths, are on display in museums in Belgrade.

The Iron Gates barrage itself, some six miles downstream from Orşova, is an uninviting place. The road across the crest of the dam, linking Romania and Serbia, is a busy international crossing point, and throughout the day the place is besieged by rows of heavy trucks waiting to clear customs. Officials do not encourage people to linger. A heavy police presence surrounds the dam and customs houses, and much of the area is closed off behind a barricade of high fences, arc lights and grim-looking police facilities that seem like a throwback to the days of the Iron Curtain.

## DROBETA-TURNU SEVERIN, KLADOVO, AND TRAJAN'S BRIDGE

Beyond the barrage the countryside on either side of the Danube flattens out. By the time the river flows past the Romanian town of Drobeta-Turnu Severin there is little hint of the spectacular terrain through which it has just forged its way. The town is only six miles downstream from the barrage; on the opposite bank, across the wide river, the Serbian town of Kladovo was developed as a dormitory settlement to house the dam's builders. There is no bridge across to Kladovo now, or even a ferry—but there was once. In fact, the bridge that linked Drobeta-Turnu Severin and Kladovo some nineteen centuries ago was one of the most important ever to span the Danube.

During the first century AD the territory lying north of the Danube as it made its slow way towards the sea—modern-day Romania—was controlled by the Dacian tribes. The Romans coveted the territory of the fiercely hostile Dacians because of the valuable reserves of gold in Transylvania. The first serious campaigns against the Dacians, waged by Emperor Domitian, ended in stalemate and a peace treaty signed in 87 AD. Fourteen years later, Emperor Trajan was determined to subdue the Dacians and punish their king, Decebalus, for flouting the terms of the peace treaty. In 101 AD Trajan crossed the Danube with an army and engaged the Dacians in battle at Tapae in the Carpathian mountains. Although Trajan claimed victory his troops suffered a mauling and he was forced to pull them back across the river.

A counter-attack by Decebalus led to another Roman invasion, which this time resulted in the capture of the Dacian capital Sarmizegethusa. (It is unclear how the Romans crossed the Danube during these early campaigns.) But the Dacians proved themselves tenacious foes and Decebalus attacked the Romans once again in 105. This time Trajan was determined to inflict a decisive and crushing blow on the Dacians. He instructed his architect, Apollodorus of Damascus, to build a bridge across the river that would allow a substantial invasion force to cross. Apollodorus chose the Dacian settlement of Drobeta as a suitable bridgehead. A garrison was established at Kladovo, on the south bank, and within a year the bridge was complete. In 106 a huge invasion force marched across the bridge, complete with carts laden with supplies and hundreds of horses, and engaged the Dacians in a final, conclusive battle. Soon a bounty of gold, silver, copper, corn, honey, salt, wood, hides, cattle and slaves was crossing back the other way, to satisfy the remorseless appetite of the Roman Empire. The defeated Decebalus committed suicide and his severed head was jammed onto a spike and displayed above the steps to the capitol in Rome. Roman victory meant that Dacia became the sole province of the empire north or east of the Danube; Decebalus, meanwhile, has been adopted as a Romanian hero—hence the giant carving of his face set into the cliff of the Kazan Gorge, a few miles back upstream.

The conquering of Dacia was just one of Trajan's many military triumphs. Under him the Roman Empire reached its greatest extent. After his military conquests in Europe, Trajan turned his sights towards the east and brought modern-day Jordan, Armenia and Iraq under Roman control. In

Rome the euphoric senate commissioned Apollodorus to design a column in Trajan's honour that celebrated his remarkable achievements; the column still stands today, in Trajan's own forum. The frieze that spirals up the column, over a length of 625 feet, contains the earliest pictorial representation of the Danube. Trajan himself appears 59 times on the frieze, fighting with his soldiers, crossing the river with them and feasting with them in riverside encampments. A river god also appears, emerging from the Danube to confer divine blessing on Trajan's campaign.

On his death, Trajan was deified by the senate and his ashes were buried under the column. His legacy has bequeathed him an almost godlike status: in medieval times Pope Gregory I, through divine intercession, supposedly resurrected Trajan from the dead and baptized him in the Christian faith, while in the nineteenth century the historian Edward Gibbon popularized him as one of the "five good emperors". Roman control of Dacia was to continue for more than a century and a half after Trajan's defeat of Decebalus. It ended when Emperor Aurelian withdrew Roman forces in 271 in the face of ruinous incursions by Asiatic tribes. The famous bridge was scuttled on the orders of Hadrian, who feared that Dacian tribes would utilize it for an easy assault on the empire.

Turnu Severin today is a restful town, with an unhurried air about its shady streets. (The prefix "Drobeta" was the name of the former Dacian settlement on this site; "Turnu Severin" in Romanian refers to the long-vanished Tower of the Emperor Septimus Severus.) The place has evidently tidied itself up since Negley Farson came here. He complained that "the cafés were dirty, the streets poorly lighted, and the whole place seemed down-at-heel. The atmosphere was—Europe, badly in need of repair, model French." But this writer saw the influence of the Romans in the clothes people wore. According to Farson, local fashion was a "blend of Dacian with Roman. The trousers still have the wide, free Dacian swing and look like modern pyjamas. The belted-in-tunic, buttoned at the throat, reaches to the knees. It was introduced to the Danube by Trajan."

The town has no riverside promenade, but the wooded banks of the Danube are scattered with Roman and medieval remains, which makes up for the fact that the heart of the town is a good 600 yards from the water. All that is left of Trajan's bridge are two rectangular stone stumps on the river bank, jammed beside a single-track railway line that runs alongside the water's edge. The bridge consisted of wooden arches built onto stone piles, so it is not surprising that only a little of it remains. In the town's museum an outstanding model shows how the bridge would have looked: its surface, fashioned from wooden beams, was wide enough for a whole phalanx of soldiers to march across, and its length was getting on for half a mile.

Other bankside remains in the town include the crumbling foundation walls of a Roman fort that guarded the bridge, and some Roman bath houses, which like the fort are slowly biting the dust; a more substantial medieval citadel, with collapsing walls to scramble over and precipitous drops to avoid, leaves less to the imagination, and was built over the remains of a second Roman fort. Evidence of the former bridge can also be seen on the opposite bank at Kladovo, but remains are even more scant than in Drobeta-Turnu Severin. Kladovo was a Roman garrison town and just upstream from here, in the Serbian riverside village of Karataš, are the scant remains of a fortress built by Trajan that served as a frontier post; another stone tablet with an inscription commemorating that emperor's exploits has been uncovered here.

# Chapter Eleven
## TOUCHING BULGARIA

### EAST FROM DROBETA-TURNU SEVERIN TO VIDIN

When he came to map of the course of the River Danube, the nineteenth-century-cartographer Guillaume Lejean, who had already successfully mapped the Nile, stumbled upon a problem. He found that he could obtain virtually no information relating to the river's course in Bulgaria. In fact, he could find more information relating to the Nile's journey through Africa than he could regarding the Danube's through south-east Europe. Lejean's difficulties came as a result of Bulgaria being one of the least-known countries in the whole of the continent. Patrick Leigh Fermor discovered this for himself as he travelled through southern Romania in 1933. "I had never met anyone who had been to Bulgaria. [Romania and Hungary] looked westwards to Vienna, Berlin, London and Paris, and the benighted region of the Balkans remained *terra incognita*... in the eyes of everyone living north of the river, [Bulgaria] seemed the darkest, most

backward and least inviting country in Europe except Albania." Bernard Newman approached Bulgaria with the same trepidation the following year, on his bicycle. In *The Blue Danube* he dubbed Bulgaria a "barbaric country, which had hitherto been to me no more than a strange name. Guns booming or outlaws murdering one another—villages raided and women screaming—this was the picture of Bulgaria which I had seen painted so often."

In the twenty-first century, Bulgaria still lies somewhat below the tourist radar. In the days of the Cold War the country developed a reputation for cheap seaside holidays in cheerless Black Sea resorts, and for skiing holidays in the Carpathians where prices and facilities were both well below those of Alpine competitors. Nowadays city sightseers flock to Plovdiv, on the Thracian plain, where Ottoman-era mosques and Byzantine churches provide a bigger draw than the rather drab capital, Sofia. But the Danube, in the north of the country, sees far fewer visitors. Flowing across an area of wetland plains, its broad valley fringed by low hills, the river has a low-key presence and the region through which it passes often seems a forgotten part of the country. Settlements are widely spaced and the major roads linking them do not run along the river. In fact, it is hard to associate Bulgaria with the Danube, despite the fact that a couple of major cities, namely Vidin and Ruse, are situated on its banks. The problem boils down to geography: the Danube forms Bulgaria's northern border with Romania for nearly 300 miles, but never actually flows through the country. So Bulgaria has somehow never been allowed to join the club of riparian states to which its Balkan neighbours, Serbia and Romania, unquestionably belong.

The gently undulating *Dunavska Ravnina*—as Bulgarians call the Danube plain—is an area of vast skies and rippling seas of cornfields. On the Bulgarian side of the river the low hills occasionally rise to form bluffs of pale limestone that shimmer in the bright summer sun; there are beaches too, and vineyards, and a slow pace of life in the quiet riverside settlements, all of which lend the region a pronounced Mediterranean air. By contrast, the countryside on the Romanian bank is low-lying and marshy, pockmarked with shallow lakes known as *baltas* that are rich in fish and provide a haven for an abundance of birdlife: cormorants, ducks, geese, swans, storks and herons—and even the occasional brown eagle, wheeling low over the marshes and pools in search of its prey.

Between the baltas and the limestone bluffs the channel winds between sandbanks and islands providing challenging conditions for skippers navigating this reach. "The River Danube below the Iron Gates was often like a sea," Tristan Jones recollects in *The Improbable Voyage*. "Here, he was wide, very long, and the fetches of wind and water raised seas that were as high, sometimes, as anything seen in the English Channel in any weather under a full gale." Difficulties in navigation were compounded by the scarcity of settlements. "We did not know what to expect. We might as well have been travelling down the Danube in the twelfth century... each bend of the river was an exploration... we had no idea what fuel or supplies were available anywhere. Often, very often, the officials at one place knew absolutely nothing about the next place on the route. Nine times out of ten their advice or information was utterly wrong."

A succession of agreeable towns and ancient Roman sites line the Bulgarian banks of the Danube. (The Romanian bank, by contrast, is distinguished only by the ordinariness of its riverside settlements and the unsightliness of its oil refineries.) Vidin, some ninety miles downstream from Drobeta-Turnu Severin, comes as a delightful surprise after a long reach of river distinguished only by yet another hydroelectric dam (at Prahovo). Many writers from the early decades of the twentieth century recall being amazed by this beautiful and mysterious city, the first along the Danube that seemed to be truly of the Orient. Lovett Fielding Edwards describes it as "one of those marvellous cities of eastern fairytale which, secure behind their fortress walls, are decorated with spires and cupolas and minarets piled one upon another in a fantastic medley of creeds, ages and styles." Don Maxwell, in *Across Europe in a Motorboat*, wrote of the "white minarets [that] appeared everywhere over the russet roofs" and the "picturesque figures, variously clad" thronging the streets, including Greek patriarchs in long black robes, and "Turkish women with veiled faces—all these helped to form the medley of flaming colour that one sees only towards the Orient."

Bernard Newman was similarly impressed by the "mystery and romance" of this town where domes of eastern Christian churches and the spikes of minarets shimmered in silhouette. "It was a first impression that excited the imagination," he wrote, realizing at once that his gloomy expectations of Bulgaria had been dashed. Negley Farson observed the Turkish water carriers who "come down at night and fill their brass jars from the filth of the river" while "vendors of sweets trot past with fly-covered, sticky pink trays on their heads." But he understood that he was seeing the place at the end of an era. "The plaster is dropping off the old minarets, and the muezzin has a crack in his voice," he noted sadly.

Time has taken its toll in Vidin. The fairytale spires have gone, victims of ruthless town planning in the communist era, and in their place are ranks of grey housing blocks, and a modern town that centres on an expansive flag-stoned square set back a hundred yards or so from the river. To the north of the square various historical monuments straggle along the attractive, tree-shaded river bank. Foremost among them is a medieval citadel, still in a good state of repair, whose exterior walls abut the river, and whose presence reflects Vidin's strategic importance on the Danube.

During the fourteenth century control of the fortress yo-yoed back and forth between the Bulgarian tsars, local despots, the Crusaders, the Turks and the Hungarians. In 1398 the Turkish sultan Bayezid wrested control of the fortress from the Crusaders and it remained Turkish until the nineteenth century, except for a brief period of Habsburg rule in the sixteenth century, and then a second period between 1792 and 1807 when the citadel came under the control of Osman Pazvantoğlu, a provincial governor who rebelled against Sultan Selim III.

Pazvantoğlu was something of a maverick, and a thorn in the side of the Turks. He strengthened the fortifications of the riverside citadel with the help of French engineers sent by Napoleon, who saw him as a potential French ally in any conflict with the Ottoman Empire. And he was just one of a number of hard-headed governors of Ottoman Bulgaria, all of whom staffed their own armies with fierce mercenaries known as Khardzhali who were given free rein to terrorize Christian villages in search of food and plunder. Pazvantoğlu, however, was a cynical political operator: one moment he was cutting the taxes levied on Christians to garner their support, the next he was launching a pogrom against Bulgarian priests and civil leaders when he feared they would revolt against him. Pazvantoğlu's mosque, the only one still standing in the town, is situated between the fortress and the main town, behind a strip of shady parkland by the river. With customary iconoclastic panache, Pazvantoğlu placed a tiny heart at the summit of the minaret, rather than the customary crescent of Islam, and it is still there. His tomb lies beside the mosque.

But it is the riverside citadel that Pazvantoğlu was briefly in charge of, the Fortress of Baba Vida, which holds most attention in Vidin. Baba

Vida is Grandma Vida, a mythical founder of the castle perhaps, although the origins of the name are lost in obscurity. The citadel has been in the hands of the military until comparatively recently: in 1935 Bernard Newman found the place was occupied by a brigade of Bulgarian troops. "I saw small squads of men undergoing training, while by the massive towers a whole company was engaged in affixing fuses to shells," he wrote. But now the soldiers have gone and the castle is a tourist showpiece beside the river. The cream-coloured walls are formidable, but the moat they enclose is dry; courtyards and ramparts abound within the walls but they are linked by dingy staircases and terraces overgrown with weeds. Gun emplacements with no guns overlook the wide river from on top of bulky round turrets. There is a good view across the river from the gun turrets, but the opposite bank is thick with trees, giving nothing away. (The nearest Romanian settlement, Calafat, is further upstream, and is linked to Vidin by an elderly car ferry, scheduled to be replaced by a new bridge in 2010.)

Despite the calmness of the scenery, the Danube here is something of a sleeping giant: in April 2006 heavy rain and snowmelt caused a flood wave to surge downstream along the river, causing the evacuation of several thousand people along both banks, and forcing 1,200 people into an emergency tent city in Vidin as the waters drenched the surrounding farmland and villages.

### VIDIN TO RUSE: ALONG THE EDGE OF THRACE

Vidin, like most towns in Bulgaria, was once part of Thrace. In fact, its heritage is a heady mixture of Thracian, Roman, Macedonian, Byzantine, Slav, Turkish and Bulgar (the latter a tribe that migrated here from central Asia around 680 AD). Four thousand years ago the tribal territory of the Thracians stretched from the shores of the Aegean to the banks of the Danube. Sometime around 350 BC Philip of Macedon invaded and conquered Thrace, and founded the city of Philippoplis (modern-day Plovdiv) on the plains east of today's Sofia. Philip and his son Alexander the Great spent many decades subduing Thrace and establishing it firstly as part of the Macedonian Empire, and then as a province of Alexander's vast empire, which at its zenith stretched from the Danube to the banks of the Indus in modern-day Pakistan. By around 50 AD the Romans were imperial masters in Thrace, and they began to establish military encampments along the south bank of the Danube facing the territory of the as yet unconquered Dacians. Later these camps were linked to cities in Illyria, on the east coast of the Adriatic, by means of the road built along the Iron Gates gorge.

Vidin occupies the site of the most westerly of the Thracian riverside encampments; in Roman times it was known as Bononia. Heading east, one Roman camp follows another with the regularity of the kilometre marker posts along the river. Some twelve miles downstream from Vidin is Artchar, formerly Ratiaris, the Roman capital of Upper Thrace, which was fortified by Trajan during his Dacian campaign and was one of the bases of the Danube fleet. Next is Lom, fifteen miles further on, which occupies the site of the Roman garrison town of Almus. Lom is Bulgaria's second river port, and serves Sofia, located just over sixty miles to the south. At the mouth of the River Isker, some sixty miles beyond Lom, are the scattered remains of the Roman town of Oescus. Emperor Constantine was supposed to have constructed a bridge over the Danube here, although there is no trace of it now.

The small town of Nikopol, situated at the foot of steep chalk cliffs beyond Oescus, owes its name to another emperor, Trajan, who christened the place "Nicopolis ad Istrum", the City of Victory on the Lower Danube, in celebration of his victory over the Dacians. Thirty-five miles beyond Nikopol is Novae, home to the most extensive Roman remains in Bulgaria, and situated at the point where the curling river touches the most southerly latitude of its entire journey. Novae was founded as a Roman camp in around 50 AD. Over the ensuing centuries it grew into a civilian town and finally, after its abandonment by the Romans, was adopted by the Goths as an important military and civilian centre. Novae has been substantially excavated and covers a number of separate sites, one of which stretches to the top of a steep bluff overlooking the river. As usual the remains are low outlines of public buildings, bath houses and barracks; the curving shape of a fifth-century basilica can also be identified amidst the weeds and rubble, and a barracks hospital has been partially reconstructed, with individual wards grouped around a central courtyard, and a deep culvert that removed waste from the latrines and into the river. Much of the site is overgrown with scruffy patches of vegetation, and loose piles of earth from archaeological digs are scattered all around; but Novae's size ranks it the third most important Roman site along the Danube, after Carnuntum and Aquincum.

It was not just important events in classical history that were played out along this stretch of the river. Trajan's fort at Nikopol was rebuilt by the Byzantine Emperor Heraclios in 629 and was seized by the Turks in 1393, provoking one of the most significant military entanglements in the Balkans during the Middle Ages. The Catholic King of Hungary, Sigismund, knew that Turkish occupation of the Balkans would threaten his kingdom and the rest of Christian Europe. So in 1396 he led an army down the Danube to reclaim the riverside fortress at Nikopol on behalf of Christendom. Sigismund's army set off from Buda and crossed the Danube at Orşova, taking eight days to get everyone across by pontoon and boat. They took Vidin with comparative ease and then pushed on along the river. Sigismund had upwards of 16,000 men at his disposal, drawn from all over Christian Europe, and at Nikopol he was joined by groups of Knights Hospitaller from Rhodes, who reached this remote spot on the Danube in a fleet of 44 Venetian ships that travelled by way of the Aegean and the Black Sea.

Sigismund's campaign was a crusade in all but name, and this was partly the reason for the calamity that followed. His soldiers were steeped in the ways of medieval chivalry and regarded war as a matter of personal prowess and knightly endeavour rather than mere swordsmanship. Against a well-organized and disciplined Ottoman army Sigismund's forces stood no chance, and his soldiers were routed by Sultan Bajazet's cavalry in a bloody show of force. The crusaders' horses were impaled on stakes, their riders slaughtered, and the Danube ran thick with human and animal blood. Sigismund escaped in a fishing boat and was ignominiously forced to return to Hungary via Constantinople (not then in Turkish hands) and Dubrovnik. The fortress at Nikopol survived another four centuries after Sigismund's calamitous defeat, but was destroyed by the Russians in 1810 during a military campaign against the Turks. Except for a dramatic entrance gateway it is now in ruins; there is a fine view of the town of Nikopol and the Danube from its position on the cliffs.

Finally, the Thracian reach of the river has also provided an arena for more recent historical events. The small town of Svishtov, between Novae and Nikopol, is a former ferry port built on two levels: beside the Danube is a small but dirty river harbour, while above it on a high bluff spreads a typical Bulgarian provincial town, shady and quiet on a hot afternoon in summer. One of the most distinctive buildings in Svishtov is the Holy Trinity Church, built in the nineteenth century by the noted architect Kolyo Ficheto; the unusual and distinctive curving line of the roof is supposed to imitate waves on the Danube.

Svishtov has always been a crossing point on the river and in 1916 the armies of Germany and Bulgaria launched an invasion of Romania from here, preceded by a fierce shelling of the Romanian bank from positions on the hill. In 1877 a Russian army had crossed in the other direction, to engage the Turks in a war that, a year later, brought five centuries of Ottoman rule in Bulgaria to an end. The Russian invasion was inspired by a popular uprising against Turkish rule that had broken out in Bulgaria the previous year.

Another small riverside settlement, named Kozloduj, situated between Lom and Nikopol, played an important role in this rebellion, when a Bulgarian patriot-in-exile named Christo Botiov chose it as a landing place for his small army of two hundred revolutionaries who had assembled in Romania. Famously, Botiov commandeered an Austro-Hungarian steamer, the *Radecki*, to help with the crossing. He provided the captain of the ship with a letter stating that the ship's crew were in no way party to the rebellion and were acting out of duress. The rebellion, however, was unsuccessful: the Turks had been warned by spies of Botiov's entry into the country, and within a week he was dead, his fellow revolutionaries dispersed around the country. His actions are remembered to this day in the form of bouquets of flowers spelling out his name on the river bank at Kozloduj. In recent years the spirit of Botiov has been rekindled in this town for a different purpose when protestors massed against the construction here of Bulgaria's only nuclear power station.

## RUSE, GIRGIU AND SILISTRA

Ruse, almost forty miles downstream from Svishtov, was once the largest and wealthiest city in Bulgaria. In 1648 the Turkish traveller Hadji Kalfa recorded that that its glorious townscape comprised 6,000 wooden houses, two Turkish baths and nine mosques. Before then the place had been an important Roman naval base, known as Sexaginta Prista ("Sixty Ships"). Parts of the third-century fortifications survive to this day on a bluff overlooking the river, together with a number of richly decorated tombstones. Centuries later, the Ottomans stationed their Danube fleet here, and the city became an important military base, but the Turkish fortress was destroyed by the Russians in 1810, and today Ruse is known not so much for its military past but for its attractive riverside setting, its wide streets

and spacious squares, its sunny climate and its recent reputation as a cosmopolitan centre thriving on trade and banking.

Things were very different a century and a half ago. By the middle of the nineteenth century Ruse was a byword for squalid living conditions: water buffaloes wandered the narrow twisting streets while ramshackle dwellings lined filthy alleyways and choked poky courtyards. Midhat Pasha, the French-educated Ottoman governor of the Danube Province, whose capital was at Ruse, was determined to improve the place. He bulldozed the slums and ordered opulent European-style buildings to rise in their place. The old alleys and lanes were replaced by imposing boulevards in the style of those built by Haussmann in Paris. The pasha also founded schools and hospitals and initiated the building of the first railway line in Bulgaria, linking Ruse with Varna on the Black Sea coast and part-financed with British money. Today a transport museum beside the river celebrates the line: elderly steam engines are lined up outside, including one built by a Manchester firm, alongside luxurious carriages that were once the travelling homes of Turkish sultans and Bulgarian tsars.

But Midhat Pasha was unorthodox and his ideas did not meet favour with Bulgarians since many of his initiatives were directed at uniting the crumbling Ottoman Empire rather than furthering the cause of Bulgars. And his policies also won him few friends in Constantinople; he was later transferred to the governorship of Syria, and was then murdered by Ottoman agents in Yemen in 1884. By then, however, Ruse had been transformed into the most fervently western city in the Balkans, home to merchant families from Greece, Armenia and Germany, and busy with banks, consulates and the comings and goings of cargo barges. Bernard Newman, who visited Ruse on his cycling trip along the Danube in 1934, was very dismissive of the place. "Ruse is a town of modern streets, gardens and theatres. It belongs to Europe, and not to the Balkans," he wrote. He took one look at it and decided to cross the river to the Romanian town of Giurgiu, whose scruffy port faces Ruse across the river.

The cosmopolitan, sophisticated milieu of turn-of-the-twentieth-century Ruse nurtured one of the greatest writing talents ever to emerge from Bulgaria. The family of Elias Canetti were prosperous Sephardic Jews who owned a profitable warehouse a few steps away from the riverside. Young Elias grew up speaking Ladino, a vernacular language similar to Spanish, and wrote his major works in German, the language spoken by his parents. He spoke no Bulgarian and left Ruse at the age of six to live in Manchester, after his father joined a business partnership there. Canetti's autobiography, *The Tongue Set Free* (1979), opens with evocative descriptions of life in multicultural Ruse, where "people of the most varied backgrounds lived... and on any one day you could hear seven or eight languages." One of these, of course, was Bulgarian, but it was only spoken by peasants from the countryside. The business life of the city was conducted in Turkish, Greek, Albanian, Armenian or Russian. "Seven or eight different tongues were spoken in our city," Canetti explained. "Each person counted up the languages he knew; it was important to master several, knowing them could save one's own life or the lives of other people."

The Danube was a constant presence, according to Canetti. Not only did it support the trade on which the city's commercial life depended, it also supplied the water for people's homes, in gigantic barrels carried from the waterside by mule. "The Danube was a constant topic of discussion," Canetti wrote in *The Tongue Set Free*:

> There were stories about the extraordinary years when the Danube froze over; about sleigh rides all across the ice to Romania... when it was very cold, wolves came down from the mountains and ravenously pounced on the horses in front of the sleighs. The coachman tried to drive them away with his whip, but it was useless, and someone had to fire at them. Once, during such a sleigh ride, it turned out that they hadn't taken anything to shoot with... They had a terrible time keeping the wolves at bay and were in great danger. If a sleigh with two men hadn't happened to come along from the opposite direction, things might have ended very badly, but the two men shot and killed one wolf and drove the others away.

Ruse might have lost its cosmopolitan character of a century ago (and its packs of wolves), but today it is a relaxed and attractive town, with its shady streets and tree-lined riverfront. Many of the old nineteenth-century buildings, featuring stuccoed exteriors and opulent rooms, are crumbling now, the subject of preservation orders funded by the Bulgarian government and the European Union. The phalanxes of grey apartment blocks are relegated to the background while whitewashed villas with red tiled roofs rise between the trees beside the river. All of this simply enhances the dramatic contrast between Ruse and the industry-choked Romanian port of Giurgiu, on the opposite bank of the river, which serves Bucharest, whose urban sprawl begins less than thirty miles to the north.

Lovett Fielding Edwards, whose boat was moored in Giurgiu in 1938, suggested that the port here was bigger than the great Rhine port of Duisburg, lined with "glittering arc lights that seem to go on forever", and busy with teams of "shaggy, dirty, evil-tempered water-buffaloes" used to drag the cargo between the river barges and the railway wagons. "The dock workers are among the toughest set of men I have ever seen," he went on, "with dark suspicious faces and a sullen and hostile attitude like their own water-buffaloes. They were almost naked, their rags being scarcely worth the name... [they tramped] up and down the narrow planks to a regular rhythm like eastern coolies."

Giurgiu continued to develop its heavy industry during the communist era. In the late 1980s air pollution from a chemical plant in Giurgiu caused such problems across the river in Ruse that a group was formed to protest against it, known as the Committee for the Protection of Ruse; it was one of the first popular campaigning groups organized in communist Bulgaria and, like the groups formed to protest against the Nagymaros Dam in Hungary, it provided a major focal point for political dissent within the country.

Four miles downstream from Ruse is the Dunav Most, which simply translates as "Danube Bridge". The blunt, no-nonsense name belies the fact that this is one of the longest bridges over the Danube. The box-girder structure is just short of a mile in length and carries a road on its top deck and the main railway line from Bucharest to Istanbul on the lower one. Trains clank across the bridge at walking pace, giving passengers a fabulous view up and down the widening river. When the bridge was completed in the 1950s it was known as the Friendship Bridge, a reference both to its status as an international crossing place and to the fact that the Soviets helped in its construction.

Downstream of the bridge the river once again spreads itself out between marshy islands and lagoons. The southern shore is home to Lake Srebarna, an expanse of reedy marshland dubbed the "eldorado of wading birds" by the Hungarian writer Felix Kanitz. Seventy different types of heron make their home here, along with egrets, rare Dalmatian pelicans and thousands of squawking geese. The banks of the lake are lined with marked paths and peaceful waterside hotels.

The Danube's flirtation with Bulgaria ends at Silistra, which has an appropriately end-of-the-road feel to it. Like so many towns along this reach of the river, Silistra was a Thracian settlement that was commandeered by Trajan as a fort; the Romans knew the place as Durostorum. Now, only some scruffy archaeological remains in a park beside the river, and the epigraph-rich tombstones in a musty archaeological museum, provide any evidence of this ancient past. In fact, more recent historical events chime louder in Silistra than those of two millennia ago.

Close to the Roman remains, a tank sitting on a circular plinth forms a low-key memorial to the Soviet invasion of Bulgaria that took place in September 1944. During the Second World War the Bulgarian king had been persuaded to side with the Axis powers after being promised Macedonia as a spoil of victory. The Nazis were interested in Bulgaria as they could use it as a base from which to launch an invasion of Greece. But the presence of Nazi troops here brought war with the USSR; the subsequent invasion also set the seal on Bulgaria's politics after the war. Within days of Soviet troops pouring across the Danube at Silistra the Bulgarian Communist Party had formed a new government, abolished the monarchy and declared Bulgaria a People's Republic. Appropriately enough for a place that sealed Bulgaria's status as a vassal state of the former USSR, Silistra is rather uninviting, lacking the urbanity of Ruse or the Turkish heritage of Vidin. Gloomy Art Nouveau mansions line shady streets, and a little-used border crossing provides car drivers with a back-door entrance to Romania. But the most that can be said for present-day Silistra is that its harbour provides the outlet for most of Bulgaria's copious exports of grain.

## Chapter Twelve
# THROUGH EASTERN ROMANIA

### SILISTRA TO BRĂILA

By the time the Danube flows past Silistra it has marked the southern edge of Romania for almost 450 miles. But immediately beyond Silistra, the route followed by the Romanian-Bulgarian border swings south-east while the river turns north-east: so for the first time, the Danube becomes a wholly Romanian river. Another 230 miles remain between Silistra and the Black Sea. This distance allows Romania to claim that, after Germany, it is the country with the second longest stretch of the river running wholly within its boundaries. And if the reach that forms international frontiers is included in Romania's total, the country can easily claim the greatest length of river of any of the ten countries that the Danube passes through or touches.

Appropriately, with its economic reliance on heavy industry and consequent need to transport bulky cargoes of coal and iron ore, Romania has traditionally been a big user of the river. In *The Improbable Voyage* Tristan Jones remarked on the number of Romanian barges he saw passing along the reach of the river between Passau and Linz, some 1,250 miles upstream from Silistra. He also commented on their generally decrepit condition too, even in comparison with the barges from other East European countries. Some Romanian barges even had vegetable gardens on their roofs—but Jones was told that all the produce grown this way had to be given up by the ship's captain to the authorities in charge of food distribution in communist Romania; for this reason each vegetable plant on boats leaving the country was accounted for by a commissar, and was checked again when the vessel returned from its voyage.

As it heads through Romania the river resumes its old habit of splitting to form substantial mid-channel islands. In fact, in some places the river may split into half a dozen channels of varying widths, separated by several miles of marshy islands, making it impossible to determine the course of the "true" Danube. A channel known as the Brațul Borcea diverges just beyond Silistra and flows west of the main channel, forming an

island that reaches a width of six miles, and stretches to a length three times that, before the errant stream rejoins the main channel at Hârşova, the site of a former Roman camp that is also home to a ruined Turkish fortress. As the Braţul Borcea rejoins, another side channel, this one known as the Dunărea Veche or Old Danube, diverges from the main channel, and the river becomes little more than a thread of channels separated by marshland. Diverging channels and marshes are, of course, nothing new. But as the river flows into Romania, it does something remarkable that it has never done before: it turns on its heels and heads due north, a bearing it has not followed for any substantial distance along its entire journey.

This northward-heading reach of the river, from Rasova to Galaţi, is around ninety miles in length. The course of the river runs parallel to the Black Sea coast and between these watery boundaries is an area of dry, undulating plains known as the Dobrudzha. This politically contested region is part of the great Eurasian steppe land that girdles the north of the Black Sea and stretches eastwards into central Asia. During the Middle Ages the area was a dustbowl under the loose control of wandering bands of Tartars. Then in 1416 it was conquered by Turkish Sultan Mehmet I, who populated the area with Turks simply because it was so empty. His settlement policy did nothing to alleviate the poverty of the area. Negley Farson, passing through here in the 1920s, recalls seeing "flights of geese and ducks rising and pitching again into some hidden water. And like some animal hidden in the scant cover of bare willows we came upon the mud huts of a village. Pathetically primitive! Peasants emerged from the mud-coloured huts and stared at us blankly. They did not answer our wave."

Sacheverell Sitwell, travelling in this part of Romania in the following decade, also recognized its other worldliness. "It is this portion of Romania that bears no resemblance to any part of the western world," he wrote in his 1938 travelogue *Romanian Journey.* "Travellers have compared these last reaches of the Danube to the Yellow River, flowing into the China Sea... The boat was anchored off a low shore of forest that might well have been the Mangrove swamps of Africa."

In the twentieth century, control of the region switched back and forth between Bulgaria and Romania. When the Romanians took over they forced Bulgarian peasants at gunpoint to abandon their farms to allow new settlers to move in. In 1941 Bulgaria regained part of the region and in the 1980s launched a controversial policy known as *Vazroditelniyat protses*, which required the area's Muslim population to speak Bulgarian and adopt Bulgarian names. Thankfully such bullying from both sides is now consigned to the past, and the Dobrudzha has settled down as a quiet region of wheat fields and scattered multi-ethnic villages. Conditions are still severe, however, with parched, torrid summers and icy, wind-blasted winters the norm.

## THE DANUBE CANAL

The great dog-leg formed by the Danube means that at Cernavodă the river is only 25 miles from the Black Sea coast as the crow flies; and yet, flowing north rather than east, the river still has over 180 miles to cover before it empties into the sea. Trajan was unwilling to fortify this last stretch of the river and instead he built a defensive line of forts and towers linking the bend in the river at Cernavodă with the shore of the Black Sea. Nineteen centuries later, the great kink in the river's course, and the extra journey it created for ships, meant that it seemed a good idea to construct a canal between Cernavodă and the Black Sea that would follow a similar route to Trajan's wall, saving barges time and fuel.

Work started on this monumental project in 1949, only to be abandoned in 1953 and then restarted in 1973, this time along a slightly different route. The workforce that built the second canal consisted mainly of forced labourers—those who had fallen foul of the brutal regime of Nicolae Ceaușescu, including political prisoners, critics of the Communist Party, farmers who resisted collectivization, the clergy, and those who had attempted to flee abroad. Around 50,000 workers died during the construction, and the canal was subsequently nicknamed the *Canalul Mortii*, or Canal of Death. The channel these unfortunate workers blasted through the Dobrudzha finally reaches the Black Sea at Agigea, just south of the great Romanian seaport and resort city of Constanța.

Most accounts of journeys along the canal portray it as little more than a grimly functional furrow of industrial proportions. Tristan Jones brought his catamaran along it in 1986, shortly after its opening:

> Like most modern construction works, the Black Sea-Danube Canal looked as if the designers had not had the human race in mind when they dreamed it up, but only machines. It was a long concrete ditch, bordered by extensive tracts of muddy clay, interspersed with a few jetties

on which stood monstrous cranes lit by cold arc lights at night. On each side of this water-filled trench of concrete, artificial hills of mud had been thrown up to a height of around a hundred feet, so it was impossible for us to see what lay beyond them.

At Cernavodă itself, where the new canal diverges from the river, the Danube is spanned by an elegant bridge which, when it opened in 1895, was the longest in Europe. The structure stretches over 13,000 feet, crossing part of the floodplain and numerous side channels as well as the main flow of the river itself. Its cantilever design, comprising a rising and falling upper line of girders, makes it a very distant cousin of the Forth Rail Bridge in Scotland. The bridge was built to carry the main railway line from Bucharest to Constanța and, in the days before the canal, this was the only access to the Black Sea for freight when the lower reaches of the river were frozen over. Although still standing, the distinctive structure is now disused, and the railway line and busy motorway now cross the river on an adjacent bridge opened in 1987.

### Brăila and Galaţi: the Scent of the Sea

In 1829 a Russian victory against the Turks, and the consequent signing of the Treaty of Adrianople, brought the present-day Romanian province of Moldavia under Russian protection. Previously the region had been ruled by corrupt Ottoman administrators who did little more than bleed the place dry. But with Russian rule, Moldavia turned its eyes towards western Europe, and its riverside cities of Brăila and Galaţi quickly developed into busy ports. Both were accessible by ocean-going vessels, and trade could thus flow from them westwards along the Danube as far as Germany, and eastwards through the last reach of the river to the Black Sea and beyond. Early twentieth-century travellers were alive at once to the vibrant mood and international outlook of both towns—particularly Brăila, with its hectic harbour and prosperous merchant community.

In *Across Europe in a Motorboat*, published in 1915, Henry Rowland wrote that he had "never seen as many different national ensigns so intermingled in any port of the world, except Constantinople. Port Said and Singapore are lonely compared to it... Brăila draws about it the usual parasites of abundant, quickly acquired gold, and the theatres and casinos

and plazas are gay with the most cosmopolitan crowd of Europe, while enormous sums change hands nightly over the gaming tables in the club." Negley Farson saw ships from Liverpool, Stockholm, Trieste, Split, Bremen and Antwerp in Brăila's harbour, "grim, great, and rusty with the salt of white seas".

It was in this milieu that the renowned Romanian novelist Panait Istrati grew up. He was born in Brăila in 1884, the illegitimate son of a Greek smuggler, and like his near-contemporary Elias Canetti he lived a peripatetic life that took him as an adult to Bucharest, Istanbul, Cairo, Naples, Paris, Moscow, Greece and Switzerland. During the early years of Istrati's life Brăila was a free port and shipped vast quantities of grain from the surrounding Bărăgan plain to western Europe. Merchants lined the streets with elegant villas and cultural life flourished. But there was a dark side to Brăila's prosperity: many of the dock workers were Gypsies, exploited in conditions of virtual slavery, whose community nonetheless grew to be the largest of any city in Europe.

Brăila shuns the river today. The docks are silted up and the riverfront, some distance away from the leafy and expansive main square, is not much more than a collection of rusting hulls gradually sinking into a muddy backwater. The villas have crumbled into the dust, but the Gypsy population is still there, lending the town a distinctive bohemian feel.

Galaţi, twelve miles downriver, has fared a little better. Ocean-going ships can still reach its busy port, and from here to the sea distances along the river are measured not in kilometres, as they have been since the start of the navigable Danube at Kelheim, but in nautical miles. The shipyard at Galaţi is the busiest in Romania, busier, even, than the one in the great seaport of Constanţa.

Like Brăila, Galaţi has a proud history as a trading station and passenger port. In Bram Stoker's 1897 novel *Dracula* Jonathan Harker and Godalming travelled here by train to catch a steamer along the Siret river to the castle of Count Dracula, deep in Transylvania. But extensive bombing during the Second World War flattened the old town, and Galaţi had to be rebuilt from scratch during the 1950s and 1960s. In 1970 its brooding steelworks opened, relying heavily on the river for delivery of raw materials. Nowadays the few remaining nineteenth-century buildings are marooned amidst industrial sprawl and the usual rows of communist-era tenement blocks. Ceauşescu saw Galaţi as a showcase of Romanian in-

dustrial prowess; today it is a byword for the economic and environmental damage inflicted on the country by his regime. Not surprisingly, even the most broad-minded of guide books have little positive to say about the place.

### THE DANUBE NAVIGATION COMMISSIONS
Galați, with its role as a port both for Black Sea shipping and for riverborne barges, has a unique place in the history of navigation on the Danube. In 1856 the town was selected as the home for the first body set up to regulate traffic along the river. Peace in Europe, and the consequent increase in river traffic, made the creation of such a body—the European Commission of the Danube—a necessity. In fact, its establishment was enshrined within the provisions of the Treaty of Paris, which ended the Crimean War. Initially the commission's powers and interests were limited to the stretch of the river from Galați to the Black Sea. But representatives from eight nations sat on its board, and in 1919 the Treaty of Versailles

also granted Britain, France and Italy representation. Two years later, the commission assumed responsibility for the entire navigable length of the river, from Ulm to the Black Sea—a distance of over 1,500 miles. The commission's duties were ended in 1939, when the war made them unworkable.

In 1946 a council of European foreign ministers meeting in New York announced the creation of a new body, the International Danube Commission, whose headquarters were established not in Galați but in Budapest, where they remain to this day. At first it was only eastern bloc countries, along with Yugoslavia, that formed this new body; Austria joined in 1960 but Germany did not become a member until the fall of communism. At the time of the International Danube Commission's creation, eight countries claimed an interest in the river, by virtue of controlling a stretch of its shore. With the break-up of the Balkans in the 1990s, that number has risen to ten, with Slovakia succeeding Czechoslovakia, Serbia and Croatia succeeding Yugoslavia, and Moldova and Ukraine succeeding the USSR.

There is no other river in the world whose navigable length is of such international complexity, which was why the creation of the European commission at Galați was needed in the first place. But in many ways this panoply of frontiers and flags makes no difference to the traffic that plies the river. "As on all great rivers, it does not really much matter on the Danube what your nationality is," John Marriner wrote in *Black Sea, Blue River.*

> The main thing is that you are there. The river is your life and to some extent your country too. Whether you are Austrian, German, Czech, Hungarian, Yugoslav, Russian, Romanian or Bulgarian is a secondary matter. One goes up and down in a continuous rhythm, known to all after a short while and accepted into the Danube family. You are of course conscious that your country may have its entity and even disagree violently with the others. But that is the affair of people far removed from your own existence. You have made your peace with the world and the men you meet are part of the life you have all mutually accepted. There are no barriers between those whom the river has drawn together. It is a sort of European foreign legion where no questions are asked. There is only one common enemy and friend—the Danube itself.

## East from Galați

At Galați the river abandons its northerly bearing and turns abruptly east. Galați itself, occupying a raised bank on the left bank of the river, overlooks the bend, one of the sharpest on the lower course of the Danube: it is as if the river suddenly shakes itself out of a dreamy reverie, remembers that its geographical destiny is the sea, and that the end will not come without a headlong change in direction. After another dog-leg just outside Galați, an east-south-easterly course towards the delta is set firm. Marshes and pools lie on both sides of the river now. The floodplain stretches as far as the flat horizon; settlements shun the banks and spread over the higher ground, away from the threading channels. As the river curves away from the dog-leg, the Prut river, the Danube's second longest tributary after the Tisza, joins from the north. Immediately downstream of the confluence, a junction of international boundaries allows a triangular wedge of the Republic of Moldova to push determinedly into the river.

This wedge is the tapering tip of a long, vaguely banana-shaped nation: the Moldovan bank of the Danube measures just 1,300 feet, but this is enough to secure Moldova a place at the table of the International Commission of the Danube in Budapest. Upstream along the Prut is Moldova's Giurgiulesti port, and on the banks of the Danube itself are the jetties, railway sidings, storage tanks and loading facilities of a combined oil, grain, passenger and container terminal that forms landlocked Moldova's outlet to the sea. There are no concessions to scenic river views here: Moldova must squeeze all the economic benefit it can out of its tiny portion of Danube shoreline. Beyond the concentration of industry, Moldova widens out and stretches north for some 190 miles. At one time a province of Romania, and then a Soviet Republic, Moldova declared independence from Moscow in 1991 in a fit of nationalistic optimism, but today it is one of the least-known and poorest countries in Europe, beset by economic woes, endemic corruption and security problems in the breakaway province of Trans-Dniester that have rumbled on since the early 1990s.

Another bend in the river, and another country on its north bank: Ukraine claims roughly 45 miles of Danube shoreline, and a little way beyond the Moldovan port facility at Giurgiulesti is Reni, a similarly grim Ukrainian oil and cargo terminal. Beyond Reni the countryside is arid and sparsely settled. The only town of any size is Isaccea, on the Romanian shore, which has been a frontier town for thousands of years. Roman and Byzantine soldiers once peered across the river from here towards land held by Barbarian tribes, and on a crumbling cliff above a broad curve in the river are the few remains of an ancient Roman fort named Noviodunum, the former headquarters of the Roman fleet that patrolled the lower Danube. In 396 AD Emperor Flavius Valens crossed the river here by means of a pontoon bridge, to engage the Goths in combat on the other side. When the gothic chieftains sued for peace, the treaty was signed in a boat bobbing in the middle of the river. Later on the Byzantine emperors made Noviodunum their main naval base on the Danube. But Slav settlers had little use for the place and during the Middle Ages Noviodunum's walls crumbled into the dry mud. The site is little more than banks and ditches now, although archaeologists are making the best of things and actively digging out some ancient Christian tombs from the dusty hillside. The Ukrainian bank opposite the Roman site is deserted, and the countryside stretches in all directions towards a featureless horizon.

*Chapter Thirteen*

# THE DELTA AND THE BLACK SEA

## A LAND OF REEDS AND MARSHES

Fifteen miles beyond Noviodunum the river splits again. But this time the channels will never rejoin: instead they fan out to create the lush triangle of the Danube Delta, the gateway, at last, to the sea. Claudio Magris calls the delta "one great dissolution, with branches and rivulets and ramifications that wander off on their own, like the organs of a body on the point of succumbing, each of which shows a decreasing interest in any of the others... the Danube is everywhere, and also its end is everywhere."

This region of reeds and marshes and ever-shifting sandbars covers an area of over 1,500 square miles—nearly twice the size of Luxembourg. The multiple channels are the result of the river becoming sluggish as it meets the ebbing tides of the Black Sea. As it slows, the silt is deposited, and the river chokes up its own course and is forced to thread yet more channels through the mud banks and islands. The silt deposited is the finest that the Danube carries, and it comes from any number of locations, from the hills of the Black Forest to the plains of Hungary, from the Alps around St.

Moritz where the Inn rises to the remotest peaks of the Carpathian mountains in the Ukraine that feed the Tisza. Much of the silt is deposited right at the mouths of the various channels, making the Delta appear as a bulge on the Black Sea's western coast. In fact, the feature is steadily growing into the sea, creating some of the youngest land in continental Europe. In 1476 the town of Chilia in the northern delta repelled a sea-borne Turkish invasion, yet it now lies over 25 miles inland.

Not surprisingly, the delta is a haven for wildlife. More than 300 species of birds make their homes amidst the wandering creeks between the muddy islands. Many of these waterfowl are found nowhere else in Europe; they include herons, ibis, eagles, red buntings, whooper swans, arctic grebes, egrets and mandarin ducks from China. Lone cormorants can often be seen perched on the banks of creeks, their wings spread wide to dry in the sun, while distant flocks of pelicans often appear as a white shimmering smudge on the horizon. Sacheverell Sitwell mistook these pelican colonies for something completely different when he first set eyes on them in 1937: "Far away, white cities gleamed and sparkled upon the horizon," he wrote in *Romanian Journey.* "It was the Orient of white domes and minarets... And then the truth came. Those were white pelicans, towns of white pelicans camped upon the islands."

Along the older reaches of accumulated silt, known as *grinduri* in Romanian, oak, willow and poplar flourish, providing stable habitats for otters, wildcats, foxes, boars and mink. And more recent silt deposits, inundated by the floods of spring and autumn and known as *plauri*, create muddy homes for wading birds and breeding grounds for one of the most famous creatures of the delta—the mosquito. In the past these airborne bloodsuckers were a malaria-carrying menace. "They began the attack around six o'clock and fought on until the early hours when, satiated, they would retire, leaving their human victims scratching and swollen until the next evening feast began," John Marriner wrote. "And it was not only the mosquitoes that ate us. Every form of undesirable small flying thing seemed to join in the attack... of course, the locals never notice the insects at all and go around just as if nothing were happening. I suppose they are conditioned to the bites when they are quite young; we noticed they also drank the Danube water with impunity."

Don Maxwell recalled the "vast cloud of mosquitoes... [that] rose and fell like layers of smoke" and decided that his passage through the delta to the sea was now "a race against malaria" (to which he succumbed, but survived). The mosquitoes are less noticeable these days but guide books still advise copious application of insect repellent for those venturing into marshy areas at night. Besides the mosquitoes there are many other inhabitants of the creeks that are less of a nuisance. At night the streets of delta villages resound to a cacophony of croaking frogs, while in the water, pike, carp, tench, bream, perch and freshwater herring glide among the reeds, and sturgeon still swim up from the Black Sea, though not in sufficient numbers to make their catching commercially viable.

Traditionally, the economic life of the delta has revolved around the bounty of the water. Land-based farming has been virtually impossible because of the floods, and each time that the waters recede, the geography of the delta is completely changed, with old mud banks swept away and new ones arising where before there were only pools. Ceauşescu looked on the delta as needlessly uneconomic wasteland and tried to convert the swamps into productive farmland. Here and there his efforts have paid off, with a number of *grinduri* divided up into fields for grazing or wheat cultivation. But apart from the produce from these farms, only one crop has ever been harvested in the delta: reeds. The strands from these plants were traditionally used in the construction of roofs and fences; nowadays

reeds are harvested commercially and processed in factories in Brăila and Tulcea to make paper, cellulose and building materials.

Commercial reed farming, like agriculture, has only made a few inroads. In 1991 the entire delta was declared a Unesco World Heritage site, winning the region the same international status as Australia's Great Barrier Reef and America's Grand Canyon. Now much of it is a biosphere reserve, closed off to casual visitors, allowing wildlife to roam free and undisturbed. And, of course, both human and animal inhabitants must survive the extreme conditions that the delta endures: summers are torrid, while in winters the delta shivers in the icy-cold blasts that howl all the way from northern Russia.

There are few roads in the delta. Many of the villages, with their thatched roofs and rudimentary jetties for fishing smacks, are still only accessible by boat. The town of Tulcea, at the apex of the delta triangle, is where the main roads and railways terminate, and where goods and passengers transfer to water-borne craft. These days, tourism is one of mainstays of the delta, and the harbour at Tulcea throngs with boats of all sizes, from sleek catamaran ferries to luxury cruise liners, from ocean-going yachts making a brief call to bobbing motorboats, from tourist vessels with

gaudy sun awnings to juddering passenger boats that the locals catch to reach the supermarket.

Away from the busy harbour front, Tulcea is a rather charmless jungle of high-rise blocks and bland pedestrian plazas. John Marriner found it "uninteresting and ugly. Its two hotels rejoiced in the names of number one and number two." But he was ignoring the town's setting, which is a handsome one, on the outside edge of a graceful curve in the river; and he also failed to look beyond the drab town centre, to the part of the town where hills rise along the water's edge, dotted with villas clustered among the trees. (Nothing remains of the Roman fort of Aegissus that stood here, or of the port established before that by the Greeks.)

Beyond Tulcea, the three main channels of the delta divide to form the characteristic webbed-foot imprint that is so distinctive on maps and satellite photos of the region. Each channel carries the Romanian prefix *Brațul*: to the north is the Brațul Chilia, to the south the Brațul Sfântu Gheorghe, and between them flows the Brațul Sulina, whose partially canalized channel provides most ships with their access to the sea.

## THE BRAȚUL CHILIA AND ISMAIL

The Brațul Chilia is the longest of the delta channels and discharges more water into the sea than the other channels put together. Diverging from the main river just upstream from Tulcea, the channel winds for fifty miles through a spongy landscape of lakes and marshes, and is weighed down by so much sediment that as it nears the sea it splits up to form a mini-delta of its own. Fishing has been the mainstay of life for thousands of years. In the 1930s Sacheverell Sitwell noticed the "fishermen's houses, raised on piles, and bearing an exact resemblance to the fishing villages of New Guinea. Each has its boat drawn up by its side, in caricature of the Austin Sevens in their sheds all along the arterial roads in England. The fishermen are black bearded and hatless, completely Russian in aspect but with the appearance of aborigines."

Those fishermen were members of the Lipovani community, ethnic Russians who had settled in the delta in the seventeenth century following their persecution at the hands of the Orthodox Church in Russia. These hardy dissenters exiled themselves to the remote swamplands of the delta so they could continue to speak Old Russian, maintain their tradition of crossing themselves with two fingers instead of three, and wear their beards, all of which were opposed by the radical new teachings of their Church. Their name derives from the *lipo* or lime forests of the Ukraine through which they passed on their way to find new homes. Once the Lipovani lived all over the delta; now they are mainly confined to towns and villages along the Brațul Chilia, including the Romanian village of Periprava and the Ukrainian town of Vilkovo facing it across the water.

Lipovani can be recognized by their blond hair, blue eyes and prominent beards, by their prodigious consumption of vodka and by their vehement abhorrence of cigarette smoking. Traditionally they have been the fishermen of the delta, harvesting reeds in the autumn and storing ice in thatched barns in winter to keep the fish cold and fresh. Now they supplement their income from fishing by ferrying tourists around in pleasure boats, tending gardens of vegetables, plums, pears and grapes, and keeping pigs and bees. In the 1960s, before tourism in the delta had made any real inroads, John Marriner spent time with Lipovani in the village of Mila 23 in the heart of the region. In a remote inn he watched them down copious quantities of vodka that made "their songs become louder, wilder and more continuous. [But] there was something very sad and faraway in the songs, as though they had been handed down from father to son over the ages, recalling a dim region of the mind where once their forebears had lived."

The border between Romania and Ukraine is drawn along the centre of this northern channel. The main settlement beside the water, Ismail, on the north bank, has been fiercely contested for centuries. Since the 1940s the town has been in Ukrainian territory. Before that it changed hands time and again between Romania, Russia, Ukraine, Turkey, Moldova and Bessarabia, the latter the dry steppe land province girdling the north coast of the Black Sea that has been under both Russian and Romanian control. Byron's *Don Juan* tells how Ismail was recaptured from the Turks by the Russians in 1790, a bloody and pointless massacre that left 40,000 Turks dead. The name of the town is Turkish (after an Ottoman emperor, the Grand Vizier Ismail), but its distant origins are Greek and Roman. In *The Blue Danube* Bernard Newman called the place "another racial mix-up" and watched as "three sailing ships from Italy, France and Egypt [were unloaded] by Romanian, Russian, Turkish, Bulgar, Greek and Gypsy labourers. A Jew did the checking and on the deck of the Italian boat a Chinese cook prepared a meal." But ten years earlier Negley Farson noted none of this cultural pluralism. Instead, he wrote that "Ismail is as

Russian as any tale of Chekhov. Prodigiously wide, cobbled streets; flat-roofed, one-storied houses. A flat horizon under a great dome of grey sky. Naked, shivering trees. Impressively dreary."

Today it appears that little has changed: Ismail is a busy port and a drab industrial centre ignored by guide books, which tend to point Ukraine's tourists in the direction of the Crimea or Kiev rather than this out-of-the way outpost on the Danube. But the port is vital politically as it gives Ukraine access to the river, and before 1991 this was the principal Soviet toehold on the international waterway. During the Cold War era Soviet barges plied the entire length of the Danube, from Ismail to southern Germany, and were equipped for their voyage both in terms of politics and provisions, as Tristan Jones noted. "All the Russian ships carried political officers who were in charge of the crew, and the captain was on board merely to steer the ship," he recalled being told by a Hungarian barge captain. "The Soviet ships spent nothing all the time they were on the river, because they brought with them from Ismail all the stores and fuel they would need for the whole voyage up and down the river, no matter how far they went." Jones thought the ships' bristling antennae meant that they played a role in Soviet eavesdropping on western activity. Certainly, the Soviet crews kept their knowledge of the river closely to themselves. "In Budapest I was told that the Soviets had surveyed the whole river in their domain quite recently, and had issued some of the new charts to their friends," Jones stated ruefully. "But to the public, or to those whom they mistrusted, the charts were simply not available. We might as well look for a plan of their missile sites."

From Ismail it is still around fifty miles to the sea. The countryside through which the sluggish channel flows is rich in pelican colonies, while falcons, white-tailed eagles, boars and wildcats make their homes in thick and largely undisturbed forests of oak. Larger settlements are still confined to the Ukrainian bank: Kilija (or Chilia in Romanian) traces its origins back to the Greeks, who named the place Achilea, after Achilles. Like Ismail it was fortified in turn by Genoese merchants and then by Turkish militias. A little further downstream is Vilkovo, a watery town surrounded by lakes and marshes that has claimed for itself the unlikely sobriquet "the Venice of Bessarabia" because of its canals. Sitwell wrote of the "web of waterways" he saw when he came here: the "little canals [were] so complicated in plan that it would be nearly impossible to map them. The town exists in the midst of a forest of willow trees and the tortuous waterways wind amongst those groves."

Beyond Vilkovo the mini-delta begins, but the border is still drawn along the main channel, allowing Ukraine to claim around a tenth of the entire delta region as its territory. The threading streams finally empty into the sea through an expanse of arid sand dunes, where lizards, tortoises and vipers scuttle and burrow through the scrubland.

## THE BRAȚUL SFÂNTU GHEORGHE AND HALMYRIS

The delta's southerly arm is also its least used. Instead of splitting and dividing around mid-river islands, as the northern channel does, the course of the Brațul Sfântu Gheorghe twists its way around a tortuous weave of tight meanders that ensure commercial shipping rarely ventures this way. About thirty miles beyond Tulcea, just before the channelside roads peter out and turn into muddy tractor paths, the ruins of the ancient city of Halmyris rise above an ocean of swaying corn fields. When the Romans berthed their ocean-going fleet here, the coast of the Black Sea was only a few hundred yards distant, accessible by a long-forgotten arm of the Danube. Nowadays the coast is still another thirty miles further on, beyond 2,000 years' worth of silt accumulation.

As with many Roman sites along the Danube, all there is to see today in Halmyris are crumbling stone ramparts, half-buried gateways and earthy ditches. The most famous find in the site are the tombs of Epictet and Astion, two Christians from Asia Minor who refused to renounce Christianity and were executed here in 290 AD. One of the martyrs' judges was so impressed with their resolve that after their execution he secretly gave their remains a decent and marked burial. Constantine later founded a basilica at Halmyris and the remains were re-interred within the new church, to be discovered in 2001 when a crypt under the basilica's altar was found to contain two skeletons guarded over by a faded fresco that bore the word "Astion". Little remains of the basilica now, save the off-limits crypt and the tumble-down foundations protected from the elements by a makeshift awning of corrugated iron. Any other secrets the site of Halmyris has yet to yield lie buried under the surrounding oceans of cornfields.

Beyond Halmyris the channel eventually empties into the sea at Sfântu Gheorghe, a Lipovani village of brightly-coloured reed and mud houses famous for its *icre negre,* or black caviar, the spawn of the sturgeon that were once caught in great quantities here. Approaching this channel from the Black Sea, John Marriner got his yacht "confused in a series of nets and floats. It was like being in a minefield. These were the famous sturgeon nets of the lower Danube… the boats come out to sea at dawn, check on where the great fish are caught and slash them to death with their knives before pulling their bodies into the boats. Most of this goes on in the springtime, when the females bear the greatest spawn—the black gold of the Delta."

Bernard Newman, writing thirty years earlier, came here on his two wheels and recalled that he saw "two or three magnificent specimens [of sturgeon], the size of a man." Some fish are still caught in Sfântu Gheorghe to this day, though not in the numbers they once were. The main draw here these days is the expansive and normally empty beach stretching north along the coast from the village. But Sfântu Gheorghe is only accessible by boat or tractor, limiting visitors to the especially hardy and the unusually curious.

## THE BRAŢUL SULINA AND THE BLACK SEA

Since the nineteenth century, sea-borne commercial shipping on the Danube has used the Sulina Channel to transit between river and sea. In the 1860s a long process of canalization began that saw many sections of this channel deepened and straightened. By cutting off numerous meanders, the distance from Tulcea to Sulina, where the channel empties into the Black Sea, was reduced by a quarter, to just over 35 miles. The channel is dredged to this day to allow for navigation, and ocean-going freighters are a regular feature along its dead-straight reaches, the ships' high bridges and massive on-board loading gear coming as a stark contrast to the low-slung profiles of the Danube barges seen everywhere else along the river. Out at sea, a further six miles of dredged deep water channel, marked by buoys, allows ships to guide themselves safely towards the mouth of the channel and into the river.

Sulina itself is a former Byzantine and Genoese port and a haven for Black Sea pirates during the Ottoman period. The Crimean War allowed the British to drive out the Russians from the town, in the process destroying the place and leaving only the church and the lighthouse standing. In later years the town prospered after the European Commission of

the Danube established offices here, and a busy multinational community similar to that in Ruse and Brăila began to take root. Between the town's main street (actually the riverfront) and the sea, a remarkable cemetery pays testament to the British community that made its home here during the nineteenth century. Fading, moss-encrusted Victorian gravestones that would look instantly familiar in a parish churchyard in England commemorate those who drowned in disasters at sea or on the river, or who fell victim to diseases that raged through the muggy delta in summer.

But just as the graveyard was becoming established, Sulina's days in the sun were numbered: Constanţa began to emerge as a preferred Romanian seaport and when John Marriner visited Sulina in the 1960s he gained "the impression [that the town was] simply falling to bits for lack of interest and too few people." Nowadays the place makes its living from the tourists who speed here every day from Tulcea on fast catamarans. But in truth, visitors have little to occupy themselves. There is a row of low-rise guesthouses and holiday-oriented restaurants along the riverside, and a squat lighthouse open to the public, although the delta's remorseless expansion into the sea has made it long redundant. Its modern replacement lies at the end of one of the twin 13,000-foot-long parallel jetties that extend the Sulina channel far into the Black Sea. As they pass the blunt ends of these jetties, ships finally throw themselves onto the roll and swell of the sea, and put the river behind them.

Also behind them, and to starboard, is a busy sandy beach that stretches along the coast from the landward end of the southern jetty: the wind tugs at the parasols, disco music blares from stalls, and the snack stands do a roaring trade. The hinterland of the beach comprises scrubby sand dunes rather than high-rise hotels; Sulina's lack of road access means that mass tourism of the destructive kind has yet to arrive.

❧

The sea into which the Danube spills was given its grim and melancholic appellation by the Turks. They saw it as a place of treacherous waters and frequent storms; the black depths were still and dead, while on the sea's shores, widows dressed in the traditional colour of mourning bewailed those the cruel waves had taken from them. Oddly, the Romans dubbed the same sea the *Pontus Euxinus*, the "Hospitable Sea", but the Turks were never as confident mariners as their Roman forebears. Along with the Black Sea's notorious storms comes a unique oceanography: the emptying of so much freshwater into the sea, principally from the Danube, but also from three great Russian and Ukrainian rivers, the Don, the Dniester and the Dniper, means that the Black Sea is far less salty than the majority of the world's oceans. Its average water level is also higher than the Mediterranean, which accounts for the strong current that tears through the Bosphorus, some 250 miles south of the delta.

From the beach at Sulina, even on a sunny day, the water of the Black Sea is muddy-brown rather than the usual oceanic blue. That is because the water is mainly river water—and not even here is the water of the Blue Danube the "right" colour. The discolouration continues for tens of miles into the choppy waters. The American adventurer Henry Rowland noticed this back in 1905: "More than ten miles offshore the Danube water debouching from the delta makes a sharp line of colour demarcation with that of the Black Sea, the former being an absinthe frappe colour and the latter a deep sapphire."

As Rowland and all other mariners realize at once, the boundary between sea and river is not fixed. Instead, it is an ever-changing and unchartable zone where silt-bearing freshwater mixes with the saltwater of the sea, a place where tides and currents engage in a remorseless and unwinnable battle. The marker in Sulina that announces "kilometre zero" is only the official point where the Danube ends: a sop to cartographers and navigators. The river could just as easily be said to end at the tip of any one of the delta's fingertip channels, at Sulina town or in Sulina harbour or at the end of the great twin jetties that jut into the Black Sea just east of the town, or even at some hard-to-determine point in the Black Sea itself. After all, the river's current continues to deposit its sediment in a great fan on the floor of the Black Sea for miles beyond the delta mouth. But the Danube's real finishing point is impossible to determine because, like all great rivers, its end is a messy unravelling rather than a triumphant arrival at a terminus.

Furthermore, the Danube trumps all the other great rivers in the world by another aspect of the vagueness of its geography: because not only does it have no firm ending, it has no firm beginning either. Arguments about the finishing point of the river echo the arguments between Donaueschingen, Furtwangen and the confluence of the Breg and Brigach as to which is the river's true beginning. In the end, the point where the river ends is as impossible to determine as the point where it begins, more than 1,740 miles upstream from the swamplands of the delta, half a world away amid the lush countryside and wooded hills of the Black Forest.

# Bibliography and Further Reading

## General Books on the Danube

*Danube*, by the Italian academic and German language scholar Claudio Magris, is probably the best-known book covering the cultural history of the Danube and the countries through which the river flows. This dense, lucid, occasionally frustrating but always enlightening book was published in Italy in 1986 and has not been updated, so it describes a journey and a river that passes through countries that no longer exist such as West Germany, Czechoslovakia and Yugoslavia. But Magris is less interested in the politics of eastern Europe than he is with philosophers, poets and writers who have lived and worked in this region from Roman times to the twentieth century. His book, which blends travelogue, history, philosophy and literary criticism, often wanders far from the Danube valley: with its descriptions of the Tatra Mountains in Eastern Slovakia, and excursions to cities that lie off the river's course such as Bucharest, the book is more a literary history of eastern and central Europe than a trip down the river itself. Magris' knowledge of European culture is vast, his curiosity infectious, his interests satisfyingly arcane. But he is primarily concerned with the spread of German culture along the Danube, and an English-speaking readership will be surprised, for instance, to find that Magris breezes through the Austrian Wachau without mentioning that Richard the Lionheart was imprisoned in a riverside castle there. And *Danube* rarely gives the impression that the river is a working one, thronged with barges and lined with smoke-belching industrial plants. The most recent English language edition of the book, translated by Patrick Creagh, was published by Harvill in 2001.

Rod Heikell's *The Danube: a river guide* was invaluable in researching this book. Published in 1991 it gives a kilometre-by-kilometre commentary on the river from Donaueschingen to its emptying into the Black Sea, blending history and geography with practical advice for those skippering boats along the river. No lock, marina, castle, monastery or tributary escapes Heikell's attention; the maps are detailed and there are many photographs and engravings along with more travelogue-style accounts of Heikell's own journeys along the river. The book is first and foremost a gazetteer and a practical guide, however, and its usefulness is limited somewhat because of its datedness: Heikell's Danube, like that of Magris, still flows through Czechoslovakia and Yugoslavia. The book is published by Imray, Laurie, Norie & Wilson Ltd and is easily available from specialist travel bookshops and from online retailers in both hardback and paperback.

Patrick Leigh Fermor's books *A Time of Gifts* (1977) and *Between the Woods and the Water* (1986) describe a journey on foot across Europe, from London to Constantinople, undertaken in the early 1930s when the author was barely a young man. Leigh Fermor's rich prose, descriptive prowess and love of anecdote have elevated these two books to the status of twentieth-century classics of travel literature. *A Time of Gifts* follows the author's progress from Holland to Esztergom, on the Slovak-Hungarian border, while *Between the Woods and the Water* recounts his journey south from Esztergom through Hungary and into Romania. The third volume in the series, describing the author's journey from Romania to Turkey, has yet to be written. Leigh Fermor initially set out to follow the valley of the Danube but his wanderings frequently took him far from the river and, in both books, the river features less prominently in the narrative than readers might expect. Ulm, Passau, Linz, the Wachau, Vienna, and Bratislava all feature in the first volume, while the Danube Bend, Budapest, and the stretch of the river around the Iron Gates gorge are encountered in the second. Both books were reissued by John Murray in 2004 and are easily available in paperback.

Many other twentieth-century travellers have written of their journeys along the length of the Danube between southern Germany and the delta. In *A Cruise across Europe* (1907) Don Maxwell describes a trip from England to the Black Sea, by way of the Rhine, the Ludwig Canal and the Danube, on a sailing boat named *Walrus*. The book was republished in January 2009 by Kessinger Publishing. Ten years after Don Maxwell's book came *Across Europe in a Motorboat* (1915), an account by an American named Henry C. Rowland of a similar journey in a boat named *Beaver*. This book is virtually impossible to obtain nowadays; however, yet another account of a similar journey, Negley Farson's 1926 *Sailing Across Europe*, was republished by Century in 1985 and is available from second-hand online book retailers. Farson was an American journalist and in this very readable book he catches vividly the unstable mood of Europe between the two world wars. Bernard Newman's 1935 account of his cycling trip along the length of the Danube, entitled *The Blue Danube*, can be obtained from online second-hand retailers, although it has not been reissued since 1935 and copies are expensive. In contrast, another book that can be easily and cheaply obtained online is John Marriner's *Black Sea and Blue River* (1968) which recounts a journey along the Danube that was unusually made upstream, from the Black Sea to Vienna, in a boat called *September Tide*. Marriner paints an extraordinary portrait of central Europe under communism and provides one of the last accounts to be written of a Danube voyage before the construction of the great dam on the Iron Gates gorge and the flooding of the island of Ada Kaleh.

Twenty years after Marriner's voyage, as communism was showing the very first signs of unravelling, the writer and sailor Tristan Jones navigated a boat from London to the Black Sea and recorded his experiences in a pugnacious book entitled *The Improbable Voyage* (1986); Jones writes in an accessible, punchy style and recalls his battles with east European bureaucracy and rotten winter weather with humour and a down-to-earth wit. The book was reissued by Adlard Coles Nautical in 1998. Rather gentler in style is *Back Door to Byzantium*, an account by veteran sailors Bill and Laurel Cooper of their journey by barge from northern France to Istanbul through the canals of northern Europe and then along the Danube. The Coopers made their journey during the troubles in Yugoslavia, which resulted in some interesting experiences as they navigated their barge *Hosanna* from Hungary to Belgrade and beyond. The book was published in 1997 by Adlard Coles Nautical, and, like Tristan Jones's book, it is easily available from internet book retailers. The latest author to publish a travelogue-style account of a trip along the river is Andrew Eames, whose book *Blue River, Black Sea* was published by Bantam in 2009.

## PRACTICAL GUIDEBOOKS

As well as the rather dated guide by Rod Heikell described above, which is aimed primarily at those skippering their own craft along the river, there are a few practical travel guidebooks to the Danube. *The Danube* (JPM Guides, 2006) covers the Rhine-Main-Danube canal, the Danube from Kelheim to the delta, and cities within striking distance of the river such as Bucharest and Salzburg. It is a brief, pocket-sized guide full of good maps and photos but short of practical information or much in the way of detailed historical background. Another JPM guide, *The Danube – to Budapest*, published in January 2008, covers the stretch of the river from Passau to southern Hungary plied by most cruise ships. Cicerone Press publishes a guide to the cycle route that runs the length of the Danube, entitled *The Danube Cycle Way* and written by John Higginson (2006); another guide, *Danube Bike Trail*, by Roland Esterbauer, is published by Verlag Esterbauer (also 2006).

Books in the *Rough Guides* series on Germany, Austria, the Czech and Slovak Republics, Hungary, Romania and Bulgaria provide excellent coverage of the Danube as it passes through these countries; meanwhile Bradt Publications publish guides to Slovakia and Serbia. Plenty of guides to the two scenic and popular regions of Germany through which the river passes, Bavaria and the Black Forest, are also readily available. Those looking for city guides to Vienna and Budapest will find plenty to choose from, while Bradt publishes city guides to Bratislava and Belgrade.

### BOOKS ABOUT SPECIFIC REACHES OF THE DANUBE

*A Thousand Miles in the Rob Roy Canoe,* by John MacGregor, originally published in 1866, describes a journey by canoe along the rivers of Germany, Switzerland and France. Part of MacGregor's trip takes him along the uppermost reaches of the Danube, from Donaueschingen to Ulm. The book was republished by Utah-based Dixon-Price Publishing in 2000 and is easily available from online booksellers. Dr. Charles Burney, a musicologist who travelled throughout Europe in the 1770s to research his book *History of Music*, also published an account of his travels, *Doctor Charles Burney's Continental Travels*, which includes the description of a trip along the upper course of the Danube in one of the crude rafts equipped with a shelter that were used for passenger transport at that time. The 1927 edition of the book is available from online booksellers, but is quite pricey.

*The Song of the Nibelungs* has received a number of translations into English. The quotations in this book come from the English translation by Burton Raffel published complete and in a single volume by Yale University Press in 2006. Hitler's life in Linz, and his architectural plans for that city, are described in Ian Kershaw's magnificent one-volume biography *Hitler*, published in 2008 by Allen Lane. The horrors of Mauthausen are described at length in Martin Gilbert's monumental study *The Holocaust*

(HarperCollins, 1989). Umberto Eco's novel *The Name of the Rose* is published by Vintage Classics in paperback. Edith Bone's memoir of her imprisonment in the notorious prison at Vác, *Seven Years Solitary*, is available from online retailers; the most recent edition of the book dates from 1966.

*Danube Stream*, written by Lovett Fielding Edwards and published in 1940, recalls a trip by tug and cargo steamer along the Danube downstream from Belgrade to the Romanian port of Giurgiu, and upstream from Belgrade as far as Apatin. The book has not been republished since its original Travel Book Club edition; however, it seems easy to obtain through online retailers. *Romanian Journey*, by the writer and critic Sir Sacheverell Sitwell, originally published in 1938, includes many accounts of visits to sites along the Romanian Danube, especially in and around the delta. The book was republished in 1992 by Oxford University Press. Elias Canetti's autobiography *The Tongue Set Free* is published in paperback by Picador.

Finally, Signal Books, the publisher of this book, publishes three books in its *Cities of the Imagination* series on cities along the Danube. *Belgrade* by David A. Norris, *Budapest* by Bob Dent and *Vienna* by Nicholas T. Parsons investigate the cultural and literary history of each capital, and make for ideal background reading before or after visits.

# Index of Literary & Historical Names

# Index of Places & Landmarks